PEPPERCORN
HIS LIFE AND LOCOMOTIVES

Tim Hillier-Graves

First published in Great Britain in 2021 by
Pen & Sword Transport

An imprint of Pen & Sword Books Ltd
Pen & Sword Books Ltd Yorkshire - Philadelphia
47 Church Street
Barnsley
South Yorkshire
S70 2AS

Copyright © Tim Hillier-Graves, 2021

ISBN 978 1 52672 985 9

The right of Tim Hillier-Graves to be identified as Author of this work has been asserted by him in accordance with the Copyright, Designs and Patents Act 1988.

A CIP catalogue record for this book is
available from the British Library.

All rights reserved. No part of this book may be reproduced or transmitted in any form or by any means, electronic or mechanical including photocopying, recording or by any information storage and retrieval system, without permission from the Publisher in writing.

Typeset by SJmagic DESIGN SERVICES, India.
Printed and bound in India by Replika Press Pvt. Ltd.

Pen & Sword Books Ltd incorporates the Imprints of Pen & Sword
Archaeology, Atlas, Aviation, Battleground, Discovery, Family History,
History, Maritime, Military, Naval, Politics, Railways, Select, Transport,
True Crime, Fiction, Frontline Books, Leo Cooper, Praetorian Press,
Seaforth Publishing, Wharncliffe and White Owl.

For a complete list of Pen & Sword titles please contact
PEN & SWORD BOOKS LIMITED
47 Church Street, Barnsley, South Yorkshire, S70 2AS, England
E-mail: enquiries@pen-and-sword.co.uk
Website: www.pen-and-sword.co.uk

or

PEN AND SWORD BOOKS
1950 Lawrence Rd, Havertown, PA 19083, USA
E-mail: Uspen-and-sword@casematepublishers.com
Website: www.penandswordbooks.com

CONTENTS

	Introduction and Acknowledgements	6
	Prologue	9
CHAPTER 1	Born to be an Engineer	14
CHAPTER 2	Growing to Maturity	53
CHAPTER 3	All Change	80
CHAPTER 4	Peppercorn in his own Words	113
CHAPTER 5	Rising to the Challenge	137
CHAPTER 6	Chief Mechanical Engineer	193
CHAPTER 7	Finale	239
	References and Sources	254
	Index	256

INTRODUCTION AND ACKNOWLEDGEMENTS

Arthur Peppercorn tends to be remembered for two things – being the LNER's last Chief Mechanical Engineer and two classes of Pacific that appeared at the end of his career. One of these, engine No. 60530, *Sayajirao*, is pictured here in all her weathered glory towards the end of her operational life in September 1962, when only fourteen years old. These A2 locomotives and the A1s that began arriving in 1948 are thought by many to be two of the finest Pacifics to run in Britain. It was their misfortune to arrive as BR finally grasped dieselisation and electrification, which soon rendered them obsolete. (*THG*)

From my earliest days I was often taken by my uncle, to King's Cross Station to see and admire many wonderful locomotives storming away under Goods Way and on to Gasworks Tunnel, or watch arriving trains as they slipped, often with barely a whisper, into its rather dingy platforms. This went on, much to my delight, until steam disappeared, which, by chance, coincided with a family move from London to Bath. Until then these visits, plus others to Euston, Waterloo and engine sheds across the city, had become a regular part of my life as had the LNER's Pacifics.

Everyone has favourites for reasons that aren't always clear. For me as a child it was always the A4s, Stanier's Coronations and Bulleid's Pacifics, but I became more discerning with the passing of years. By chance, during a family visit to Hadley Wood, I was delighted to find that the house in which we stayed sat very close to the LNER's main line. It was a summer Saturday and express trains flew past at regular intervals. For some reason, one came to a halt within thirty or so yards from where I stood – a Peppercorn A1, No.60149, *Amadis*, by then a Doncaster engine. The fact that the driver and fireman called a greeting and both waved made me an instant fan of them and their locomotive. From that moment, I longed to travel behind one of these A1s but it wasn't to be while BR operated steam locomotives. In fact, I had to wait until the reborn A1 *Tornado* was visiting the West Somerset Railway fifty years later for this particular wish to be granted. I wasn't disappointed.

So it was with a sense of keen anticipation when John Scott-Morgan, Pen and Sword's commissioning editor, asked me to write a series of books about the LNER with particular reference to the lives and work of its three CMEs. I could, without fear of criticism, allow my fascination with their work to absorb me, which it has for two years whilst these books were being written.

During this process, I was given much help by staff at the National Railway Museum, the National Archives and the Institution of Mechanical Engineers. To everyone involved in these invaluable places I give my thanks. But there were many others who played a part in this book. In particular I must mention Dorothy 'Pat' Mather, who was married to Arthur Peppercorn and became his widow in 1951; Pat died in 2015. She was happy to share memories of her late husband and always promoted his work in such a positive way. Then there is Richard Hardy, who knew some of the key characters described and was very open, balanced and honest in his assessments of their work and personalities.

Peppercorn A1 Pacific No. 60149, *Amadis*, which became the author's favourite after a chance encounter with engine and crew in the summer of 1962. (*THG*)

No list would be complete without my old friends Jack Constantine and David Neal. Jack, who lives in New Jersey, knows a great deal about railway history, particularly in his own country and happily shares this knowledge and the material he has acquired over many years. In the Fifties and Sixties, when so much was being destroyed, David collected many unique items relating to the LNER, including a number of Edward Thompson's albums and papers and material relating to Arthur Peppercorn. He sent me copies of these and gave me permission to use them as I saw fit. To this can be added the efforts of my late uncle, Ronald Hillier. He spent nearly forty years doing the same thing as David and continued seeking material up to his death in 1984. He also met or corresponded with many who were part of the LNER's history and could add interesting details to the story. Sadly, this didn't include either Thompson or Peppercorn, but, by luck, he did harness Bert Spencer's thoughts on some matters. In due course, everything my uncle and I have collected will be donated to Search Engine at York so that others can make use of this material.

Last, but not least, is the Watts family, who have carefully traced their family's history, which highlighted and recorded much of Arthur Peppercorn's life and background. My thanks to them and especially to Peter Watts, who gave me permission to use this material.

In producing photographs for this book, preservation work has been necessary. In some cases their sepia finish, foxing and dilapidated condition could not be entirely overcome. However, because they are often rare pictures or have some historic significance they have been included despite their condition. I hope this doesn't spoil your enjoyment of the book.

All things must pass. In early 1964 A1 Pacific No. 60147, *North Eastern*, was found at York in a cold state. From here she was shortly to be condemned and sold for scrap. Stripped of her nameplate, but still with a tender full of coal, presumably so that she can substitute for another engine should it fail, she still looks impressive. The tragedy of steam's demise was the destruction of so many locomotives with decades of effective life left in them. (*THG*)

PROLOGUE

Arthur Peppercorn sits for an official photograph in the 1940s. In this candid shot he looks uncomfortable and unamused. One might be forgiven for thinking that he possessed a difficult, if not truculent personality from his expression. Clearly no one reaches the position of eminence in any industry as he did without being able to exercise authority effectively and, at times, ruthlessly. Yet he appears to have done so with good grace and an understanding of human nature. In fact, when reading accounts of his life and career it is difficult, if not impossible, to find a harsh word said against him. Such a man is worthy of closer study to understand how it is possible to run a huge and demanding business successfully without rancour or unnecessary conflict. *(PR/RH)*

The London and North Eastern Railway existed for twenty-five years and in that time had only three Chief Mechanical Engineers. First came Gresley, who dominated the scene for eighteen years with considerable success. Then came Edward Thompson, inheriting a chalice poisoned by war and lack of opportunities, but also a sense of expectation promoted by Gresley's many triumphs. Despite all the problems he faced, Thompson still moved the LNER forward during his five years in charge, though he received little credit for his achievements in the years that followed. With nationalisation facing Britain's railways, Arthur Peppercorn became CME and in the few years left to him probably enjoyed far less freedom than Thompson, let alone Gresley. Despite this, he set to with great purpose and sought to improve the locomotives he had inherited. At a time of such uncertainty and change this showed a determination to take steam technology to its limit. But there was little time left to do so and in very short order the LNER was swallowed up by British Railways and their distinctive flavour was consumed by the mass. Very quickly, individual identities of all the railway companies began to disappear, surrendered to a new corporate brand and a search for rationalisation and standardisation. Soon Peppercorn, and many other champions of the 'Big Four', would also disappear, choosing to leave before all they had worked so hard to achieve was swept away in the pursuit of a political principle.

Looking back, one wonders where Peppercorn might have taken locomotive design if, for example, he had succeeded Gresley in 1941 or earlier? Given many more years as CME would he have followed a similar path to the master or taken the route followed by Thompson? It is a moot point, because so much that happened post-Gresley was driven by the war and concerns expressed by the General Manager and the Running Department over the deteriorating state of many Gresley locomotives. For the actions he took, Thompson has been roundly criticised for destroying a legacy out of spite, at worst, or from incompetence, at best. And those who have expounded this view then seem to have concluded that all would have been different under Peppercorn. Although an interesting thought, it is one that can never be developed to any great extent because it hangs on the belief that Thompson's work was ill-conceived, unnecessary and ultimately a failure; three conclusions which available evidence does little to confirm and probably deny.

To a certain extent, any company moves in a new direction each time its leader changes. Emphasis may be re-directed, and this will be overlaid by the influence of fluctuating market forces. Quite quickly, a policy followed with some success over many years may become redundant or seem misplaced. This is nowhere

A1 Pacific No. 60120, *Kittiwake*, at speed in the early 1960s, the driver and photographer exchanging glances. In a few short years the familiar sights, sounds and smells of this world will all be gone. (*THG*)

more apparent than in the railway industry. Gresley was lucky to manage at a time when there was greater freedom to experiment and invent, leaving a substantial legacy in the process. But neither Thompson or Peppercorn enjoyed this freedom or patronage so their efforts were muted by comparison and, consequently, their design credentials could not really be tested or improved. So, it is inappropriate, even unfair, to compare the achievements of these three men. Much better to judge them as engineers and leaders by their achievements in the circumstances in which they found themselves. And here we must remember all Thompson and Peppercorn's contributions before becoming CME. Both men spent decades in the giant shadow cast by Gresley, but these were hardly wasted years. They achieved much of substance in this period which added greatly to their leader's legend.

No one person in such a vast industry can be solely responsible for success. However, to the leader will go the credit for steering an organisation to glory, but so will criticism and brickbats for any failures. Yet behind them sit many others whose contribution may be anonymous and rarely glimpsed, but are, nevertheless, essential to the group's success. In volume one of my LNER books, I argued that Gresley could not have achieved all he did without the intelligent and dedicated support of many others. From men such as Robert Thom, Arthur Stamer, Oliver Bulleid, Bert Spencer, Tom Street, Francis Wintour and more, Gresley drew great strength. They were a team of specialists who could take his often sketchy ideas and turn them into reality. They were only the tip of an iceberg that contained many thousands of people who contributed in varying degrees to the success of each project.

Thompson and Peppercorn were also key players in this tale, each contributing in no small way to the LNER's story before becoming CME. But they did so from a variety of positions and locations, gaining in seniority and experience as they progressed to the top. Throughout this period, they became thoroughly

A peaceful scene at Newcastle in the late 1950s as a Gresley Pacific and a Peppercorn A2, both with 'Queen of Scots' headboards, pause. Neither smokebox number plate is visible so the names are not known. Even in this limited view of both engines, it is interesting to compare their designs and appreciate the evolutionary nature of the work that took place between the 1920s and 1940s. (*THG*)

Towards the end of steam as the mass cull of numbers quickly took hold it was a joy to find an engine in good condition ready to be steamed if required – sometimes with its nameplate still attached. This was just such a case with engine No. 60156, *Great Central*, which for the last year of her life operated from York. On 10 May 1965, she was condemned and scrapped by Clayton and Davie of Dunston, a yard near Gateshead more used to cutting up ships, but took the opportunity to take a number of BR's locomotives to provide fill-in work for its employees. (*THG*)

conversant with all aspects of the CME's work, except in the specifics of locomotive design. They sat beside the experts in this field, even managed their 'pay and rations', but neither worked in a drawing office for any length of time or gained the skills of these specialists. So only when reaching the pinnacle of their careers did they truly exercise authority in this field of endeavour. Undoubtedly they had gained a broad appreciation of this work and sought some more direct involvement, but it was, more often than not, deemed to be a subject that was the sole province of Gresley, his technical assistants and draughtsman. We have seen in volume two how Thompson dealt with these issues and the many challenges he faced. Now it is Peppercorn's turn.

Today, he is best remembered for his three years as CME even though his career before that was one of great substance. So it is important to take his life as a whole, consider events and influences, unwrap and analyse his experiences and opportunities to assess the completeness of his achievements. It is important to do this, because locomotive design was only one part of his job and his accomplishments. Beyond that there is much more to evaluate and understand if we are to see him clearly as a highly skilled leader and engineer.

For Gresley, Thompson and Peppercorn there are a number of locomotive memorials that still grace Britain's preservation movement. They don't have the grime or hard worked look of their heyday and they

Tornado, the final A1 Pacific, which was completed in 2008, working hard on the long rising slope from Westbury Station on the way to Salisbury. Always a pleasure to see and a fitting memorial to Peppercorn and his talented team of engineers. (*THG*)

have no other purpose than to pull those wishing to experience a time which many could not possibly have known. It is only an echo with little to truly evoke the world they served. But despite this tenuous link I am still glad to see them, a reminder of my early years and all that is gone. Hopefully this book and its companion volumes may capture more than the fleeting passage of a preserved or newly built LNER Pacific as it slips by.

CHAPTER 1

BORN TO BE AN ENGINEER

The direction in which any life evolves is influenced by nature, nurture and opportunity. Without intelligence, hard work, enduring support, a strong character, sound education and good luck, success can prove elusive. Arthur Peppercorn was blessed with all of these elements and much more. His life followed a path which took him from a cloistered and fairly privileged background to one of eminence in a field as far removed from his background as it was possible to get. Being the son of a classics scholar and the vicar of St Luke's Church in Herefordshire, with older brothers who also became ministers, he might have been expected to follow a similar path. Yet from an early age he seems to have embraced the world of engineering and railways, though few, if any, could possibly have guessed where this fascination would lead him.

The late Victorian era into which he was born is so distant to us now to have become a 'foreign country', where 'they do things differently' as L.P. Hartley declared in his book *The Go-Between*. Now it is hard to imagine lives spent without a welfare safety net, other than the work house, and few civil liberties or employment rights. In fact, you would have been lucky to have a job capable of sustaining the most basic level of subsistence, let alone produce a surplus. Such was the parlous state of most lives at that time, each social blemish being accepted without universal condemnation. And yet there were signs of change – albeit a microcosm of what would follow in the next century – and these were mirrored by Peppercorn's life and career. Womens' suffrage was slowly finding a voice and employers were being challenged over poor pay and working conditions by a small but growing number of increasingly resolute workers. Yet in both cases these efforts tended to be fragmented, poorly planned and met by a ruthless response from employers and the state. Yet these reformers wouldn't be assuaged and, in time, political will would underpin these campaigns allowing progress to be made towards a fairer society. The Victorian ruling class saw this as an unnecessary erosion of the obedience they had come to expect, whilst the mass sensed their own rights finally being recognised.

Arthur Peppercorn stands behind his mentor and friend, Herbert Nigel Gresley. When this picture was taken in the 1920s Gresley was CME of the LNER and at the peak of his powers, whilst the younger man, and heir apparent, was just beginning his rise to the top. (*LJ*)

At the time of Arthur Peppercorn's birth, these struggles were just beginning to make their mark. During November 1887, a protest in London against unemployment in Britain and the suspension of civil rights in Ireland resulted in a mixed police and army force being used to control demonstrators. The ensuing melee led to numerous serious casualties and 400 or so arrests with more unrest and civil disobedience following as protestors slowly found their voice. These took the form of mass demonstrations that now began to focus on specific issues involving a single employer. This was the case in

1888, when staff at the Bryant and May Match factory, in Bow, London, withdrew their labour over poor working conditions and pay, compounded by the levy of punitive fines for minor transgressions or missed targets.

Theirs was a victory of sorts, with improvements in working conditions being achieved and the system of fines abolished. More importantly, a grievance procedure was established allowing employees to seek some redress. In so doing, this protest established a model that would slowly spread and grow across British industries. However, the working environment at Bow still left a lot to be desired, even by the standards of the age, but Bryant and May's workers had shone a light on many common employment abuses. In this way, they highlighted the need for change and the strength and potency of organised resistance. It was movement that grew, slowly and inexorably, creating industrial democracy and the health and safety legislation we have come to accept as a natural part of our working lives today. A major strike a year later by dock workers, seeking a minimum wage of 6d per hour, strengthened this movement and led to the formation of stronger trade unions.

The drivers for social and political advance could come in many forms though. This was nowhere more apparent than on the railways and 1889 contained an event which had a long term impact on the way a largely un-regulated industry was operated. In the explosion of new lines that marked the nineteenth century, before boom turned to bust, safety was often compromised for profit. Without a basic level of regulation, and a Railway Inspectorate lacking the power to order change, many companies skimped on safety and accidents were frequent and casualties, amongst workers and passengers, excessive. All this came to a head on 12 June at Armagh in Ireland when a heavily overloaded train stalled on a steep incline. It was decided to divide the load and take the first five carriages forward, leaving the ten cars in the rear section resting on their non-automatic vacuum brakes. Sadly, this was insufficient to hold this portion of the train which rolled back down the hill colliding with an oncoming locomotive killing 80 and injuring another 260 in the process.

Faced with clear evidence of poor safety standards, the Board of Trade took action to implement change. In August that year, parliament passed into law the Regulation of Railways Act which is now considered to be the moment that ushered in the modern era of rail safety. 1889 wasn't the pinnacle of this work but it was certainly a key point in the process.

It was into this rapidly changing Britain that Arthur entered on 29 January 1889, the tenth child of Alfred and Agnes Peppercorn. It was a country dominated by industrial might and a sense of Empire that would shape his career and in which he would play a significant part. Yet by the end of his life, all that had become familiar and all he had striven to achieve was being swept away by the sacrifice of two world wars and the strongest desire for social change. The slow haemorrhage of power and prestige, the loss of wealth and the growing strength of foreign markets ensured that a position of pre-eminence was forfeited. The Victorian ideals which Peppercorn had been born to accept as a right were indeed hard to give up and his life mirrored this decline.

The Peppercorn family were firmly rooted in the middle class. Arthur's paternal grandfather, William, was a solicitor who practiced in St Neots, Cambridgeshire, and was sufficiently wealthy to allow his four children to receive an education well above the norm for the time. This allowed the studious Alfred, who was born in 1851, to attend Uppingham School then study the Classics at Jesus College Cambridge. He then followed his two older brothers into the Church of England, attending Gloucester College in 1875 from where he was ordained as a deacon two years later, soon moving to the parish of Crudwell in Wiltshire. It was here that he married Agnes Ann Watts, the eldest child of Thomas and Ann Watts and two years later, in 1879, the first of their fourteen children was born.

Agnes Watts was the eldest child of Anglo-Australian parents and was born in Queensland during 1855. Her father, John, hailed from Gloucestershire and her mother, Jane, from Ipswich, Queensland. They married in 1855 and Agnes arrived in the same year, the first of their five children – three girls and two boys. The last of these, William, was born in 1863, but sadly, Jane died two weeks later, presumably as a result of complications arising from the pregnancy. Three years later John took a new wife, Caroline Sparkes, who had been recently widowed herself.

Of all Arthur's ancestors, John Watts is perhaps the most intriguing. He seems to have had a strong entrepreneurial spirit which led him down many interesting paths. The son of Thomas Watts, a surgeon, and Ann, he was brought up in Frampton and educated in Paris and

St Luke's Church Stoke Prior as it appears today. In the 1890s, it was the centre of Arthur Peppercorn's life, his father, Alfred, being the rector of the parish. With a population of only 450 or so people, this farming community was a place of peace and apparent calm, but this didn't reflect the social upheaval in Britain at that time. The interior of the church is little changed from the days in which Agnes Peppercorn, her numerous children and servants worshipped and watched Alfred preach from this pulpit. Only two Peppercorns appear to be buried in the churchyard, John, one of Arthur's older brothers, and his wife. Many more lie in nearby Leominster. (*THG*)

Stoke Prior's Rectory in 2019 framed by long established trees and rolling fields leading down to the centre of the village and St Luke's Church beyond. Here Arthur, and some of his siblings, were born. It isn't hard to imagine the children playing in the house, adjacent stables and surrounding grounds of this idyllic estate. The railway between Leominster and Hereford lies a mile or so to the east. (*THG*)

John Watts, Arthur Peppercorn's dynamic and entrepreneurial grandfather, and his daughter Agnes shortly before her marriage to Alfred Peppercorn. (*WF*)

then Bath in Somerset. In 1842, at the age of 21, he travelled to Australia on an unspecified business venture in which he lost £500, forcing a return home. Not deterred by this, and with his father's support, he tried again in 1847 this time with more success as a 'pastoralist' working on Felton Station in Queensland breeding sheep and cattle in large numbers. Here he would remain until 1868, becoming a local magistrate in the process and being elected to the Queensland Parliament which was formed in 1860. Along the way, he acquired 40,000 acres that quickly grew in value as prices boomed, plus considerable wealth, developing business interests in both Germany and Britain in the process. And so his rise continued, but the call of his home country remained a strong one and in 1868 he sold some of his assets and returned to Britain, living in Gloucestershire with his family. It was here ten years later that Agnes met and then married Alfred Peppercorn.

Undoubtedly John's wealth cascaded down to his children, allowing them to lead comfortable lives. With Alfred and Agnes producing fourteen children, nine girls and five boys, between 1879 and 1894, only supported by a country parson's 'living' for income, her father's assistance would prove invaluable and probably ensured that their sons, at least, received better education.

As the family grew in size, Alfred was appointed to different parishes. From Crudwell the family moved to Ashmansworth in Hampshire in 1879, East Woodhay a year later and then Stoke Prior in Herefordshire, a parish which included Docklow. Here Alfred remained until his death in 1908 at the comparatively young age of 56 and his youngest child only 14. It was at the Rectory in Stoke Prior that Arthur Henry was born.

With three older brothers and five older sisters, the sixth having died in 1880 when only three months old, life wouldn't have been dull, but as the children of a rector their behaviour would have been moderated in respect of their father's position. With a mother spending most of their young lives pregnant, their care would have fallen to domestic staff. In 1891 this consisted of a nurse, a housemaid, two nursemaids and a page, their wages met, or so it seems, by the Church and by John Watts, until his death in Dorset during 1902. Agnes then inherited £2,500 from her father and this must have helped considerably in the upkeep of such a large family. Nevertheless, funds must have been tight at times and would have required some economies as a later event would suggest.

A scene Arthur Peppercorn would have known well as he grew up – Stoke Prior captured in a postcard of the time. (*THG*)

The children's early education seems to have been managed at home, records not revealing if they attended any local schools, state or otherwise until they were older. It was not unusual for this to happen at that time, social status often being preserved by establishing a degree of separation. There may also have been doubts about the standard of education that local schools could offer and also the broader question of health. Then and now the closed environment of a school can be an incubator for many illnesses. But in the late nineteenth century this list included many 'killers' unknown in this country today – smallpox, cholera and typhoid amongst them, with the ever present danger of tuberculosis also close by. When joining the Institution of Mechanical Engineers in 1912, Arthur recorded that he attended a 'Private School between 1897 and 1901', though gave no other details about the school – location or curriculum.

It is hard to say how well Arthur's primary education prepared him for the future, but it would inevitably have included reading, writing and arithmetic. Depending upon the ability of his tutors, subject matter may well have extended to Latin, a foreign language and the natural world. At the same time, his father probably provided instruction in the Classics and religion to supplement and broaden their outlook on life. However, a general scientific education was not common then, engineering, in particular, still struggling to achieve wider recognition in this post-Industrial Revolution world. But even though Stoke Prior and Herefordshire were rural communities, still largely untouched by the upheaval caused by this revolution, the growth of the railways brought a sense of these changes to the countryside. By the 1890s, an active network existed covering much of this area and linking it with the rest of Britain. However, Stoke Prior didn't enjoy its own station on the Leominster to Bromyard Railway until 1929, and so villagers had to walk two or so miles to the nearest station at Leominster if they wished to catch a train. In the year before Arthur was born, this company was taken over by the Great Western. So, as he grew up their engines would have become a common sight and featured large in his life, especially when attending Hereford Cathedral School between 1901 and 1905.

For someone who would submerge himself in the railway industry and rise to such a high position, it is probable that the fascination began early. He left no word to describe the reasons for his growing interest, but Walter Bentley, who was born in 1888 and would soon be a fellow engineering apprentice at Doncaster, did. It is probably true to say that both men experienced the same awakening. In his 1958 autobiography, Bentley wrote:

'In 1904 I had no time at all for the motor car. It was the locomotive that held my devoted love . . . The sight of one of Patrick Stirling's eight foot singles could move me profoundly. Ever since I had been conscious that the world was full of these great roaring masterpieces of engineering . . . They filled my dreams and ambitions.

'My toys matched my interests, with a strong bias towards the mechanical. I had a magnificent stationary steam engine . . . Then there was a clockwork train set, probably crude by present day standard, but I remember it as reliable and well made.

'My friend Geoffrey Thornhills was a train fiend too We spent hours together. Both our bedrooms were lined with copies of the Railway Magazine and railway books and on the walls were photographs and paintings of locomotives. We were utterly single-minded.

'In my bicycle I had the means to express this longing [for independent travel], and the fact that I usually made a dead set for the nearest railway line to watch trains is by the way.'

One can imagine Peppercorn undergoing the same awakening and one wonders how his family, particularly his father, viewed this emerging passion. A good parent would nurture such an interest as a way of encouraging intellectual curiosity, so aiding their general education. However, they might not wish to see such a hobby dominate adult life to the exclusion of other options. Alfred, as a Cambridge graduate, would probably have felt this way and hoped attendance at senior school would open Arthur's mind to other possibilities. If so, he might have been disappointed.

By the time Arthur entered Hereford Cathedral School, his older brothers had already established a strong family connection there. At this stage, the school was still a long way from being the major establishment it would become later in the century and in some ways it was struggling for its very existence, which was surprising given its long history. Through available records its antecedents can be traced back to the fourteenth century, though it had undergone a number of incarnations over

Part of Hereford Cathedral School in November 2019, much of it is little changed from when Arthur Peppercorn was in attendance there during the early years of the twentieth century. (THG)

The school crest with its distinctive colours – gold and dark blue – which also adorned the boys' blazers. (THG)

When Arthur Peppercorn arrived at Hereford Cathedral School its life was dominated by Headmaster William Henry Murray Ragg who was also the son of a vicar. Under his guiding hand numbers revived and the curriculum underwent change, although science subjects remained a minor part of the syllabus. (*THG*)

the years. By the mid-1890s it was struggling to attract 100 or so boys as boarders or day boys and wasn't in the 'top drawer' as far as public schools were concerned. Fees were essential for its continued existence but so was a sizeable contribution from the Ecclesiastical Commission each year. To try and sustain growth and ensure survival the school embraced change and in 1898 recruited a new Headmaster – William Ragg. Like Alfred Peppercorn he was a Classics scholar.

During the years since graduation in 1884 he had risen quickly through the ranks and when chosen to lead Hereford School was already a headmaster in Great Yarmouth. However, his arrival coincided with a low point in the school's life when it could only boast 72 pupils and was struggling to maintain academic standards. Change was inevitable and embraced all aspects of school life. By 1901, this included a new Preparatory School and a move to external examinations and validation, so that it could seek to attain higher educational standards and be measured against other public schools. In due course, this meant that Arthur's academic achievements would be assessed by Oxford University in their Higher and Lower examinations. These were deemed to be the best preparation for university or a career, many professions recognising these tests as an effective way of gauging suitability. By these and other means, Ragg slowly restored the school's fortunes and the number of pupils crept up to 118 during 1902.

However, the curriculum, although slowly improving, still focussed heavily on languages, which took up half the lessons, plus mathematics and scripture. Science remained on the periphery of school activity. Chemistry did slide into the syllabus with a minimal amount of time being assigned to it, increasing to two half sessions each week by 1904. For boys such as Arthur, to whom science seemed to be a natural outlet, this was a serious omission. Sadly for him a critical review, undertaken by the Oxford and Cambridge Board in 1905, highlighted this deficiency and by 1908 advances were being made. Despite this, the general attitude towards these subjects was probably best summed up by Ragg himself when he wrote, 'We have no facilities for the subject [science], no one qualified to teach it and very few boys interested in pursuing it.' And later he added in a speech:

> 'There is perhaps one point in which the Cathedral School has not yet fulfilled its duty and that was in regard to scientific teaching, but we hope to do more than we are doing which is practically nothing. For my own part, I hold very strong views on the relative value of Science and Languages as a means of education, and in giving the latter preference, I find I am upheld in this opinion by Sir William Anson, President of the Board of Education.'

This is a strange contradiction, especially in a rapidly industrialising world on the cusp of huge scientific developments. Luckily, all schools were not this backwards and were at least taking some steps to broaden their curriculum. They had begun to realise that some children had skills and development needs not met by the classics or the arts. In this, both Herbert Gresley and Edward Thompson were much luckier and better served by

Hereford as it appeared when Arthur Peppercorn attended the cathedral school. The lower photograph shows the city's railway station which would have featured in his life as he commuted back and forth to Stoke Prior. With his growing interest in engineering and the railways this must have been a magnet for the young man. At Hereford he would have seen an array of GWR locomotives operating. Today, the ground in front of the station is covered by a Morrison's superstore and car park but the station buildings would still be recognisable to Peppercorn. (*THG*)

attending Marlborough College, which, by the standards of the age, was a far more progressive seat of learning.

So during his time at Hereford, Arthur Peppercorn faced a regime that little understood his developing engineering interests and did little more than provide him with a rather basic, lopsided education. There may have been some compensating factors though, with sport and an active Combined Cadet Force providing an outlet for the boys' energies. Participation in both these activities was compulsory and, as far as the CCF was concerned, gave boys a grounding in military matters that the Great War would soon begin to exploit more fully.

Discipline in most schools at this time was harsh and a system of corporal punishment sat at its core. In this Hereford was little different. By any standards, this was a brutal and unnecessary regime, based on a misguided concept that beatings for the slightest misdemeanour created strong character. As Ragg himself stated at Speech Day in 1898, 'The training of character was more important than the training of the mind.'

As always, fair treatment tends to lead to a measured and positive response, cruelty either cowers or breeds resentment. For many this bitterness lasted for the rest of their lives as a near contemporary of Arthur Peppercorn, Kingsley Martin, who became a noted journalist, recalled in his book *Father Figures*:

'The Headmaster solemnly read out a list of boys who had done particularly well, and of others whose inattention, stupidity, bad work or other form of wickedness could only be expatiated by an exemplary whipping. They were sent to his study and came back rubbing themselves . . . It was an absurd method of reforming boys.'

And in speaking of the general standard of education they received he recalled that:

'No boy was expected to be concerned with Music or the Arts, or Politics or the world round us (the science lessons only provided comic relief). We were bored beyond belief . . . We ragged when we dared and dozed when we could.'

The state of this school led to him being moved to Mill Hill School in London by his parents, to which he was

The Hereford Combined Cadet Force during its annual camp on the Isle of Man in 1903 which the 14-year-old Arthur Peppercorn attended (details on the back of the photograph suggest that he is the boy in the back row second from the right). (*THG*)

awarded a scholarship, and then went on to Magdalene College Cambridge.

With their sons passing through public school, and with the cost of their daughters' education to bear, Alfred and Agnes must have struggled to meet all their commitments, even with support. The problems they faced were highlighted in 1901 when their sons, John and Walter, contracted measles at school. Without a sick bay in which they could be isolated and allowed to recover, both boys were shipped home, where their siblings would, no doubt, have been infected too. Alfred, quite reasonably, sought a reduction of their fees for the term, a request that Ragg rejected. His actions resulted in a complaint to the school's governing body which also proved unsuccessful. It seems unlikely that Alfred would have pursued this course of action if his finances had not been stretched.

When Arthur's turn came to consider the future, university does not seem to have been an option pursued for reasons that are not clear. He may have lacked the academic prowess necessary for such a step or may simply have expressed a wish to pursue a career where a university education was not required. At this stage, science subjects were probably better managed at some universities than public schools, but were, nevertheless, still in an early stage of development. In any event, it was common at the time for industry to meet its ever-growing need for skilled workers by the application of apprenticeship schemes, supported by attendance at local technical colleges where necessary. So for the less gifted students an alternative route into a worthwhile career existed and became greatly valued for that reason.

When considering Arthur's academic achievements, it is interesting to note that when applying for membership of IMechE he simply confirmed a period of attendance at Hereford Cathedral School and lists no examination successes. And yet he offers a wider description of attainments whilst undergoing an apprenticeship with the Great Northern Railway. One conclusion drawn from this is that his performance in the Oxford Lower Exams didn't pass muster. A career in railway engineering would, in the circumstances, have been a good alternative and appears to have been the young man's preferred choice anyway, fitting in nicely with his interests.

It is rumoured, but not confirmed, that his choice of a career caused mild friction between him and his father.

If so, it isn't difficult to understand why. Having been a classics scholar, then a man of the cloth, and having committed himself to the expense of supporting a child through public school, an apprenticeship may have seemed to be a retrograde step. This is a view more easily understood by looking at the fifteen or so boys in Arthur's year at school and the paths they followed. Quite a number went to university and few then entered the church. Two, Wilfred Askwith and Harry Ragg, in fact became bishops. Another boy, Richard Symonds-Tayler, joined the Royal Navy and became an admiral and John Richards rose to become a senior civil servant. Only two of Arthur's fellow pupils appear to have taken a scientific route. Geoffrey Marr Vevers trained to be a doctor at St Thomas's in London, saw service in the Great War with the Royal Army Medical Corps, then became a specialist in tropical medicine before moving into the field of zoology. Arthur Zimmerman studied at Birmingham University and was granted a Bowen Scholarship in 1913 to research more deeply some unspecified aspect of engineering.

With the end of school in sight, a choice about Arthur's future was unavoidable. He could have delayed this decision and stayed on at Hereford for another two years in the Sixth Form, but there would have been little point in doing this if academically he was struggling. So it remained only to choose a suitable place to train as an engineer and there were a considerable number of railway companies offering apprenticeships, with those at Swindon, Crewe, Derby and Doncaster being amongst the most prized. For some, like Walter Bentley, who had failed to find his academic feet at Clifton College in Bristol, the choice was an easy one. 'My governess had a nephew who was an apprentice at Doncaster. This fact, plus my loyalty to Yorkshire and the Great Northern, settled Doncaster for me by the time I was eight.'

No records seem to exist that describe the thought process within the Peppercorn household when choosing a suitable billet for Arthur. One can only assume that he had a voice in these discussions, may have visited a number of companies to see for himself what they offered and chose the GNR for sound practical reasons. Luckily, his family had sufficient funds to sponsor a Premium Apprenticeship and this, coupled to an education higher than the norm for the time, made him an attractive proposition for any company to recruit. The only problems that remained would have been passing an interview with Henry Ivatt, the GNR's Locomotive Superintendent, under whom he would study, experiencing separation from his family and then gradually acclimatising to this new life. However, five years away at a tough public school may have sharpened his sense of self-sufficiency and made this move less traumatic. Nevertheless, it was still a considerable jump from the 'protected' world of home and school to the cut and thrust of heavy industry where inner steel and toughness were essential for survival. From the few accounts that still exist it seems that Arthur had these qualities and was eager for the challenge that lay ahead.

On the eve of his departure to Doncaster, Peppercorn's father presented him with a third edition copy of Charles Bowen Cooke's 1893 book *British Locomotives*. Bowen Cooke was the London and North Western Railway's CME and a man of some standing in the industry whose views and thoughts carried authority. Such a thoughtful and personal gift from father to son, with its inscribed 'best wishes my son for your future', speaks of deep affection but also a desire to see him succeed in his chosen career. If he harboured any doubts about Arthur's choice, he kept them to himself once the commitment was made.

When Arthur moved to Doncaster he would have found a town dwarfed by the presence of the railway. The works were a major employer in the area and also a significant visual presence in the town's landscape, along with churches and the extensive workhouse in Springwell Lane, its dominating presence providing an ever present reminder of the price of failure or destitution in a society with few safety nets.

Accommodation for premium apprentices was found in digs usually within a short distance of the works. Peppercorn lived in a house on Bennetthorpe, according to the few surviving records of this period of his life, so only had a short walk or tram ride to work each day. He also had the town centre close by, but as Walter Bentley

Doncaster in the early years of the twentieth century and the sights that would have become familiar to Peppercorn as he found his way around the town and settled into his new life there. (*THG*)

later recalled this wasn't necessarily a good thing, if someone was seeking excitement:

> 'The gaiety and glitter of the Empire or the Palace [in London] with old friends had the charm after the severity and austerity of Doncaster. I can still remember the sound of the church clocks chiming above the silent streets and the smell of the Don wafting all over the town . . . Doncaster had lived by trains for fifty years. There was little else there but the construction and maintenance works; there were no coal mines huddled around the little town then, and almost everyone was connected with the Great Northern.'

It seems he arrived at the same time as Bentley, who left a detailed account of these early years at Doncaster and the way the company ran their lives. Both were Premium Apprentices and so enjoyed a status not necessarily given to other young men entering this trade. Conversely, any prestige they attracted as paying students would have been balanced by a greater sense of expectation, so hard work and commitment were essential. Bentley wrote:

> 'To be even 30 seconds late was an unforgiveable crime. The Doncaster regime really was a most tough one and you had to be a devoted disciple to survive it. The first session was from 6 to 8.15 am, when there was a break for breakfast; then a four-hour stretch and a final one from 2 to 5.30 pm.
>
> 'On our first morning the new premium apprentices started the day with a brief to-the-point lecture of what was going to happen, given by a nondescript little man. To utter even the curt words of welcome appeared to pain him, and he seemed relieved to pass us over, raw, bewildered and thoroughly intimidated to the first foreman, Treece. From him we received an equally chilly reception and were impressed with the standards of discipline expected of us. "At the Plant, six o'clock means six o'clock" he told us.
>
> 'The formidable Growcock, under whom we were to serve directly, seemed at first, through my seventeen-year-old eyes, to be more a sergeant-major than an under-foreman, and the two and three year apprentices like battle-scarred old campaigners, worldly, knowledgeable and rather frightening. At first I hardly dared to open my mouth when they were around.
>
> 'The purpose of this became clear only after some time . . . To the foreman premium apprentices were mostly 'softies', gently nurtured beings from well-to-do homes. That there would be some material worth developing from among them was a certainty; the difficulty was to discover it, and to save everybody's time, this must be done as quickly as possible.
>
> 'It is no use pretending that there wasn't a barrier between the apprentices – sons of men who had lived all their working life on the GNR – and us. They were paid five shillings a week from the day they started; we paid our way in, a £75 premium for five years slogging, though we did get this back in wages. I was ragged for my accent, even ribbed for being a snob. How you responded was watched carefully; if you came through the barrier dissolved and that was that.

Walter Bentley at the time he and Arthur Peppercorn were serving together at Doncaster as apprentices. Soon after qualifying, Bentley left the railway business to find fame and fortune designing cars and aero engines (in particular the Bentley Rotary that powered the Sopwith Camel). In his book *W.O.* he confirmed his friendship with Peppercorn and described in great detail their lives together with the GNR. (*WB*)

Bennetthorpe as Peppercorn would remember it during his apprenticeship. He lived in digs here. (*THG*)

Newbridge in Doncaster and the ever present influence of the railways. (*THG*)

The sprawling mass of the workshops at Doncaster as they appeared under the LNER's jurisdiction. It had changed little from Peppercorn's time there as an apprentice. (*THG*)

'Later I began to understand not only how to get on with the working man, but also his mind: his pride, his conscientiousness, his loyalty, his attitude to life and his generosity.

'The hierarchy at Doncaster in 1905 was impressive. The Locomotive Superintendent was Henry Ivatt. He had been responsible for the first Atlantic-type locomotives to be built in this country . . . He was tall, thin, much respected but not much liked because of his severity . . . His main quality was his awareness of his own limitations, and because of this he knew he could not afford to make a mistake. This was in the strongest contrast to Nigel Gresley, then Superintendent of the Carriage and Wagon Works and due to succeed Ivatt. He made mistakes, but they were mistakes of a genius and an original creator.'

Bentley then went on to describe day to day life in the Works and the way each apprentice passed through the shops gradually learning a range of skills. Arthur only recorded that in his five years this included 'the Machine, Erecting Shops, &c, plus the Drawing Office'. However, he then added a short description of the extra-curricular activities he undertook as part of his apprenticeship, 'Technical Education: Doncaster Technical School (evening classes) Machine Drawing, Mathematics, Applied Mechs, Steam, &c'. Underpinning all this was direct tuition by Ivatt and Francis Wintour, the Works Manager, and a growing friendship with Oliver Bulleid, who had completed his apprenticeship in the year Arthur arrived, and was appointed assistant to F. Webster, the Locomotive Running Superintendent, shortly afterwards.

Bulleid had forged a very close association with Ivatt when commencing his apprenticeship. In due course he became a family guest and would marry Ivatt's youngest daughter, Marjorie, in 1908. It seems that selected apprentices were also invited as guests by Ivatt and Arthur Peppercorn was one of them. Bentley makes no mention of this happening to him and so one wonders whether Ivatt may have been identifying the most

Doncaster Technical College, which Peppercorn, Bentley and many other apprentices attended, mostly during evenings, came into being during the last quarter of the 19th Century. However, its creation was more a whimper than a bang, its role and influence growing only very slowly over thirty years as the need for further education was gradually realised. The workshops would teach the practical but not the theoretical in great depth, so a gradual investment of time and money sought to overcome this shortcoming. Initially classes were held in drawing and machine construction using the facilities of St James' School (otherwise known as the Great Northern Railway School), which, apparently, was close to St James' Church, otherwise known as the 'Railway Church' due to its close proximity to the Works. It is believed that Peppercorn was a regular attendee at the church. (Top)This picture portrays this area at about the time Peppercorn and Bentley were undergoing training, by then the number of courses offered had expanded considerably and steps were being taken to build a new, larger centre, near St George's Minster (below). This opened in 1915 and serviced the training needs of GNR and then LNER apprentices, including Bert Spencer, for many years. (*THG*)

H.A. Ivatt (left) as he would have appeared to the 1905 intake of apprentices and Herbert Nigel Gresley, seen here posing in his office when promoted to replace Ivatt when he retired in late 1911. (*RH*)

promising students and those likely to rise to senior rank in the company. If so, it was a custom practiced widely then as now.

For these apprentices, attendance at suitable evening classes was deemed compulsory, which for some young men like Walter Bentley, who had struggled academically, could present insurmountable difficulties. Not so Peppercorn, or so it seems. From the first he took to this work and quickly established a sound record of achievement, both practical and theoretical. This may explain why some of his apprenticeship was spent in the Drawing Office at Doncaster under the expert eye of the Chief Draughtsman, William Elwess. Here he would have been actively involved in all the latest tasks and begun to understand more deeply all aspects of locomotive design. No record appears to exist describing his contribution while learning this aspect of his trade, which would have been peripheral at best. However, he would have carefully observed all that went on around him – both practical and managerial – and learnt a great deal from this.

Although most of their training focussed on workshop tasks, it was expected that they would also gain footplate experience at some stage. However, this was restricted somewhat following an accident on 19 September 1906 which claimed thirteen lives. An express train running between King's Cross and Edinburgh, pulled by Atlantic Class engine No. 276, ran through Grantham at too high a speed, missed a 'red' and was derailed by points set against them. On this occasion, the recently widowed 45-year-old driver, Frederick William Fleetwood, was supported

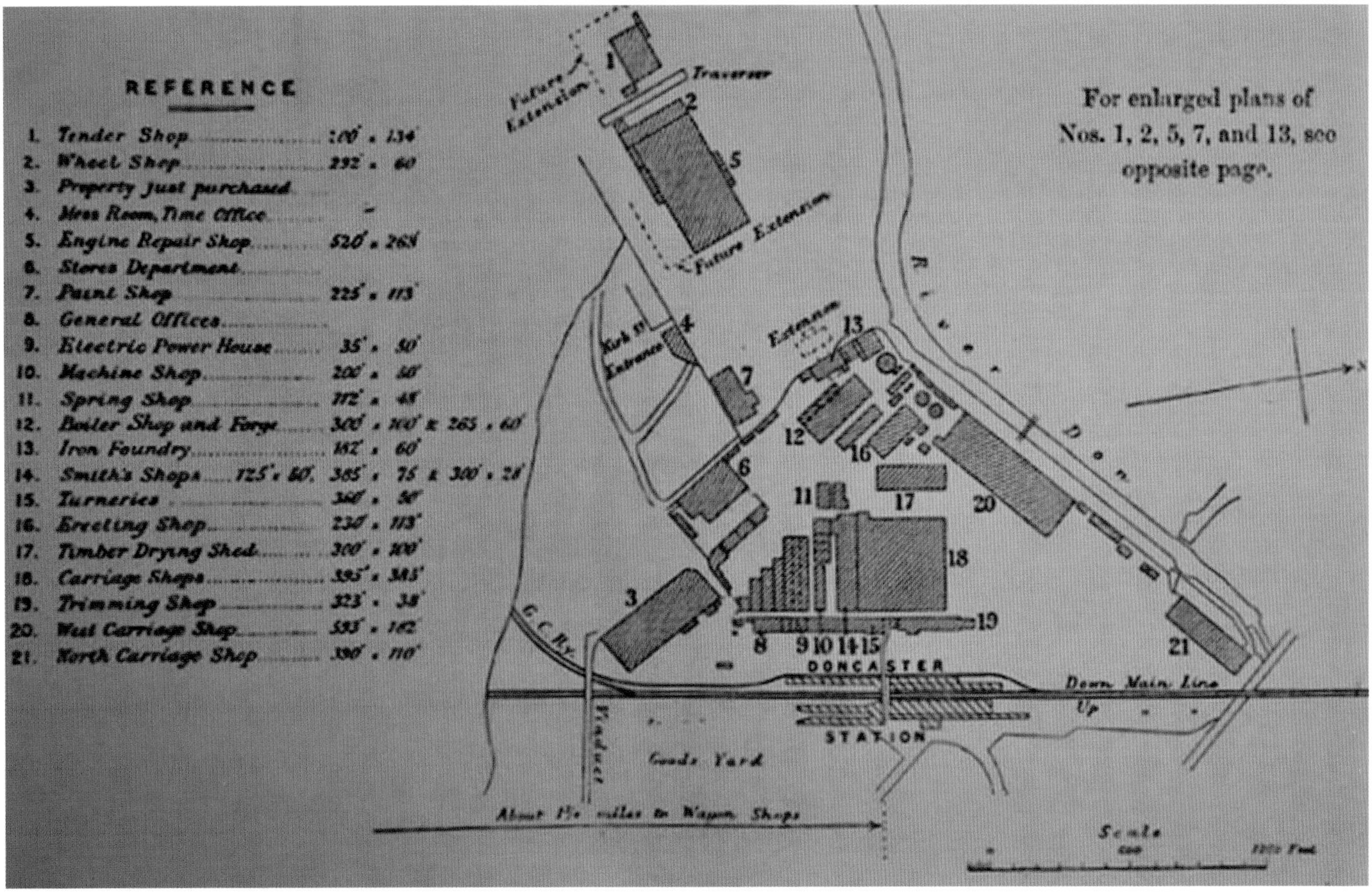

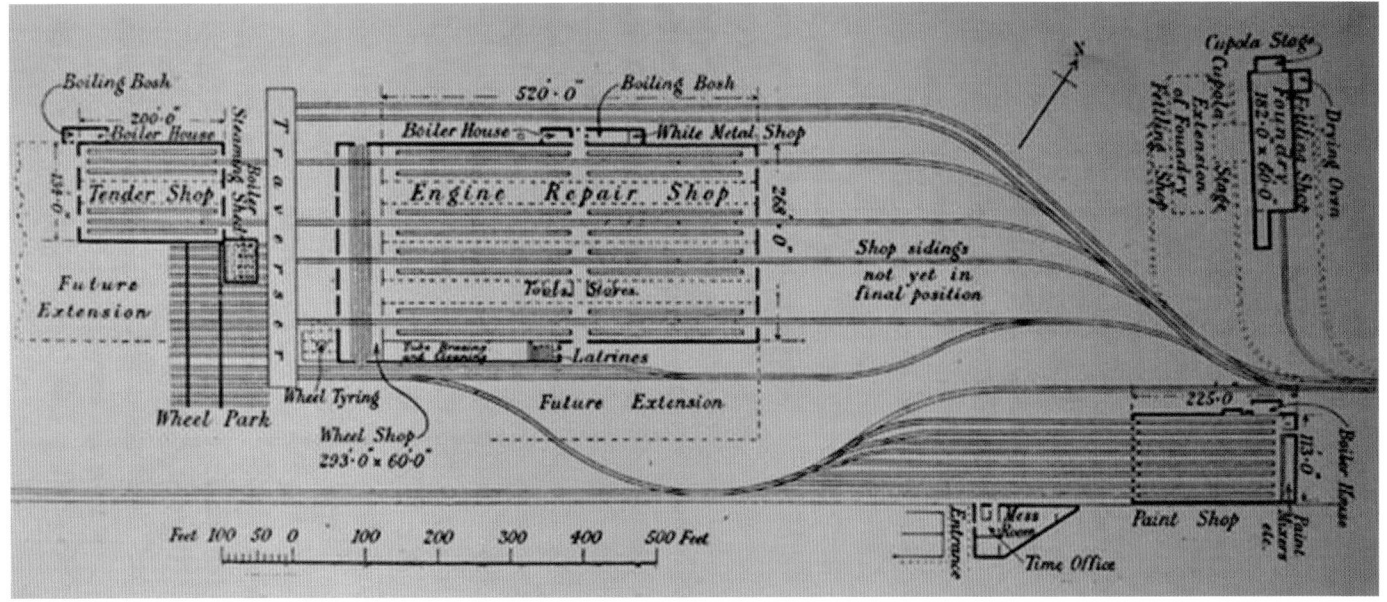

In 1903, a group of IMechE members undertook a tour of engineering workshops in Yorkshire, including Doncaster. To aid their visit the GNR produced a series of drawings and provided a detailed description of the site and the workshops it contained. Two of these are reproduced here. Premium Apprentices, it appears, did not always follow the same route through the workshops during their training. As the course drew to a close there was even a degree of specialisation. In Peppercorn's case this led him to the Drawing Office and a focus on locomotive and rolling stock design. (*RH*)

The sobering results of the Grantham crash on 19 September 1906 in which the driver and fireman were killed. This photo captures engine No. 276 shortly after being salvaged and ready for inspection. In this state the locomotive would have been of great interest to the 1906 intake of apprentices including Peppercorn. The fireman, Ralph Talbot, was a fellow premium apprentice who had completed his time at Doncaster and was undergoing a prolonged period of footplate work. His loss led to a review of this practice and restrictions being placed on young men at this stage in their training. (*ET/DN*)

on the footplate by Ralph Talbot. He was a newly qualified premium apprentice who had become a trainee inspector, however, he was also eligible to act as fireman although was not overly experienced in this role. Both men died in the crash and in their absence the cause of the accident remained a matter of conjecture, although some unconfirmed concerns over Fleetwood's sobriety and health problems came to the fore. In reacting to the Board of Trade's inconclusive investigation and report, the GNR decided to restrict footplate access for young engineering apprentices, as Bentley recalled:

'The disaster made a tremendous impact on us at Doncaster, of course. More experienced men than we argued hotly on the cause . . . The one positive result it had was to prohibit premium apprentices from the footplate except as second fireman.'

Undoubtedly, Peppercorn would have been affected by all this, as was Bulleid, who still talked about the tragedy many years later when CME of the Southern Railway; Talbot had been his contemporary and friend. He is recorded as having been a talented and intelligent engineer who might have risen to senior rank. Even when training, he displayed leadership qualities and had become something of a mentor to the younger men passing through Doncaster, as Bentley recalled years later in several letters. So his loss was both a personal and professional one, and led to a significant reduction in the time apprentices could spend on the footplate studying the end result of all their training.

The GNR at this stage was an active place to be for those wishing to design and construct locomotives. Under Locomotive Superintendents Patrick Stirling, then Henry Ivatt, the company had advanced considerably in engine development as volumes of passenger and goods traffic increased. When serving on the shop floor or in the Drawing Office, Peppercorn would have seen the fruits of their labours as well as the wide variety of locomotives necessary to meet all the railway's commitments. He would have also studied the various magazines and engineering journals available at the time and observed developments elsewhere in this industry. Most notably this would have included the GWR, now under the ever growing influence of George Churchward who became its Chief Mechanical Engineer in 1902. For a trainee it was an exciting time to enter this trade.

In terms of design philosophy, many CMEs and their senior engineers were not always open in recording or discussing their thought processes and few chose to write their memoirs, Ivatt included. Membership of professional institutions was often the only forum for discourse and debate that they exploited. For this reason, guesswork is often our only means of establishing how these men formed and developed their ideas. This is so in Ivatt's case and in June 1900, at a meeting of the IMechE, he came close to defining the factors he thought important in design, the problems faced and possible solutions. As Peppercorn would be under his tutorship at a most impressionable age, Ivatt's words are doubly important, because they suggest how he may have directed his young premium apprentices. In response to a paper on French locomotive practice he is recorded as saying:

> 'The measure of the power of a locomotive is the boiler ... It is no use having large cylinders, and figuring the power of the engine from the cylinders, unless one has a boiler that will keep the cylinders properly supplied.
>
> 'One of the difficulties which locomotive engineers have to deal with is trying to pull very big trains at very high speeds. When a locomotive engineer makes an engine capable of pulling a church, he is at once

Ivatt's first 4-2-2 as it appeared in 1898 (A4 No. 266). This design was a departure from Stirling's 'singles' having its 18 ¼ inch diameter cylinders placed inside the frames. A report written at the time added the information that 'in the matter of boiler power, Mr Ivatt has been more liberal than his predecessor, achieving a heating surface of 1,269.6sqft'. It was a theme he explored further with the A5s when they appeared two years later.

Ivatt's second 4-2-2, No. 267, as it appeared when built in 1900. This was the first of eleven A5s to be constructed. They differed from No. 266 in 'having cylinders 19in. in diameter with balanced valves on top, the movement of the link motion being transferred by means of a rocking shaft. The valves are balanced by strips on the Richardson system, and the exhaust takes place straight through the top . . . this engine also had a deeper frame at the forward end.' (*RH*)

asked to hitch on the school as well. What is required for running heavy fast expresses is to start with an engine of the dray horse type, capable of exerting great tractive force and quickly getting up to about 50 miles per hour; then to take that engine off, and put on another of the quick trotter or high flyer type.

'Of course that is impossible in practice, but it seems to me that the four-cylinder compound, with plenty of adhesive weight, is likely to be the solution of the difficulty. A four-cylinder compound, with a boiler big enough to allow all four cylinders to work by high pressure, not for short distances only, but for many miles when necessary, fitted with a simple arrangement which will allow the engine to be worked at will, might perhaps assist in the direction I have tried to indicate.'

But how far did he take these ideas in practice?

Under Ivatt, the 4-4-2 Atlantic concept was explored to good effect and his years in office saw this class quickly evolve, taking over from his predecessor's successful 'Stirling Single', or 'eight footer' 4-2-2s as they became known. By the time Peppercorn arrived, the 4-2-2s were no longer being built; nevertheless there had been a final flurry of activity between 1898 and 1901 with twelve more being constructed at Doncaster; a single A4 and eleven A5s. In addition to this, Ivatt rebuilt a number of Stirling 4-2-2s when major maintenance became due. His aim here was a simple one – to extend their lives but also to 'extend their spheres of usefulness' as it was described at the time. In essence, these modifications focussed on the provision of new boilers with larger fireboxes capable of generating higher steam pressure. This worked up to a point, but, as a contemporary report put it, 'these fine single-wheelers have for some time been hopelessly outclassed in express work'. And so, in the years before the Great War, the type had become obsolete and were fast being superseded by the Atlantics. However, they would have been a familiar sight to Peppercorn during his apprenticeship and were a type on which he undoubtedly worked as he passed through the workshops learning much in the process about design and evolution. Pushing back boundaries in science is so obvious a requirement that one forgets that it has to be taught and demonstrated. Encouraging a sense of curiosity, so allowing the mind to explore new concepts, is a key part of anyone's education, none more so than in the world of design engineering.

With the 4-2-2s unable to meet increased traffic demands, Ivatt's decision to experiment with the

A scene that would soon become familiar to Peppercorn as he travelled back and forth to Hereford and as his apprenticeship gradually developed – Doncaster Station in the early years of the twentieth century with the Works to one side. (*ET/DN*)

potential contained in the Atlantics is understandable. By this stage, the concept was still in the early stage of development, particularly in the USA where the first tender version was built during 1888 at the Hinkley Locomotive Works in Boston to a design prepared by George Strong. This experimental locomotive was deemed a failure and was soon scrapped, but other models soon followed in the States, Japan and South Africa. But all this work was pre-dated by William Adams, then Locomotive Superintendent of the London and South Western Railway, who designed a 4-4-2 tank engine for the London, Tilbury and Southend Railway for their heavy suburban trains. Construction began in 1880 and continued on until 1898, by which time thirty-six had been built. It proved so popular that other classes – the 37, 51 and 79 – soon followed with thirty-four of all these types being built by 1909. Meanwhile, the LSWR, through Adams, acquired their own 4-4-2Ts in the form of the 415 Class, with 71 being built between 1882 and 1885. However, tank engines were one thing, a tender version was quite another and here Ivatt's work would prove crucial.

Before the Atlantics began appearing, a pressing need for other types of engines dominated his thinking, each reflecting the diverse needs of the GNR's loco fleet. These designs also reflected Ivatt's desire to achieve some standardisation and so benefit from the economies offered by having commonality of parts. Inevitably, this was a long term plan though, dependent upon a company's will to build new engines and having the funds to do so. From the beginning of Ivatt's tenure, the GNR seemed willing to invest and the programme was a substantial one. First came the D2 4-4-0 in 1896, with 51 being built by 1899, then ten E1 2-4-0s, 133 J5 0-6-0 tender engines and then 85 J13 saddle tank engines which all began entering service in 1897. Undoubtedly planning for the 4-4-2s ran alongside these other projects but the first models didn't see the light of day until 1898 and involved both tender and tank engine designs, designated C1 and C2 respectively. In due course, the C1 became the C2 and the C2 was translated to C12 by the LNER and a new C1 appeared.

Over the next few years, Ivatt would take this concept and seek to develop it further, in the process achieving a number of incremental advances in an effort to draw out the design's potential. Whilst he continued to work on other classes and ideas, the Atlantics seem to have become his raison d'être as an engineer and his main attempt at creating a masterpiece by which he might be remembered. For this reason, and for the effect such a development could have on the minds of the young premium apprentices in his care, this is worthy of closer analysis.

The programme of Atlantics with tenders came in a number of phases and resulted in the construction of 116 locomotives, plus 60 tank engines, by the time Peppercorn arrived at Doncaster. The C1 broke this new ground. It had outside 18¾in diameter cylinders, which were set at a slight inclination with 10ft connecting rods which drove the rear 6ft 7½in driving wheels. The boiler was described at the time as being 'of exceptional pattern and dimension', the author adding:

Ivatt's 4-4-2 C1 tender engine and C2 tank engine as they appeared in 1898.

'The barrel, which was pitched with its centre line 7ft 11in above the rail level, measured 14ft 8⅝in in length, with a diameter outside the smallest ring of 4ft 8in. This extreme length, however, was not utilized exclusively for the tube heating surface, as the leading end of the barrel was recessed so as to provide an extension of the smokebox capacity, and this arrangement shortened the length of the tubes to 13ft between the end plates. The tubes were 191 in number. The firebox casing had a length of 8ft and a depth below the centre line of the boiler of 5ft 6in in front and 5ft at the back. These ample measurements allowed the use of a firebox having the very generous heating surface of 140sqft and a grate area of 26.75sqft. The total heating surface equalled 1,442sqft, the tubes contributing 1,302sqft and a working pressure of 175psi was provided.

'In full working order the engine weighs 58 tons. An unusually large tender was provided having a capacity of 3,670 gallons of water and 5 tons of coal . . . It has proved so successful that ten new engines have been built of practically similar size and dimension. It may be interesting to note that Mr Ivatt has placed the regulator in the steam dome, and has reverted from the standard GNR push and pull handle to the two-armed pattern moving across the back of the firebox in a sector plate.'

With the prototype, No. 990, proving successful, ten more C1s were added. As always, a good designer doesn't stand still but continues to develop the concept and Ivatt took the opportunity to refine the idea still further with the next eleven built. Although of the same general dimensions there were a number 'of external points of difference in such detail as the framing at the leading end and a modification of the sanding arrangement'. The engines were also fitted with 'a novel arrangement for locking the reversing gear in any desired position'. In addition, the brake blocks on the tender were positioned at the front of the wheels instead of the back. All small changes, perhaps, but incremental advances nonetheless. Originality and major step changes have their place, but it is a process that has to be governed by a well-developed business sense that balances risk with potential gain. However, Ivatt did begin an experiment in 1901/02 which sought to push back boundaries and experiment with this design concept, which George Bird, a noted railway author, recorded in 1910:

> 'A few years ago almost every locomotive superintendent of note designed a four-cylinder high pressure engine for express traffic, more or less as a protest against the introduction of the compound system, and in 1902 Mr Ivatt built such an engine – No. 271.'

This single locomotive resembled engine No. 990, but the similarities lay on the surface only. The four in line cylinders, each 15in in diameter, directly drove the first pair of coupled wheels. It had piston valves and inside valve gear, a longer smokebox, a 15ft 4¼in boiler barrel containing 141 tubes, a grate area of 24½sqft and weighed 15 cwt more than engine No. 990. However, these changes didn't achieve the improvements in performance Ivatt hoped for though, so he continued to experiment. In 1904, Walschaerts valve gear was fitted

Engine No. 989, the last of the second batch of C1s produced by the GNR in 1903. The differences between the two batches was minor but demonstrated the gradual evolution of design that underpinned the work of good engineers.

Engine No. 271 as designed and in reality. In the lower picture Ivatt (left) and Douglas Marsh, the Works Manager at Doncaster and Ivatt's Chief Assistant, pose for the photographer on the engine's footplate. Marsh's contribution to design and production of new locomotives for the GNR has slipped from view, but was undoubtedly of significance. He left the GNR in 1905 to become Locomotive Superintendent on the London, Brighton and South Coast Railway just as Peppercorn began his apprenticeship. However, the regime he had created absorbed him and directed his training over the next five years.

and in 1908, during a major overhaul, a boiler of the standard 990 class was fitted. With nothing more to be gained from these tests, or so it seems, the locomotive was rebuilt in 1911 to conform to the 990s.

By 1902, with twenty-two of these engines, plus No. 271, in or soon to enter service, the next phase of Ivatt's Atlantic programme was taking shape. And here the words he expressed in 1900, about the need to have a boiler capable of keeping cylinders properly supplied, found a voice. The 990s had been built with sufficient stretch potential to take a bigger boiler and it was an obvious step to take advantage of this flexibility in their design. The first engine when it appeared in December that year caught the attention of the railway world as Bird again recalled eight years later:

'It is to the modern GNR what Mr Stirling's famous 8ft singles were to the same railway's stock of 40 years ago. This noteworthy engine, No. 251, is the prototype of the standard GN express engine of today.

'So far as the general dimensions of cylinders, wheels and length are concerned it is practically the same as No. 990, but it is fitted with a much larger boiler, with a total heating surface of 2,500sqft, and this innovation, which increased the adhesion weight by several tons, has rendered it a far more powerful machine than the earlier engine.'

The boiler barrel consisted of two rings made from ⅝in steel plate and had a total length of 16ft 3⅞in. The section nearest the smokebox was 8ft 6¾in long, with a diameter of 5ft 4¾in, and the other 8ft 1in long and 5ft 6 in diameter. The length of the boiler between tube-plates was 16ft, with a smokebox 5ft 9in long. The firebox was 'a design not hitherto adopted in Great Britain, curving out from the shape of the barrel at top to a wide base resting on the main engine frames . . . In order to clear the driving wheels both the throat-plate and the lower part of the firebox tube-plate were sloped backwards at an appreciable angle. No. 251 weighed considerably more than No. 990

The C1 as developed through the introduction of engine No. 251 in late 1902. The drawing above easily captures the step change created by the larger boiler and the sense of power it generated. There is little wonder that it caught the attention of the industry and the press at the time (below – a postcard of 251 which was published to coincide with the engine's launch). (*THG*)

(the engine alone being 68 tons 8 cwt, so more than ten tons heavier and produces the same tractive effort).'

This locomotive remained the sole member of the class until 1904 when twenty more were added, followed by 24 in 1905 and another forty-four by the time the programme came to an end in 1910. With such a large number of these powerful locomotives in service, the class found wide use and gathered headlines as they dominated the GNR's premier services. Despite their success, the company continued to seek improvements and in July 1904 authority was given by the Board to procure a compound locomotive to test its effectiveness on the network.

Ivatt doesn't seem to have been a strong advocate of this policy, presumably seeing it as a distraction from his primary tasks, especially with the large boilered C1s proving so successful. Nevertheless, he was overruled by Oliver Bury, the General Manager, who was,

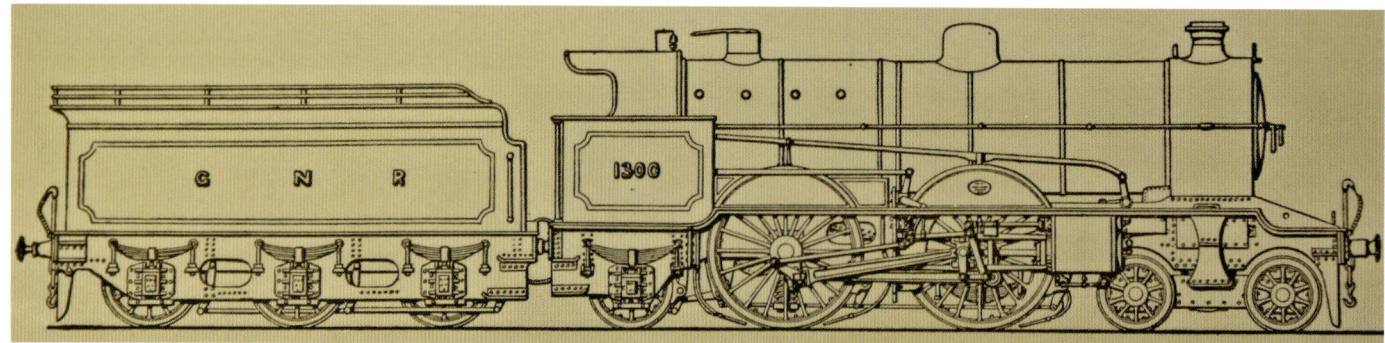

(Above) The Vulcan built compound Atlantic which arrived in July 1905, but due to some teething problems didn't enter regular service until October that year. After Gresley took over from Ivatt in 1912 this non-standard engine continued in service for a time but was eventually rebuilt as a two-cylinder engine in which state it is seen here (below). The unique shape of its cab meant that it could not be mistaken for an Ivatt engine. (*RH*)

by all accounts, attracted by the potential economies offered by compounding. As a result, five companies were asked to submit their ideas in an open competition. In due course, an engine designed by Vulcan Foundry Limited at their works in Newton-le-Willows, was chosen, ordered and given the number 1300 when delivered. At the same time, Ivatt set about designing and constructing an in-house compound Atlantic for reasons that are not entirely clear, but probably centre on comparability. So, with the aid of his Works Manager and Chief Assistant, Douglas Marsh, he produced an experimental four-cylinder Atlantic, No 292. However, despite taking the lead in this work most of the task fell on Marsh's shoulders, Ivatt being absent for three months on sick leave, thought to be brought on by stress.

With both these engines in service, and with any teething problems resolved, it was decided to hold comparability trials between them and a freshly built, second batch Class C1 engine, No. 294. These were held during 1906 between London and Doncaster and would have provided an object lesson in design and testing for the recently arrived premium apprentices, including Peppercorn. What better, when still a fledgling in this field, to witness such an exercise in motion and be briefed by senior staff on the process and the results. In this case, the trials proved that when all running costs were calculated, the C1 was marginally the most effective producing a total cost per engine mile of 2.88d, against 3.125d and 2.9d for No.1300 and No.292 respectively. The margins were narrow and took no account of comparable construction or

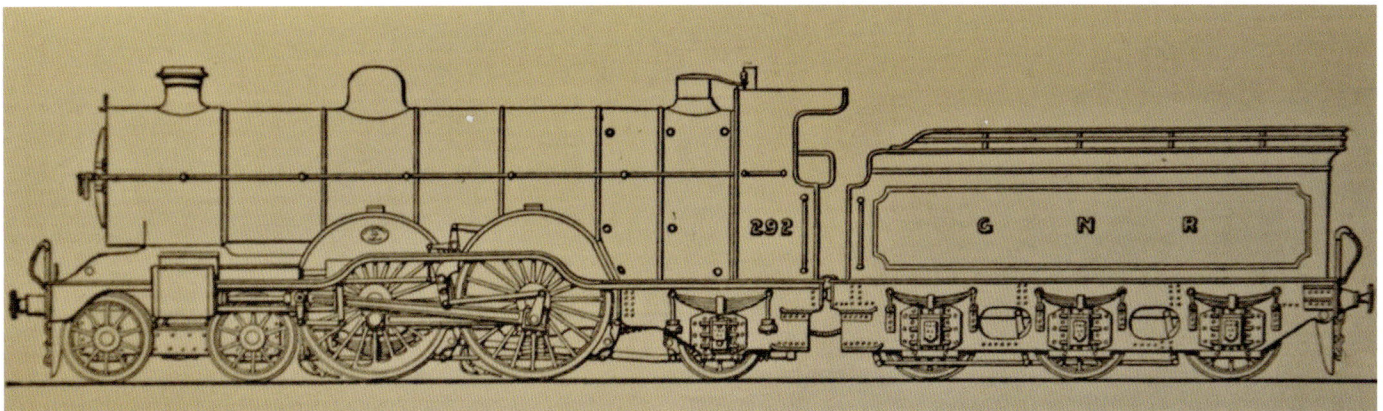

Engine No. 292 as designed and in reality. The Vulcan built engine and 292 would undergo comparability trials in 1906 along with the latest C1 Atlantic, in this case engine No. 294 which entered service during May 1905. (*RH*)

maintenance costs, so the picture that emerged was an incomplete one. However, it was probably sufficient for Ivatt's purposes and only one other compounding experiment was attempted in 1909. This involved engine No.1421 which was constructed along the lines of 292, but was fitted with low pressure cylinders increased in size from 16 to 18 inches. In his book *Master Builders of Steam*, Henry Bulleid, perhaps reflecting Ivatt, his grandfather, and father's thoughts, recalled that 'No.1421 did seem to have something extra, but not such as to justify the extra first cost and maintenance.'

Although there was much to observe at Doncaster during an apprenticeship at this time, no aspiring engineer would simply look at developments locally. With a proliferation of engineering and railway journals

Ivatt's last experiment of note with compounding. No. 1421 as it appeared in 1909. Despite showing some promise the proliferation of so many C1s made further work on these alternative Atlantics something of an unsustainable luxury. It was a brave attempt to push back scientific boundaries but ultimately the policy, if not the concept, was flawed. In due course Gresley would oversee the rebuilding of Nos.1300 and 1421 as two cylinder engines. (*RH*)

highlighting advances across the industry it was relatively easy for those seeking to broaden their knowledge to do so. Peppercorn and his contemporaries would have been encouraged to study the work of other designers, with Churchward's locomotive designs at Swindon drawing particular attention. Here was a man imbued with the spirit of Brunel and a man more than capable of identifying, analysing and exploiting new ideas with great success. In the first decade of the century this meant following the development of his 4-6-0 engines, culminating in the GWR Class 2900 (Saints), his single Pacific (*The Great Bear*), attempts at standardisation and the process of locomotive testing he introduced, aided by the construction of a specialist facility that included a rolling road at Swindon. His was a model worth considering and following.

Gresley was known to be an admirer of Churchward and it appears that there was regular contact between the two men, especially after he succeeded Ivatt in 1912. In view of the close association that would grow up between Gresley and Peppercorn, which seems to have its origins during the younger man's apprenticeship, it seems likely that he would have drawn his attention to Churchward's work. But Gresley and Ivatt may also have encouraged these newly minted engineers to study the designs of other leaders in this field, at home and abroad.

Two of these were known to be the North Eastern Railway's Wilson Worsdell and his assistant Walter Smith, who had developed their own V Class Atlantics having noted the GNR's success in this field. They also produced a compound version in 1906 mirroring Ivatt's own work in this field, but here the two engines built, Nos. 730 and 731, seem to have out-performed their conventional sisters. In his book *The North Eastern Railway,* Cecil Allen records that 'their superiority was

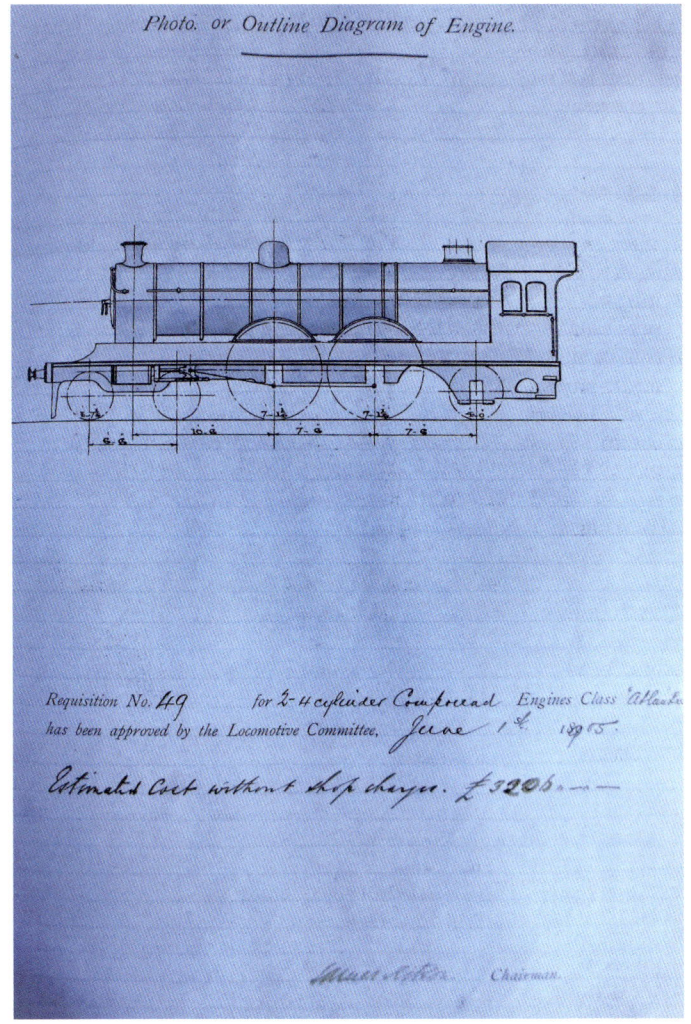

How far did the work of other railway companies influence the thoughts of engineers under training? Case studies then and now are the basis of education in specialist subjects. Bert Spencer, who trained at Doncaster shortly after Peppercorn, and would become Gresley's assistant in time, recalled that his training was interspersed with such studies and kept many papers to help inform his own work. The picture above, which captures the NER's work on compounding, is one example. Peppercorn would have been similarly trained and influenced. (*BS/RH*)

appreciable in both tractive power and economy in fuel consumption'.

When Bert Spencer, who would rise to become assistant to both Gresley and Peppercorn, was under training in the works at Doncaster, and attending the local Technical College from 1914, he remembered that:

'Our attention was drawn to the chief designers who had worked for the GNR but also the likes of Churchward, who Gresley greatly admired. Although learning of his work with 4-6-0s, of greater interest to me personally was *The Great Bear*, which seemed to me worthy of closer study especially when both the GNR and NER were designing their own versions. But we also learnt about Wilson Worsdell and his Chief Draughtsman Walter Smith and their work on Atlantics. We were made aware, by Gresley, of Worsdell's time in the United States working for the Pennsylvania Railroad at Altoona and the influence this had on his work. Smith died in 1906 before he could fully develop his compounding ideas, but we were encouraged to study this work and I kept drawings and specifications of their compound Atlantics amongst my papers. In fact, Worsdell addressed a number of apprentices, after he'd retired, and talked at length about his work. Such was the way our skills were developed, with membership of learned institutions being encouraged from the first.'

As Peppercorn's apprenticeship gradually progressed, there were four other classes of locomotive being developed by Ivatt that would have drawn his attention. They didn't have the obvious glamour of the Atlantics, being more utilitarian in purpose, but probably better represented the broader trading function of the railway. The first of these was the 0-8-0 K1 tender engines designed to pull ever-heavier mineral trains. These began appearing in 1901 and continued in production until 1909, by which time fifty-five had been built. George Bird described them as possessing 'immense tractive and adhesive power, having cylinders 19¾in by 26in, eight coupled wheels, with 3in tyres, a diameter of only 4ft 8in, and a total weight available for adhesion of more than 54½tons, whilst its capacity to raise sufficient steam to supply those big cylinders is evidenced by the ample size of the boiler.'

These engines proved successful with some remaining in service until 1937. It was to be expected that during their lives they would undergo modification and this proved to be the case, though the basic sturdiness of the design meant that the changes did not result in complete rebuilds. In some of them slide valves replaced piston valves, superheating was introduced, variable blast pipes appeared on several, as did the Klinger forced system of lubrication. But beyond this they remained largely untouched by either

The third K1 0-8-0, No. 406, as built in 1902. There were fifty-five of these powerful goods engines in service by 1909. Ivatt, left, poses with Archibald Sturrock who held the post of Locomotive Superintendent at Doncaster from 1850-66 and whose presence and work would have been well known to Peppercorn. This picture was taken in 1903 when Sturrock was an active 87-year-old. He died six years later in London. (*ET/DN*)

The prototype L1 as built in 1903 and in full PR mode to advertise its appearance on London's Metropolitan City Line. At this stage the engine was painted in primer grey but would soon adopt more traditional company colours. (*RH*)

Ivatt or Gresley, eventually being re-classified by the LNER as Q1, Q2 and Q3s depending upon the modifications undertaken.

Next came the L1 0-8-2 tank engines which first appeared in 1903 and continued in production until 1906 by which time forty-one had been built. It was loosely based on the K1, in an effort to achieve some standardisation, and was designed specifically for use on London's Metropolitan City Line for both goods and passenger traffic, underground where necessary. Shortly after entering service Bird reported that 'this powerful and otherwise successful prototype engine was found to be too heavy for the line, and in response to the requirements of the Permanent Way Department, Mr Ivatt undertook to modify the design materially to reduce the gross moving load . . . He replaced the boiler and reduced the firebox to 6ft 2in. in length. At the same time the side tanks were reduced lessening their capacity from 2,000 to 1,500 gallons and only 3 tons of coal were carried (down from 4 tons).' These changes resolved the problem but, in due course, the engines' suitability for commuter services was questioned, particularly their low top speed. As a result, they were gradually transferred from London to Colwick and Ardsley to work freight trains. This move was made possible by the arrival of the N1 0-6-2 tank engines which were better suited to the needs of the GNR's suburban lines.

The development of the N1s coincided with Francis Wintour succeeding Douglas Marsh in 1905 as Works Manager and Chief Assistant. Before moving to Doncaster, he had been District Locomotive Superintendent at King's Cross. In this post, he would have acquired first-hand knowledge of the specific needs of inner city commuter services. So it is quite possible that his input to the design of the N1 was more than simply overseeing their construction. Perhaps more importantly he arrived at the same time as Peppercorn began his apprenticeship, so would oversee his development, possibly more directly than Ivatt himself.

In the N1, the GNR acquired a sturdy and reliable engine. Yet at the beginning, the prototype gave some cause for concern. Like the L1s (later redesignated R1s by the LNER) it proved to be a little too heavy especially at the leading coupled wheels. To correct this, the rear

Engine No. 152 following its construction in 1906 at Doncaster with modifications to lessen its weight (boiler, firebox and side tanks reduced in size to meet weight restrictions on London's Metropolitan line). Some remained in action until 1934 though not on services for which they were first designed. Here they were replaced by the N1 0-6-2Ts. (*ET/DN*)

A common sight around the North London commuter belt as the N1s began displacing the L1s in 1907. (*ET/DN*)

frames were lengthened and the wheels moved further back. This also allowed a larger bunker to be provided and the side tanks shortened, though without a drop in water capacity. In this form, the other fifty-five members of the class were built, all engines, except Nos. 1592 to 1595, with condensing apparatus to allow them to work the Metropolitan's underground lines. Construction began in 1907 and continued on until 1912. Post-war a pressing need for more passenger tank engines led to the development of the N2 0-6-2s. Here again Wintour played an important role in the development programme overseeing the production of the bulk of the 107 engines built, either at Doncaster or by contractors, by the time he retired in 1927.

In many ways, the next locomotives built by the GNR evolved from the N1, using many common parts. 0-6-0 tender engines were the staple part of any company's mixed traffic fleet and two classes of these useful engines were produced by Ivatt as the decade drew to a close. In fact, they were probably designed when Peppercorn was working in the Drawing Office at Doncaster, as part of his apprenticeship, so he may have had some involvement in their development. The first of these engines was the J21, twelve of which were built in 1908. Like the N1s they had 5ft 8in driving wheels, a wheel-base of 7ft 3in between leading and driving wheels, two inside cylinders measuring 18in in diameter by 26in stroke, a working pressure of 170psi, a firebox of 120sqft, a grate area of 19sqft., tubes of 1,130sqft and a tractive effort of 18,427lbs.

They were designed for fast freight as well as passenger services and proved successful in both roles until withdrawn from service nearly forty years later in the early 1950s. However, the next 0-6-0s did deviate slightly from this model. In 1909, the first of twenty J22s appeared. In all respects they were identical to the J21s but were primarily goods locomotives and so received smaller (5ft 2in) driving wheels which made them more suited to this type of work. Like the J21s, they had long and successful lives and, like their sisters, survived until the mid-1950s.

No matter how settled life might appear, events can often conspire to unsettle and distract and Alfred Peppercorn's sudden death on 14 February 1908 was

Peppercorn would have closely observed the development of the highly successful N1 class of 0-6-2 tank engines, designed specifically to run on London's congested and fast moving commuter lines. Although these duties lacked glamour and prestige they provided a significant and growing part of the GNR's income. Here the prototype engine makes its first public appearance shortly after construction in early 1907. This engine was initially allocated to Hornsey Shed in London, but transferred to Ardsley in 1927 and then Copley Hill in 1941, being condemned in December 1956 and scrapped shortly afterwards. (*ET/DN*)

J21 No.12 as it appeared when built in 1908. (*THG*)

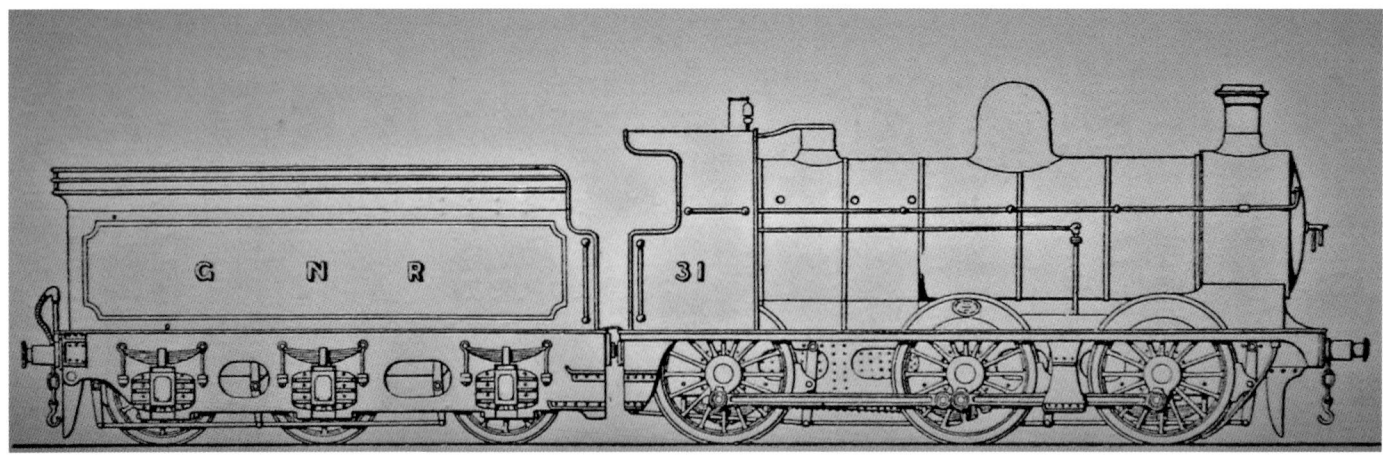

The first J22 0-6-0 tender engine as designed. Peppercorn, or so it seems, was working in the Drawing Office when these engines were in planning. The J22s (later reclassified J5 by the LNER) were almost identical to the J21s (later the J1) but had smaller driving wheels deemed more suitable for pulling slow moving goods traffic.

Class C1 No. 278 at speed near Barlby Bridge in Yorkshire during the early years of the twentieth century. (*RH*)

one of these occasions. History doesn't record how close Arthur was to his father, but filial love and loyalty is difficult to ignore even in the most trying circumstances. In this case, the fact that the son kept and treasured an inscribed copy of 'Hymns Ancient and Modern', that his father presented to him in 1906, for the rest of his life suggests there was some affection. On one page Arthur has underlined the words in Hymn 7, *Christ, Whose Glory Fills the Skies*:

> 'Dark and cheerless is the morn,
> Unaccompanied by Thee;
> Joyless is the day's return,
> Till Thy mercy's beams I see;
> Till they inward light impart,
> Glad my eyes and warm my heart.
>
> Visit then this soul of mine,
> Pierce the gloom of sin and grief.'

So the sadness of loss would seem to have afflicted him making his last year as an apprentice a difficult one, especially being so far from home at such a difficult time.

Probate of £4,384 on Alfred's estate was granted to Agnes on 30 April, which was of small compensation for the loss of her husband, her home and income. The church would have allowed her to stay at the Rectory for a time, but the new vicar would soon have needed to take up residency and leave she must. In due course, she moved to Lulham Court, near Madley six miles west of Hereford, which Arthur registered as his own home for a number of years, taking temporary lodgings wherever the GNR posted him.

With four children still at home requiring support, and Arthur still with one year to run as an apprentice, the family, never rich, would have lived in straightened circumstances. It seems that Arthur, in particular, took on responsibility for supporting his mother financially, a role he fulfilled up to her death in 1934, as he did for several of his sisters as his Will later makes clear. As he rose rapidly through the ranks of the GNR, then LNER, this became easier to achieve, but in the beginning it must have been a struggle to find sufficient funds to do this and meet his own needs. This is hard at any age, but at 19 could present insuperable problems for such a young man just starting out in the world. And yet he seems to have shouldered this responsibility with great maturity and with little thought for himself.

Yet the loss of a parent can have a polarising effect that provides impetus to a young life. John Mortimer probably captured this best in his work *Voyage Round My Father* when he wrote that there was a 'sudden freedom. Growing up. The end of dependence. You step into the sunlight where no one is taller than you. You are in no one's shadow.' As can so often happen, death can sharpen and deepen a personality. When a son loses a father it can be a defining moment in life and it seems to have been so for Peppercorn, bringing with it a determination to succeed in his professional life. He had been lucky in finding a profession and a vocation that suited his skills and personality, but as 1910 dawned, and his training came to an end, he needed to find full time employment – success as an apprentice granting no right of permanent employment with the GNR.

The best trainees might be retained, but often it could be a case of establishing some level of patronage and exploiting the influence that might be exerted through such a connection. Those who rise to the top tend to be people who have well developed personal skills, as well as high professional standards, and so are able to stand out from the crowd. Peppercorn seems to have been so imbued and was lucky in that the GNR possessed, in Ivatt and Gresley, men capable of granting favours to those who had caught their attention. Gresley in particular, being only in his early thirties, was clearly destined for higher rank. It had become his habit to identify young men with potential and seek to accelerate their careers as his assistant or in other selected positions. It was a process that increased when he was promoted to replace Ivatt. In this way Oliver Bulleid benefitted from his patronage, as would Arthur Peppercorn and Bert Spencer in due course.

So in 1910, as his five-year apprenticeship came to an end, what had Peppercorn learnt and what skills had he developed that marked him out for high office? His apprenticeship would have taught him many basic engineering and workshop skills. He would have seen and participated in the construction and maintenance of locomotives and rolling stock from the ground up, learning how to handle an array of equipment in the process. It was a proud boast of many young apprentices that they could handle workshop machinery as well as their permanent operators. True or not, it did underpin the

In October 1909, towards the end of Peppercorn's apprenticeship, Doncaster became the scene of a week-long Aviation Meeting which was widely advertised by the GNR. Walter Bentley, in later correspondence, recorded his attendance with his fellow premium apprentices, including Peppercorn. Although in a fledgling state, aircraft were a great draw and would, in due course, attract a number of railway engineers to the ranks of their designers – including Bentley and, more notably, R.J. Mitchell. There is no indication that Peppercorn was attracted to this experimental and less certain field of engineering. However, he remained in contact with Bentley in the decades that followed, which may simply have been an act of friendship or a continuing fascination with aviation or the automobile. Either way, the event in 1909, captured here in these two photographs, must have been an interesting one in an age where few had seen an aircraft let alone fly in one. (*THG*)

depth of training they received over five years of hard graft. But they learnt much more than this.

Time was spent on the footplate of different classes of locomotive, though this was reduced following the death of Ralph Talbot. This would have taught them the rudiments of engine handling and, for the observant, the effect of design on the lives of footplate crew – both good and bad. The ergonomics of engine design were in their infancy in this pre-Great War period and during Peppercorn's career would advance considerably. There was also the question of workshop management and layout to study and understand and how this could impact on flow rates and overall efficiency. Once again, it was a science in an early stage of development. Very soon, eyes would look towards the United States where production line methods and technology were, in Henry Ford's hands, making their mark on the fledgling motor industry. These methods would soon impact on railway workshops across Britain so had to be studied and evolved. Yet another task that would seriously impact on Peppercorn's working life as he reached senior rank in the LNER.

Managing people and learning how to command are harder skills to acquire because they are deeply rooted in personality and temperament. No matter how clever the mind or skilled an engineer, a lack of understanding of human nature is a significant block to progress, especially when linked to business needs. The old adage that 'you can't put in what nature hasn't provided' bears many grains of truth. Certainly experience helps, but my belief is that this only enhances natural talents. Sadly, a poor manager will remain a poor manager no matter how much experience they gain and when tested will most probably be found wanting. From the information available, I think it is safe to assume that Peppercorn was imbued with well-developed management skills to

As Peppercorn's apprenticeship came to an end, Ivatt's impact on the GNR's locomotive fleet was only too apparent, with his Atlantics dominating the scene. Gresley would begin to change the emphasis of design post 1912, but even when the LNER came into being during 1923 the Ivatt Atlantics could still present a picture of power and prestige. Here engine No. 4413 (ex-GNR 1413 built in 1905) is captured at King's Cross after amalgamation. Their reign would last until the Gresley Pacifics arrived in large numbers, but even then the Atlantics found a useful role until withdrawals began in 1943. The last remained in service until 1950 and one, No. 251, has been preserved as part of the national collection. (RH)

which experience added many new layers in the years ahead. Some would shout, others would rant and bully, but he measured the task and the people working for him then balanced their working capacity with budgets and business needs with a sure touch. These are quite rare skills, especially when coupled with his engineering abilities, all of which would be sorely tested in the years ahead.

The one element of his professional development not tested to any great extent in these early years lay in the creative field of design. Undoubtedly, his interest in this area of work would have been stimulated by many things, amongst them participation in workshop tasks, footplate work, the period of his apprenticeship spent in the GNR's Drawing Office and courses run by Doncaster Technical College. But there is no indication that he participated directly in the conceptual thinking and experimentation that underpins design. This wasn't unusual, especially amongst those who would become Chief Mechanical Engineers, suggesting that most apprentices received training more suited to production engineering. So how did some and not others make the leap into this field? Was it simply a matter of opportunity or the recognition of some skill that made them stand out from the crowd?

In Peppercorn's case, the years ahead would see him posted to workshops and general management posts superintending the railway's daily operations, but not areas in which he could demonstrate any ability for invention or innovation. In this he differed from Gresley, Bulleid and Spencer, who spent considerable time enhancing their scientific credentials with much original thought being given to the science of locomotive design. If Peppercorn harboured any ambitions to develop new engines, and I am sure such a good engineer would, many years would pass before an opportunity would come his way to allow this to happen. In the meantime, there was much more to occupy his mind.

CHAPTER 2

GROWING TO MATURITY

As Peppercorn's apprenticeship came to an end an event took place that no promising engineer on the GNR could ignore. Competition between railway companies was unavoidable, even though they may not have been direct rivals for trade. There was the public relations aspect to be exploited by showing that your products were the latest and the best, but rivalry could also be driven by the simple need to demonstrate scientific prowess or superiority of one's designs. Either way, this could occasionally lead to comparability trials being held in which engines from different companies were tested against each other. In 1909, this resulted in such an exercise, co-sponsored by Charles Bowen Cooke, the recently appointed CME of the London and North Western Railway at Crewe, and Ivatt. George Bird again captured details of the event:

> 'An interesting series of trials was instituted between engines of this class (Ivatt's C1s) and standard LNWR express locomotives during the summer of 1909. No. 1449 was "lent" to the LNWR and put to work on the traffic between Euston and Crewe. The engine was worked by its own driver and fireman, with an LNWR driver as pilot-man. During the same period the LNWR locomotive No. 412, *Marquis*, a four-coupled bogie engine of the "Precursor" class, was at work on the GNR main line running between King's Cross, Doncaster and Leeds on alternate days, in competition with No. 1451. No official figures are forthcoming as to the results of these friendly trials, which naturally aroused considerable interest in the railway world.'

When Bird wrote these words in 1910, any information emanating from the trials was restricted, but within a year more detail was revealed. Most of the trials took place in June and July, but they also involved *Cardean*, a 4-6-0 Class 903 from the Caledonian Railway, which only worked the line from Crewe to Glasgow and not over the East Coast main line at all, so precluding any

Rail travel to the seaside grew in popularity during the years before the Great War, though was quite often beyond the means of most families even for day trips. It was not a big money spinner for the GNR or other companies either. Nevertheless, images of golden sand and blue sky featured heavily in their PR campaigns and helped sell the concept of rail travel that would grow exponentially post-war. (*ET/DN*)

Engine No. 1449 during the exchange trials between the GNR and LNWR in 1909. On this occasion the engine is hauling fourteen carriages as it leaves Euston Station. The GNR locomotive is recorded by George Ivatt as having tackled the Camden Bank without assistance despite the size of its load. The inference drawn from this is that such a feat was unusual at the time for LNWR express locomotives. (*THG*)

comparison with the Atlantic. On a number of occasions, Ivatt rode on *Marquis*, whilst his son, Henry George, then an apprentice at Crewe, worked on No. 1449's footplate during a journey from Euston. These tests showed that the Atlantic, whether running on the LNWR's lines or its home network, was marginally better on coal consumption than the Precursor – 0.128lb per mile ton compared to 0.140lb from Euston and 0.145lb as opposed to 0.154lb from King's Cross. Young Henry, known as George, who knew both classes well, was clear in his praise of the Atlantic, although some of this may have been down to filial loyalty. Nevertheless, his summary is interesting, as recalled by F.A.S. Brown in his book *From Stirling to Gresley*:

'We had 400 tons behind the tender, which was a very heavy load for this size of locomotive. We climbed the 1 in 75 bank out of Euston without assistance and between Rugby and Stafford ran many miles at 75mph. This demonstrated that this locomotive had pulling power and was capable of high speed running.'

George Ivatt and Peppercorn were near contemporaries and appear to have known each other through both Henry Ivatt and Oliver Bulleid, Peppercorn being an occasional guest in both households. It was a relationship that continued as they both climbed through the ranks of the LNER and LMS. In fact, they would both

The LNWR locomotive No. 412 *Marquis* in the early years of the twentieth century. It was a member of the 130-strong Precursor Class designed by George Whale, the Locomotive Superintendent, and his team and was built in June 1904. In essence, it was an extended version of Francis Webb's Improved Precedent Class. The GNR Atlantics seem to have outperformed the Precursors, though did not lead to the 4-4-2 configuration being adopted by Whale, who, by 1909, had moved towards the 4-6-0 concept with his Experiment Class, building 105 between 1905 and 1910. However, the information he acquired during the trials does seem to have influenced Cooke when contemplating a new 2-6-4 general utility tank engine. It was the custom amongst designers to 'cherry pick' ideas at times and attempt to mould them together into new designs. In this case he was sufficiently impressed with the two 'foreign' engines to reflect upon the reversing gear and extended smokebox used on the GNR locomotive and the sloping firebox and well at the bottom of the feed tank from *Cardean*. It seems that even the most creative minds could benefit from observing the work of others, supported by the work of the IMechE, the soon to be formed Institution of Locomotive Engineers (1911) and other professional bodies. (*RH*)

become CMEs of these two companies in 1946, though they remained in these posts for comparatively short periods – three and five years respectively. In many respects, their careers followed similar paths, though Ivatt probably spent more time in the design field. They would also serve together during the Great War on the Western Front with the Royal Engineers in the Directorate of Transport. As the years unfolded it is interesting to observe how the careers of these two ambitious and gifted men unfolded and how, when armed with similar tools and resources, they worked and developed their ideas on design.

The first step in a career, when training comes to an end, is often a difficult one. There can be a worrying pause while the individual looks for a suitable post then enters a competition to acquire it. But even when successful, many problems remain, not least of all gaining the acceptance of co-workers, many of whom you are obliged to manage. Then there is the need to make a good impression on your superiors, especially if you are saddled with a trial period or a short term contract. Peppercorn was saved some of these worries, being chosen by his GNR managers for further employment when his apprenticeship came to an end in 1910. From the few papers that remain, it seems that Ivatt was impressed enough by the young man to offer him a permanent post without a trial period. However, this led him to operational duties, not an appointment in the Drawing Office where he had spent a part of his apprenticeship, a natural destination for anyone contemplating a career in design. What does this suggest?

It seems that Peppercorn had impressed as a trainee, helped by direct access to Ivatt and Wintour as a premium apprentice. This could be a doubled edged sword, though. A poor student would be quickly exposed by the direct scrutiny of such senior managers, who might be less likely to forgive transgressions or poor performance than lesser mortals. But the indications are that both men found in Peppercorn an intelligent young man both willing and able to work hard. He also seems to have acquired the necessary engineering skills to enable him to fulfil a number of different roles. And yet this didn't lead to a design post but to Colwick Locomotive Depot on the edge of Nottingham. In his 1912 application to join the Institution of Mechanical Engineers, he described his duties during this period as 'shed fitting, firing, &c, offices and assisting Foreman – 2 years and 5 months'. The date of his application is significant,

Two views of Doncaster during Peppercorn's time as an apprentice. (Top) A mixed group of workers pose on Doncaster built engine No. 209. This was a Stirling E2 Class 2-4-0 that was rebuilt under Ivatt's leadership and then reclassified E1. In this guise some of the 117 constructed between 1874 and 1895 were absorbed by the LNER post-1923, though not No. 209 which was withdrawn in 1922. (Bottom) A mass of men and boys of many different skills and trades leave the Works at the end of a working day. A single afternoon was recorded by a cine camera in the late 1900s. With many thousands employed on the site the film has to run for many minutes to get them all through. By this simple means the cameraman has captured an impression of time, place and period very well. It is a scene so typical of Edwardian Britain and its reliance on heavy industry. More importantly for this story it was a world that absorbed young Arthur Peppercorn, formed his character and professional life and which he served for forty-four years through many social, political and economic upheavals. (*ET/DN*)

because it coincided with Gresley's promotion to Locomotive Superintendent and Ivatt's departure. It also corresponded with Bulleid's return to the GNR after a brief sojourn to Westinghouse and the Board of Trade between 1908 and 1912.

Here it is interesting to speculate on the role both men played in the early years of Peppercorn's career. Gresley became the GNR's Carriage and Wagon Works Superintendent in 1905, his arrival coinciding with the start of Peppercorn's apprenticeship. However, no part of his training seems to have been undertaken in Gresley's department, yet he seems to have taken him under his wing, if comments made by H.C.B. Rogers in his book *Thompson and Peppercorn* are to be believed. In quoting a letter from J.F. Harrison, who later worked for Gresley and Peppercorn, he reported that 'Gresley took a great liking to the young apprentice. He was always sending for him. Arthur got to know the Gresley boys and girls very well and was treated as one of the family.'

Gresley, throughout his career, seems to have been a good judge of character and carefully selected those with potential for senior rank, even when he might not see eye to eye with them in some cases. Clearly, he saw possibilities in the young Peppercorn and he might also have felt some sympathy for his predicament. They were both sons of clergymen whose fathers might have preferred them to enter university and not the rougher world of heavy industry. Gresley would have understood the hard nature of an apprenticeship and the loneliness of being far away from home when so young. He also demonstrated, throughout his career, a deep interest in these training schemes and actively involved himself in them. So despite Ivatt's role as leader, Gresley would most probably have taken some young recruits under his wing, teaching them and offering encouragement whenever he could. But this level of interest doesn't appear to have extended to all premium apprentices. Certainly Walter Bentley makes no mention of it in his book and papers, suggesting that Peppercorn was one of the lucky few.

Ivatt was also known to invite a few selected young men into his household. In due course Peppercorn would also become a regular visitor to the Bulleid household suggesting another close personal and professional link. Did all this aid his career in any way or simply reflect a gregarious and convivial personality? No one of intelligence and ambition would pass up opportunities to socialise with senior managers and establish strong links with them. It is all part and parcel of a successful career. But Peppercorn seems to have been a genuine and very likeable man who looked beyond the needs of career and liked people, happily fostering friendships along the way. If he had simply sought advancement by inveigling himself into Gresley, Ivatt or Bulleid's lives they would undoubtedly have seen through this mask very quickly and slapped him down, damaging his career in the process.

Peppercorn's transfer to Colwick, which did not share the premier status of Doncaster or King's Cross, where Bentley was posted as his training drew to a close, suggests that he was being treated as just another apprentice at this time. But whether at Colwick or King's Cross they would both have spent a considerable amount of time on the footplate or in the workshops as general 'dogsbodies', as Bentley recalled much later:

'Work at King's Cross was about the filthiest I ever got involved in during my apprenticeship. Routine maintenance was carried out in the running sheds, more serious overhauls at Doncaster. Examining fireboxes not only made you filthy, but roasted you as well. Fireboxes take a long time to cool down, too long to wait before the job has to be done.

'My first footplate work was as second fireman on local goods trains, but I couldn't have cared if it had been local shunting . . . Firing locomotives isn't a matter of just throwing shovelfuls of coal into the box when the fire begins to look low. It would have taken me years to master the art, but I did learn something about keeping the pressure just right, anticipating requirements before coming, say, to a long gradient, about dealing with coal, a dirty boiler, injector troubles and so on. I learnt a little about the art of driving too, but only a little, for it requires uncommon skill. I have been on the footplate out of King's Cross in wet weather when, in the smoke-laden tunnels, the wheels have started to slip and, unless I leant out to feel the tunnel wall there was no way of telling whether you were moving backwards or forwards.'

He then went on to describe the allure of this life and what it meant to him to be involved so directly:

'How lucky I was that the sensation of being on the footplate of a GNR Atlantic, heading an express north

Colwick Locomotive Depot prior to the Great War and in the early 1920s showing its size and the extent of the locomotive fleet it supported. It was here that Peppercorn began his career and would spend nearly 2 ½ years after completing his apprenticeship at Doncaster. (*RH*)

out of London, was more thrilling and wonderful than I had ever thought it could be. I was fascinated by the feeling of power…There was nothing I know to compare with the sensation of rushing through the night without lights and with the soothing mechanical rhythm beating away continuously, even leading to a dangerous tendency to surrender to the power quivering beneath the steel floor.'

It seems fairly certain that Peppercorn would have felt the same way as Bentley, but his developing career would unfold in a place without the dynamism or kudos of King's Cross. However, Colwick was still a place of some importance to the GNR, though its chief focus was more probably on the carriage of goods rather than people with the obvious economic dominance of the East Midlands coalfields in the area. In 1908, the Nottinghamshire fields alone were producing 11 million tons of coal a year, employing more than 35,000 people and, at any one time, had 30 or more collieries in operation. With the railways being the sole means of bulk movement available, the profits to be made from the coal industry, here and elsewhere, were significant and of the greatest importance to the GNR's profitability.

As the mining industry expanded in the mid-nineteenth century, so the railways supporting it grew. This resulted in a small engine shed being opened at Colwick on the edge of Nottingham in 1858, followed later by a marshalling yard to the south. Expansion of both facilities took place over 50 years and at its peak the depot would support 200 or more locomotives. The sheds had 16 roads, 100 metres of which were under cover. In addition, it would be fitted out with an Erecting Shop, repair facilities for locomotives and wagons, offices, a coaling plant, turntable, housing for workers, a social club and a bowling green. So when Peppercorn arrived in 1910 he would have found a bustling centre of activity with freight work dominating daily duties and a locomotive fleet reflecting this work.

By any standards, the inventory would have contained a mixed bag of engines with many from different eras still in evidence. Although Archibald Sturrock ceased being the Locomotive Superintendent in 1866, some of his engines may still have been running, but their numbers would have been fast dwindling to be superseded by a mass of new engines built during Patrick Stirling and Ivatt's reigns. From the 1860s, there would probably have been some of Sturrock's

A pre-Great War view of Colwick taken from the coaling stage showing the variety of engines handled by the sheds. (*RH*)

Class 400 0-6-0s, seventy of which were built, perhaps even the earlier Class 308 0-6-0s, though now very long in the tooth. From Stirling there was a concentration of J Class 0-6-0s and F2 0-4-2s, whilst all of Ivatt's class L1 0-8-2s and twenty-two KI 0-8-0s would appear there in the years before the Great War. In addition, Ivatt's newly built J5, J21 and J22s added to the stock of other 0-6-0s there until more than a hundred were in evidence by 1922. These were supplemented by a number of his 4-4-0s for passenger work, transferred to Colwick when Nottingham's London Road (low level) shed closed in 1906. To these would be added a variety of other engines, some of which were simply visiting. For a budding engineer, the intensity of operations and the variety of locomotives handled, though lacking the glamour of premier passenger services, did provide a good grounding in all aspects of railway operations.

One wonders what aspirations Peppercorn harboured at this time and where he thought his career might develop post-Colwick. Having spent a time in Doncaster's Drawing Office as an apprentice, did his ambitions lie in the direction of design? He left no word to describe his thought processes, but there is a hint in a present his mother gave him for his birthday in 1911. Two books, inscribed by her to celebrate the occasion, have survived – *Locomotive Engineering* by W.F. Pettigrew and *Mechanical Drawing* by J.E. Jagger, which was first published in 1910. This suggests a continuing desire to learn more about the mechanics of design and the presentation of ideas, even though his time at Doncaster Technical College had come to an end. However, there is no indication that he pursued any academic studies post 1910. On the contrary, he seems to have relied upon learning on the job and not the acquisition of additional professional qualifications to expand his knowledge. But in this he was not alone. Walter Bentley, for one, saw no need either before deciding to leave the industry and transfer his attentions to the slowly growing world of cars and aeroplanes where he would make his name. And then there were a number of railway engineers who followed a path to senior rank without feeling the need to acquire additional qualifications along the way either, amongst them both Gresley and William Stanier.

The truth of the matter seems to be that there were limits to the extent of formal education available in this era, a situation reflected in the small number of colleges and universities offering advanced courses in mechanical engineering. Much was still in its infancy and places at colleges were limited, a situation not helped by a lack of funding for higher education and the need for potential students to work full time to scrape a living. Basically, people were too poor to consider college education. The railways, by offering apprenticeships and encouraging attendance at local technical colleges, went some way towards overcoming this, but there were limits that were hard to overcome. Some like Oliver Bulleid and Bert Spencer did find a way around this restriction and went on to study at university, but they appear to have been academically gifted men. In other cases, there were families wealthy enough to send their children to public schools and then on to university before the railways beckoned. In this way, Edward Thompson and a few others came into the industry at a more advanced level of scientific learning. But for most, an apprenticeship was all they could hope for and then acquire knowledge by observing and learning from others at work and in the study of professional journals and text books.

It was here that learned institutions, supported by an ever growing number of books written by specialist authors, such as those given to Peppercorn by his mother, played an increasingly important role in developing these sciences. These institutions actively encouraged the presentation, discussion and dissemination of ideas amongst members, whether university graduates or apprentices. Some like the IMechE were national bodies but others were locally orientated, based close to major industrial employers and centres – in Swindon, Crewe and Leeds for example. Between them, though, they offered an increasingly important forum for ambitious engineers to gain knowledge and think about their trade.

Peppercorn's rise was slightly different to many of his contemporaries in so far as his father would probably have sanctioned attendance at university. But this was not to be and his time as an apprenticeship underpinned his career. Did he suffer because of it? Obviously not in rank attained but possibly in the direction his career moved. Such a clever man might well have found the design world more stimulating than being a manager of workshops and resources. However, he did join the IMechE when encouraged to do so by Gresley which would have boosted his credentials in this more creative field. In fact, the newly appointed Locomotive

Superintendent acted as his proposer in June 1912, supported by Francis Webster and John Bazin, who was the Assistant Works Manager at Doncaster.

Within a few weeks, he was elected to this important body and had the opportunity to absorb all the papers it produced. Did these act as a spur to his creative instincts? All that can be said with any certainty is that for most of his career, Peppercorn was either wholly committed to production engineering or sat alongside designers perhaps guiding their work as any senior manager would, especially when becoming CME. However, it is clear that when his apprenticeship ended in 1910, he would never again work as a draughtsman or in a drawing office. So, arguably, he did not fully develop the intimate knowledge of locomotive design that would take the average person many years to learn and practice successfully. Nevertheless, he would, undoubtedly, have appreciated the complexities of design and developed his own ideas independent of a specialist in this field. But he wouldn't, as Ivatt, Gresley and others did, develop new ideas to the point at which patents on their work could be produced. He was not, it seems, an inventor, which suggests that his level of scientific curiosity may have been muted. Perhaps his time in Doncaster's Drawing Office demonstrated this to Elwess and Wintour and showed that his skills truly lay in production engineering. His subsequent postings would seem to bear this out.

It was during Peppercorn's time at Colwick that Ivatt retired and Gresley, perhaps the greatest influence on his career, took over. As Locomotive Superintendent, Gresley's responsibilities would now embrace the running sheds as well as the workshops. This wider authority included all staffing matters for the operational side of the GNR. In this role, he could choose where anyones' careers might develop and post them accordingly. With his advocacy of the younger man's membership of the highly influential IMechE still fresh in the mind, perhaps suggesting some broader influence growing, he appointed Peppercorn to a more senior post at Ardsley near Leeds.

Late in 1912, the assistant to the District Locomotive Inspector post fell vacant there and Peppercorn was selected to fill the position. Why he was chosen is now lost to time, but it would seem to have been an ideal position for someone deemed suitable for rapid promotion. Like Colwick, Ardsley had come into being in the mid-nineteenth century on the back of an ever-expanding coal industry in the West Riding of Yorkshire, but also on the trade generated by the large number of woollen mills operating in the area. By 1912, the main shed had eight roads and was capable of holding more than eighty engines at any one time. There was a coaling stage, a smithy, a Turning Shop and other workshop facilities sufficient to allow many repairs to be carried out on site, so reducing the need to send engines to Doncaster for all but major tasks.

As assistant to the District Inspector, Peppercorn would have spent a considerable amount of time with engine crews, arranging their work schedules and managing all their needs. For the first time, he would have been responsible for 'pay and rations', welfare, discipline and the growing influence of trades unions. There would also have been the readiness and serviceability of the locomotive fleet to manage, so ensuring that sufficient types and numbers were available to meet commitments.

Monitoring and measuring engines' performances would also have been one of his responsibilities, a task probably increased when Gresley was promoted to Superintendent. Even at this early stage in his career, he had registered the importance of testing locomotives and comparing outputs. It was all part and parcel of his sincerely held view that greater efficiency must be sought at all times and that design must seek to push back the boundaries of what is possible. Standing still or resting on past successes was not stitched into his DNA as events would soon prove. Testing would sit at the heart of all he did as a scientist and designer. Peppercorn and his contemporaries would, undoubtedly, have been coached in these techniques, analysing results and developing new and possibly better solutions as a matter of course. It is clear from studying the memories of the leading figures around Gresley that this became an essential part of their work.

Whilst Peppercorn settled into his new role at Ardsley, Gresley's agile mind, now unfettered by no longer being a deputy, began grappling with many questions of locomotive design. Soon the results of his labours were becoming only too apparent. However, it was a programme of work that would struggle to move forward during the Great War, but in its aftermath would move on at an unrelenting pace for the next twenty-nine years. He started carefully, like a good batsman playing

(Top) Ardsley Shed prior to the Great War with a mixed bag of engines on show including a 2-6-0 built by the Baldwin Locomotive Works of Philadelphia, one of twenty purchased from the American company in 1899/1900. Ardsley was a smaller establishment than Colwick and had a less intense workload, but it was an ideal place for a young engineer to experience his first job of any substance as assistant to the District Locomotive Inspector. The lower picture shows a group of very youthful workers at Ardsley, probably cleaners or apprentices, captured in a photo taken from Edward Thompson's collection. (*ET/DN*)

Nineteen of the twenty Baldwin 2-6-0s arrived in kit form at Ardsley and were assembled there. The last member of the class was delivered to a location near Paris, constructed there and then appeared as a GNR exhibit at the Exposition in the city in 1900. During Peppercorn's time at Colwick these engines were occasional visitors, but at Ardsley they became a permanent feature of his life. These locomotives had comparatively short lives, all, it seems, being scrapped by 1915. (*ET/DN*)

Above and below: The first of the GNR's H2 2-6-0s No. 1630, in 1912. Many historians have commented that this engine introduced the 'Gresley look'. True or not, they were certainly handsome engines with a balanced, purposeful look. (*ET/DN*)

himself in on an uncertain pitch, but the changes he wrought were significant nonetheless.

His first venture produced a mixed traffic 2-6-0 tender engine designated the H2, the H1 being the Baldwin built engines. The ten built during 1912/13 contained many Doncaster features and were recognisable descendants of Ivatt's engines. They had two outside cylinders, 20in diameter by 26in stroke, Walschaerts valve gear and a 4ft 8in diameter boiler that produced 170psi and a tractive effort of 22,070lb. There were, however, some Gresley touches. The running plate was much higher than GNR locomotives that had gone before, obviously with ease of maintenance in mind. In addition, a Gresley patented double-bolster swing link pony truck was fitted, but this did little, or so it is reported, to reduce their rough riding qualities. Due to this, they acquired the nickname 'Ragtimers'. Nevertheless, they proved to be strong, reliable engines and were allocated to King's Cross, Doncaster and Peterborough's New England shed where Peppercorn would encounter them when posted there from Ardsley in 1914.

The new Superintendent developed his fleet of engines in a number of other ways in the short period between this move and the outbreak of war. The first of these, his heavy goods Class O1 2-8-0s, helped establish his big engine policy and became a rallying cry for much that happened later. Here, the influence of George Churchward was only too apparent. In 1903, he produced a two-cylinder prototype 2-8-0 goods engine that proved so successful that eighty-four were built by the GWR, so setting a precedent for others to follow. On the GNR, Ivatt's 0-8-0s had proven themselves capable engines, but loads were increasing and something bigger was needed. This programme led to the construction of five O1s in 1914 with another fifteen added by 1919. But the development went on and in 1918 another prototype appeared that demonstrated Gresley's evolving ideas.

This 2-8-0 engine, No. 461, was his first serious attempt at using three cylinders, believing that this configuration was better suited to heavy freight work. These cylinders were arranged in line abreast and drove the second set of coupled wheels. To transmit drive to the wheels, Gresley chose to adopt his 1915 patented conjugated valve gear rather than use three independent sets. It was a concept he and his team had considered during the war's lean years when simply keeping the railways going and producing munitions were their primary tasks. Innovation and experimentation were sacrificed for the greater good, but by late 1917, though peace could not be predicted, work on 461 was moving on. Drawings had been prepared and the new cylinder block had been cast and assembled, with other parts under manufacture using the O1 model as guide. Progress was unhurried and the engine was rolled out in May 1918 to begin testing, which confirmed its superiority over the

Engine No. 461 when rolled out, painted in lined primer grey, at Doncaster in May 1918. An historically important moment in time, because this engine marked the beginning of Gresley's design revolution. It was the first of his big engines and it was the first to make use of his patented conjugated valve gear. (*ET/DN*)

No. 461's cylinder and saddle block fully assembled in November 1917. The inclined angle of the cylinders is of note. This was necessary so that they could drive, through shortened connecting rods, the second pair of coupled wheels. (*ET/DN*)

two-cylinder version, though fifteen more were built in 1919/20 under contract by North British.

In 1921, sixty-six O2s were added to this heavy goods fleet with those refinements tested on No.461 by then thoroughly examined by Gresley. Once again, Peppercorn became very familiar with these engines when serving at New England in the early years of the war. Post-war he was undoubtedly influenced by Gresley's design philosophy and its practical application in 461. Many years later, Bert Spencer hinted at how strong this influence mighty have been when he wrote:

'Peppercorn often spoke of the years following his return from the Western Front when he observed the direction in which Gresley was moving. He was clearly impressed and enthused by all he saw. I remember him speaking of a brief period shortly after being demobbed when he was assigned to Doncaster while awaiting a permanent posting to Retford. He recalled a long conversation with Gresley in which he described his aims and ideas and showed him some early drawings of his Pacific which had clearly occupied his mind during the war years. Even thirty years later Peppercorn talked of these days and the strong influence they had upon him. I did get the impression that he might have liked to have worked as Gresley's assistant but Bulleid took this enviable slot instead.'

Who is to say whether more or less might have been achieved if the roles had been reversed. Bulleid, although often described as clever but erratic, probably had better credentials as a designer even at this stage, having studied engineering at university. He was also a lively speaker capable of expounding ideas and pushing them through no matter how junior his rank. If so, he was like Gresley himself and Bulleid left a number of reports of the animated and conceptual discussions the two men had over design issues in which they explored ideas together. Peppercorn was by all accounts a milder, less strident person. If so, he was less likely to shine in the same way. He had, or so it seems, a more measured personality, one that may have been better suited to the management of a large organisation rather than become a specialist designer. When both Ivatt and Gresley were observing the two men from close quarters, these differences were probably only too clear to them, hence the different directions in which their careers moved. Bulleid remained Gresley's assistant until 1937 and Peppercorn focussed solely on production and operational issues until reaching a very senior rank.

There were two other projects that Peppercorn might have observed as the countdown to war began, but these were less experimental in nature than the construction of No. 461, though did contain some Gresley refinements. The first of these was the two-cylinder J23 0-6-0 tank engine, thirty of which were built in 1913/14 with another seventy-two added in the period 1922 to 1939. These engines were constructed with very distinctive tapered side tanks and were designed to take redundant 4ft 2in diameter L1 boilers, which became available when the 0-8-2Ts received larger boilers. Later members of the class were fitted with surplus 4ft 5in units so continued this frugal theme. The prototype, No. 167, became something of a test bed for Gresley, being fitted with a Robinson superheater and balanced slide valves as an experiment. Neither adaption proved particularly successful, though, and did not find their way onto other members of this successful class.

To coincide with the introduction of the J23, Gresley presented the next stage in the evolution of his 2-6-0 tender engines – the H3. Building on the H2, he extended the wheelbase and added a bigger 5ft 6in diameter boiler and fitted a 24-element Robinson superheater. These modifications meant that these engines could produce a tractive effort of 23,400lb., an increase of about 1,300lb. over the H2s. The next stage in this programme, the H4, was a further step change that reflected Gresley's continuing growth as a designer and the gradual emergence

Gresley's first H3 2-6-0 easily distinguished from the H2 by the size of its boiler. By the time war was declared ten were in service. They proved so strong and versatile that they found ready use in this period of national emergency. Ten more were added in 1916 and twenty more in 1918, such were their proven strengths. Twenty-five were constructed post-war and the ten H2s began receiving the bigger boilers from 1920 onwards. (*RH*)

New England Shed at Peterborough where Peppercorn was posted as war began in 1914 and (right) Peterborough Station shortly after Crescent Bridge, in the foreground, was opened in 1913. By this time the Ivatt Atlantics dominated express traffic along the east coast line, as demonstrated here by engine No. 1439, built in 1908, as she makes a spectacular getaway from the city that year. (*RH*)

of his ideas. Yet with the war intervening, the H4 would not make its first appearance until 1920 and mark the beginning of the most dynamic period of his life, a fact not lost on the many talented men who were gradually gathering around this most gifted man. But if engine design was disrupted by the war years, the impact on those men of 'fighting age' in the company, and the rest of Britain, was far greater and more deadly, as Peppercorn would soon discover.

For most people in this country, the Great War came as a surprise. Far off, distant events in Sarajevo played on national ambitions and grievances in such a way that a conflict that might have been avoided turned to all-out war. The historian A.J.P. Taylor best describes these events when he wrote:

'Men are reluctant to believe that great events have small causes. Therefore, once the War started, they were convinced that it must be the outcome of profound forces. It is hard to discover these when we examine the details. Nowhere was their conscious determination to provoke a war. Statesmen miscalculated. They used the instruments of bluff and threat which had proved effective on previous occasions. This time things went wrong; the statesmen became prisoners of their own weapons. The great armies, accumulated to provide security and preserve the peace, carried nations to war by their own weight… The plans for mobilising these millions rested on railways; and railway timetables cannot be improvised. Once started, the wagons and carriages must roll remorselessly and inevitably forward to their predestined goal.

'The First World War had begun – imposed on the statesmen of Europe by railway timetables. It was an unexpected climax to the railway age.'

In August, war plans and timetables came together and largely conscript armies joined their units in an irrevocable step that no one seemed able to control – Germany, France and Russia fearing that to delay might give too great an advantage to an enemy. Britain sat on the side line of these events with too small an army, and no trained reserve, to be of any real consequence, but committed to help Belgium if attacked from any side. Germany's planners, fearing encirclement, sought to avoid a war on two fronts. So they devised a scheme whereby the greater threat from France would be neutralised before the less efficient Russian Army could muster and threaten from the east. The Schlieffen Plan, as the strike against France was called, was activated with disastrous consequences for all concerned. Their sweep westwards assumed free passage through Belgium, but when their request was denied they simply invaded this country to get at France. Unable to stand by, Britain declared war and placed its small army in the path of the German juggernaut and the slaughter began.

Although not geared up for a European war, a mobilisation of sorts did consume Britain quite rapidly. In this the railways played a considerable part. But this country's true effort lay in harnessing its considerable industry and building a large army from scratch. Both these targets would take time to achieve and in the meantime, the railways began to prepare themselves to support this herculean task. Peppercorn was soon swept up in this work and, it seems, was soon transferred from Ardsley to the major railway centre at Peterborough.

For many, the Great War became the defining moment of their lives. It is not difficult to see why. The coming years would lay bare all elements of their lives and all they had come to accept and believe. It was a war of unparalleled brutality which allowed no quarter and offered little compassion to those swept up in its maelstrom. Those who survived would forever be marked by its passing, their characters forever translated by its worst excesses. War is always a bloody, unforgiving business but this conflict plumbed new depths of misery on an unimaginable scale. Sadly, most individual experiences of this conflict have been lost to time, a process not helped by the destruction of many personal files when the records centre at Hayes in Middlesex was bombed by the Luftwaffe in 1940. We lost a large part of this precious archive, including Arthur Peppercorn's files or so it seems. All that remains is a single 'Medal Card' which states that he served as a lieutenant then captain in the Royal Engineers (Training Battalion), but gives no dates. For his contribution to the war, he received the War and the Victory Medals, both of which he claimed in March 1926. His promotion to captain is thought to have been in an acting capacity, which was quite common practice at the time. Reversion to the most junior rank possible, when demobilisation became a reality, meant smaller discharge payments and a reduced burden on the exchequer.

When it came to railway workers, their service was deemed so essential to the war effort that reserved status was applied to them. This did not stop many from volunteering, there being no conscription until late 1915. But if they did take this path without permission, there was no guarantee that their employer would hold the post open for them. So, the wise sought consent, the headstrong just went. Being a mature middle manager, Peppercorn resisted the temptation to take up arms immediately. Instead, he found himself posted to Peterborough's New England Shed in 1914 as Assistant to the District Locomotive Superintendent. Although a level transfer, this shed is considered to have been a significant step up for any budding manager. During the conflict, this status increased further as it became the hub of so much wartime activity, particularly in the movement of men, munitions and equipment. Someone with Peppercorn's growing skill and authority was best placed to help ensure all this was managed effectively.

Like many, he probably felt pangs of conscience when witnessing soldiers depart and reading of the great battles raging in France and Belgium. Each day, newspapers would have provided a constant reminder of the lives sacrificed with long casualty lists even when the front appeared 'quiet'. So the temptation to 'do his bit' must have been strong. But duty is duty and he undoubtedly contributed much more to the war effort by remaining at New England rather than feeding the mincing machine on the Western Front. So it continued for a time as the war grew in scale and horror, sucking in more and more men and women in the process.

During the war, the role of the Royal Engineers proved crucial to the Allied victory and by 1918 over 295,000 men filled their ranks operating on all fronts. Their tasks were many and varied, but, in essence, were concerned with keeping the front line fed with men and material. A key part of this work involved the construction and maintenance of railways and the training of recruits to keep them open and running effectively. Huge numbers of men, especially specialist engineers, skilled workers, miners, labourers and more, were soon be recruited as the conflict stagnated into trench warfare. However, it took until the mid-part of 1915 for this to be fully appreciated and only then after several ill-prepared and disastrous frontal assaults by the Allied armies against German strong points. The defensive power of machine guns and artillery now dominated the battlefield. Together, they made any attack a costly and ruinous business. So the troops dug in and relied heavily on the work of the Royal Engineers to survive in something approaching fighting trim.

By mid-1915, or so it seems, Peppercorn could not deny his natural instinct to join up and sought a way of achieving release from his commitments at Peterborough. He was not alone in this. Oliver Bulleid had already gone to war and was serving in France. With his engineering background, he was soon granted a commission with the Army Service Corps and was now in command of the Second Army's ammunition railhead at St Venant in the Pas-de-Calais. Edward Thompson, being more senior than Bulleid and Peppercorn, discovered that release from the GNR was more difficult to achieve. He only found his way to France, as a Major with the Royal Engineers, late in 1916, via a posting to Woolwich Arsenal, where his father-in-law, Vincent Raven, was in command. By this stage, Peppercorn had been commissioned and was attached to the Engineers' Training Battalion, which was commanded by Lt Colonel T.H. Cochrane, a regular army officer, as an instructor. It is interesting to note that he let his membership of IMechE lapse at this time and did not renew it until 1919. An oversight perhaps, but it might reflect his attitude to the war and his chances of survival. With the Battle of the Somme fresh in the mind, with its horrendous casualty lists published daily in the press, no one but a blind optimist would have given themselves much chance of survival. This was especially so of young subalterns, who suffered a disproportionate number of casualties in front line service.

This unit, according to Engineers' official history, was set up to 'receive young regular RE officers on first commission from the Royal Military Academy at Woolwich, temporary officers on first commission or on transfer from other arms, and later, cadets on probation for temporary commission and recruits on enlistment. All these had to be trained in drill, field engineering and musketry, and dispatched, as required overseas or elsewhere.'

As the war dragged on, the Battalion received up to 150 new officers each week, which kept the number of men under training at a maximum of 3,500 at any one time. A few of these were transferred each month to other establishments for 'training in special subjects', but the vast bulk went straight to operational units. Those responsible for training, like Peppercorn, were expected to remain with the unit for the duration

Above: Recruiting posters, most notably with Lord Kitchener's face staring out at potential volunteers, a finger pointing in an accusing way, became common fare on billboards across the country. The Royal Engineers chose a more appealing approach and between 1914 and 1918 their numbers increased from 25,000 to nearly 296,000, including Peppercorn and many other railwaymen. (*DN*)

Opposite: A scene enacted on a daily basis at each of the major rail centres across Britain during the war and one that Peppercorn would have witnessed as he busied himself with his duties as Assistant at Peterborough. In the early days of the war volunteers often marched to the station accompanied by brass bands and crowds to see them off. As the struggle deepened and the numbers diminished these ceremonies became rarer and rarer. Here groups of volunteers leave Peterborough to travel to their training centre in late 1914 as part of the 7th Battalion of the Northamptonshire Regiment. The upper group was nicknamed 'Whitsed's Light Infantry' in tribute to Councillor Isaac Whitsed who toured local companies and schools seeking volunteers. The percentage of those returned home after the war from this early intake was small, with chances of survival, or not being maimed, being no more than one in three. (*THG*)

Peppercorn, third from right back row, with fellow officers when attached to the RE's Training Battalion in 1916. All the names are recorded on the back of the picture but not the location which may be either Brompton or St Mary's Barracks in Kent. (*THG*)

of the war, but in some cases 'it was found possible to accede to the requests of a few instructors to be sent overseas'. There is no official record that Peppercorn did so. However, when providing a short biography for Hereford Cathedral School in 1931 he wrote, 'From 1917 to 1919 I served in the Chief Mechanical Engineer's Department of the Royal Engineers in France at various depots. During the latter part of this time I was Technical Assistant to the CME at General Headquarters.' This would suggest that he successfully canvassed support for a front line posting. As the War Department continued to register his permanent unit as the Training Battalion, this implies that he went overseas on secondment only, with recall at any time remaining a distinct possibility. But by 1917, the Engineers were over the peak of their recruitment and training programmes and only needed sufficient numbers to make good losses and provide reliefs to those reaching the end of their tours. In the circumstances, they were unlikely to gather Peppercorn in unless the war took an unexpected turn and training programmes had to be stepped up again.

So for two years, Peppercorn fulfilled his duties with the Training Battalion. For most of the war, its main accommodation was centred in Brompton and St Mary's Barracks in Chatham and nearby Rochester. However, recruits spent time at other establishments learning more specialist skills. These included the Railway and Roads Training Centres at Longmoor and Borden in Hampshire, which would have become familiar to Peppercorn.

All in all, it would have been a pleasant way of passing such a war and many would have been happy to remain in such a 'cushy' posting until it ended. But for others it became too much to bear and they agitated for release, Peppercorn amongst them. The fact that he was an engineer and leader of some experience would have helped speed this process. The army could only sustain its drive eastwards if its infrastructure coped with a battlefield terrain virtually destroyed by high explosives. By 1917, it was struggling to do this and needed men of his experience to help it achieve its main aims, which on the Western Front meant keeping

It is reported that four standard gauge Hudswell Clarke locomotives were sold by the Midland Railway to the War Office. One of these ended up at Borden Camp where it was employed on training duties amongst other things. This engine was given the name *Kingsley* and is seen here in about 1916/17 with commissioned and non-commissioned officers, presumably instructors, posing in the foreground. The notes written on the back in pencil contain Peppercorn's name, but they do not state where he is. Judging by other photos of the period it is likely that he is in the front row second from the right. (*DN*)

Probably a daily scene for Peppercorn for two years – the Memorial Gate in front of Brompton Barracks as it appeared during the Great War. By commemorating those lost in the Boer War it provided a constant reminder of those then serving of the ultimate sacrifice they might have to make themselves. The barracks are now home to the Royal Engineers' Museum. (*THG*)

supply routes open and defences strong no matter how difficult this might have been.

By the time Peppercorn joined the staff of the Chief Mechanical Engineer, the organisation was well established. However, the CME title should not be mistaken for that used by some railway companies at the time. In fact, this department grew out of the Directorate of Fortifications and Works, which in 1914 began expanding rapidly under Lord Kitchener's guiding hand. Within weeks, many sub-divisions had been created with the CME being designated F.W.8, with Lt Colonel R. Oakes in command and based at Adastral House in London. Very soon he began recruiting civil engineers and Engineer officers with specialist skills. By 1918, staff numbers reached nearly 200 in the HQ group, with 46 commissioned and 28 civilian inspectors. Their main task was to oversee work at docks and be 'continually at work visiting and helping contractors in Britain or in the battle area conducting engineering tasks of all types', ensuring their work was completed successfully and on time. It seems that Peppercorn became one of these inspectors, hence his appearance in France. In due course, Oakes was transferred and replaced by Colonel S.J. Craster, an experienced engineer who was returned to duty from the retired list in September 1917.

Their work covered a wide spectrum of duties in back areas but also well forward into the front line. No matter where you operated, though, everywhere could be fraught with dangers, from short or long range gunfire,

Whilst on leave from the Army, Arthur attended his sister Lily's wedding in Hereford. During June she married Norman Watts, who was serving with the Australian Infantry Force. This picture captures the bride, second from left front row, and members of her family, including her mother and her younger brothers, John and Walter, who were both vicars, and sisters. Speculation surrounds the identity of the uniformed figure which resembles both Arthur and Norman, who were both Lieutenants at the time. The cap badge, which might have confirmed the regiment, is unclear, but suggest the AIF not the Royal Engineers. (*WF*)

so it was rarely possible to be entirely free of risk as the inspectors went about their business.

The Engineers' official history paints an interesting picture of how F.W.8 evolved:

'As trench warfare developed, demands were received for many new forms of plant, such as excavators and mining stores, all of which fell to F.W.8. The French railways also appealed for assistance, and later, when the Americans arrived they made large demands for machinery and stores. At the end of 1916, when Transportation became a separate organisation, the Director-General of Transportation (Major-General Sir Eric Geddes) took over the responsibility for his own stores, plant and material, for the railways, light railways, roads, inland waterways and docks, and a year later the Royal Flying Corps formed its own supply organisation.'

A picture of everyday life on the Western Front that captures the mud, confusion and intensity of trench life close to the action. The sights and sounds would have been only too familiar to Peppercorn as he undertook his inspection duties with F.W.8. (*RH*)

Each night on the Western Front there was a deadly and remorseless firework display that veterans were unlikely to forget or wish to experience again. In the forward or back areas, which Peppercorn had to inhabit on a daily basis during 1917/18, the continuous barrage exacted a heavy toll of life and depleted the nerves of those who survived. (*RH*)

It then goes on to describe some of the key projects they managed that may have involved Peppercorn as an inspector in France:

'<u>Bridging Equipment</u> – the rebuilding of broken bridges from local material. When this proved too slow pontoons were constructed and used. By 1917 this totalled some 3,000 units, with F.W.8 asked to design and oversee construction of steel bridges with spans up to 85 feet, transportable in sections.

'<u>Hutting</u> – here the work of Captain Nissen in designing semi-circular huts constructed of corrugated steel sheets on a wooden frame proved of significance. 27,000 were ordered in 1916.

'<u>Special Plant</u> – This included laundry and woodworking machinery, machine tools for engineer workshops, fire engines, destructors, disinfectors, cranes, concrete areas, boring rigs, pumps, airlifts and water purifying plant.

'<u>Shipping</u> – In connection with the shipment of non-explosive stores overseas, all such movements passed from the Army's Ordnance Department to F.W.8 in 1915. A fleet of twenty vessels was allotted by the Admiralty for this task and stores depots were established in Britain and France to handle a wide range of stores and equipment.

'<u>Water supply, mining and miscellaneous stores</u> – this included the purchase and supply of 10 million steel posts and an equal number of screw pickets, plus excavating tools, pumps and machinery to support mining operations (under enemy trenches for listening purposes or to be blown in support of major attacks).

'<u>Sandbags</u> – The total number supplied reached 1,300 million. These were provided and supplied by F.W.8.'

An inspector's task would have varied day by day and required their presence on many parts of the front to

The familiar world of those serving on the Western Front. Scenes of death and mutilation were the norm, accompanied by its ever present stench and proliferation of flies, whilst rats picked over the remains of bodies that lay unburied for weeks, even months. Such things are alien to us now and we tend to forget the deeply disturbing impression made on the minds of those who lived and died in these appalling conditions. (*RH*)

The Great War led to huge social changes in Britain. With so many men away fighting there was a chronic shortage of workers across many industries, it became essential that women fill these vacancies. The GNR were not slow in seeing the benefits of this course of action and took on many hundreds of female employees, breaking with the long assumed roles of the sexes in such an industry. As soldiers returned from the war the numbers diminished, nevertheless a prohibition had been lifted in part and the slow march to equality had begun. This picture, taken in 1917 at Grantham, captures the spirit of this new world with some of the women who serviced engines for the GNR standing by one of their steeds, a large boilered Ivatt Class C1 Atlantic built in 1908. (RH)

ensure that the items they had provided were fit for purpose. Probably one of the most dangerous duties they faced would have been inspecting equipment in use in the front lines or in the many mines burrowed beneath as each side sought some tactical advantage. Effectiveness of material and machinery could only truly be assessed by engineers witnessing it in action. In this way, they could confirm its suitability or recommend any modifications that might be made. It seems strange that quality control should be practised in such a deadly environment, but in many ways it was just another industry to be analysed and evaluated.

Wherever Peppercorn travelled in France and Belgium he would have seen the death and destruction visited on his comrades, particularly when another 'big push' was underway. If the many contemporary accounts of this war are to be believed, the sights and sounds of this conflict were deeply disturbing to even the most sturdy souls. It is beyond reason to expect anyone to know how they will react to combat or the level of stress they will be able to endure when being constantly pounded. Although not a front line soldier, Peppercorn would have observed and understood the debilitating effect of gunfire, the constant threat of injury, appalling living conditions and the reality of violent death. He like millions of others would be changed by these experiences and made more mature and, perhaps, less certain about their own immortality. Peace, when it came, would present new challenges and demand that they suppress all memories of these dreadful events.

The Armistice in 1918 brought the fighting to an end but not the war. Without a permanent peace treaty in place, the Allied Armies could not be reduced in size to any great extent. Demobilisation would be a slow process for many and for Peppercorn this meant a delayed return to the GNR. But, at least, he would have found himself back in England fairly quickly, his work as an inspector over, without the added burden of serving in the Army of Occupation to help suppress any immediate threat from Germany. And so the months passed and these men waited, some patiently, others less so, for their civilian lives to be re-established and work to re-absorb them. Being a single man probably meant a slightly longer wait for Peppercorn, but as the winter of 1919 approached, he finally left the services with a small gratuity payment. However, he did have a secure, but unidentified post waiting for him, a mentor and advocate in Gresley and the possibility of further promotion ahead. After a trying few years in uniform, he must have looked to the future with some optimism.

CHAPTER 3

ALL CHANGE

Old friendships and working partnerships on the GNR were quickly renewed in the post-war years. Bulleid and Peppercorn, who both served on the Western Front, remained close. Under Gresley's guiding hand they quickly re-established themselves in the hierarchy of the company and continued their climb to the top of their profession. Here the two men are photographed in 1924, at Hadley Common, north of London, where Bulleid lived with his family following his transfer to King's Cross as Gresley's assistant. Peppercorn, a cigarette in hand, remained a heavy smoker all his life; a habit very common amongst old soldiers to whom a 'smoke' was one way of relieving stress; it also warmed the hand on a cold night in the trenches. (*HB*)

Soldiers returning from the war found a country irrevocably changed by recent experiences, but few at home seemed to appreciate the depth of the traumas suffered in the front line. Much later, after many years of thought, some ex-soldiers chose to record their memories of this difficult time. Their accounts bear strong similarities with words such as 'they couldn't understand', 'few, if any, would listen', 'they were embarrassed if you talked of the war and quickly changed the subject' and much more. In truth, everyone was tired of the war and all its effects. Yet peace when it came did not see a sudden upswing in living standards or opportunities. Despite the hope people felt, bolstered by politicians' false words, it would not become a 'country fit for heroes' but one of economic recession and slow spreading, hard earnt equality. For those returning to the security of a job and possibly a wife, the transition might have been an easier one. For Peppercorn, there was the certainty of a job, but not the one he had left. He would undoubtedly have contacted Gresley at some stage to notify him of his imminent return and sought some advice on possible postings. It is recorded that he spent a short period at Doncaster before being appointed as District Locomotive Superintendent Retford, twenty or so miles south of Gresley's HQ. Although a much smaller facility than Colwick, Ardsley or New England it was still a promotion and a perfect way in which to resurrect his career before taking on a bigger challenge.

Although Retford was situated on the main line to London it did not have a significant number of engines on its books. With Doncaster only twenty miles away, this is not surprising. At its peak, it managed only thirty or so engines, supported by a shed with four roads, a turntable, coaling stage, two sets of heavy lifting equipment and some workshop facilities. All in all, not a major centre of activity, perhaps reflected in the type and number of locomotives stabled there, none of which were true heavyweights. In the early 1920s, this included thirteen J5 0-6-0 tender engines, seven J22s, a smaller number of E1 2-4-0s, D1, D2 and D3 4-4-0s, plus 0-6-0 J4s and J7s. In addition, there would have been the occasional visiting engine undergoing minor repairs.

Although on the main line, the engines based at Retford had little to do with this major route. As you might expect with locomotives of these types, their main duties concerned local passenger traffic, assisting through trains when in difficulty and the haulage of coal from local collieries. But they had one other duty. The GNR line and the old Manchester, Sheffield and Lincolnshire Railway, which became the Great Central Railway in 1897, crossed at Retford. The GCR also had a small shed nearby, but until amalgamation in 1923 worked independently of the other, nevertheless the GNR locomotives were called upon to transfer loads between the two lines at times.

For someone like Peppercorn, who was more used to managing work at bigger sheds, Retford does not seem to have provided much of a challenge. In fact, in 1912,

Retford Station just before the Great War. It is situated on the main line south of Doncaster. (*DN*)

when it lost a sub-depot at Newark, the Superintendent post was downgraded to Locomotive Foreman and came under the direct control of the District Locomotive Superintendent at Doncaster. So his appointment there in 1919, and the restoration of the Superintendent post, may simply have been a way of finding him a job until something better turned up. If so, it probably reflects Peppercorn's status in Gresley's eyes and the need to engage him in railway business as soon as possible.

The veterans gradually slipped back into their peacetime lives again with mixed results. Whatever they felt about the recent conflict and whatever the state of their wounds, the period of readjustment slowly passed with varying degrees of success. Peppercorn, unlike Bulleid and Thompson, had no family in the area to help in this process, but he found the company of these two old comrades, who had shared his wartime experiences, invaluable. One outlet for their energies proved to be golf. The three men constantly practised on courses around Doncaster, often accompanied by Isaac Groom, the GNR's Running Superintendent, who was a very accomplished player, if records are to be believed. This camaraderie continued even when Thompson gave up the post of Carriage and Wagon Superintendent and returned to the North Eastern Railway as the Carriage and Wagon Works Manager at York in 1920. Such was the importance of the sport to these men, that Bulleid's memories of these friendly encounters found prominence in the biography his son wrote in 1977. Here he remembered Peppercorn playing all the time 'with intense vigour'. This friendly rivalry was a simple means of letting off steam and enjoying the company of contemporaries and the common ground this created.

The script supplied with the negative describes this as Retford early in LNER days as viewed from the coaling stage looking northwards with the shed behind the photographer. The main line runs to the right of the picture hidden by sidings. The lifting gear in the foreground is of the shear leg variety most commonly used in boatyards mounted on a vessel for manoeuvrability. Retford had two such installations, one with three legs the other with four, and were both capable of lifting 100 tons or more. This picture shows Ivatt Atlantic No. 4425 which appears to have been a visiting locomotive under repair and unable to reach the workshops at Doncaster. (*THG*)

The shed at Retford as it appeared in July 1932, little changed from when Peppercorn served there. The engine, a Class D3 4-4-0 No. 4074, was typical of the types assigned to Retford. These were in sharp contrast to Ivatt's Atlantics that flashed past on the main line, let alone the products of Gresley's fertile mind that then dominated the network. When this photograph was taken the shed and station would echo to the sounds of Pacifics passing by, a constant reminder of Retford Shed's more mundane life. (*RH*)

Sport seems to have played a part in Peppercorn's life since school days. At Hereford he appears to have been a keen rugby player and cricketer. It was an active interest that continued for many years; until age pushed him into becoming a spectator. There was, in addition, a strong sporting culture in the GNR, and then the LNER, encouraged by directors and senior managers. A lot of this focussed on specific events such as inter-department competitions with the aim of encouraging esprit de corps but also good health. This attitude also spread across into the world of horse racing and here Gresley, Peppercorn and many other senior managers found a ready outlet for their social and sporting interests. Over the years, they regularly attended meetings at nearby Doncaster Race Course, with the St Leger race being a particular favourite. The company's in house magazine regularly reported these events and underpinned the social nature of sport and its ability to create harmony. This was very important in these post-war years when social and economic turmoil were spreading discord and conflict.

When the war ended, there was a sense of hope engendered by the long awaited peace, but by the early twenties this had dissipated as the true long term impact of those awful years hit home. Markets had been destroyed, the country suffered under the burden of huge debts incurred by the conflict, with an infrastructure strained to breaking point. At the same time, there was a growing clamour for improved employment rights, better housing, greater social support and equality. With riches lost and a world economy in freefall, most employers could only offer austerity and the promise of better times ahead. Clashes were inevitable but spread slowly in the twenties,

Sporting events were heavily promoted by the GNR and LNER during the post-war years with Gresley, Thompson and Peppercorn's active involvement. Athletics, cricket, football, golf and much more became major events in the company's life as witnessed here as the LNER's amateur boxers gather together with the CME to show off their trophies. The value of these sponsored events was not underplayed at a time of austerity and social disharmony. (*ET/DN*)

culminating in the General Strike of 1926. Sport, though irrelevant in day to day survival, did, at least, have the power to distract and create some unity. So it is little wonder that the GNR and LNER actively encouraged it whenever possible.

With Doncaster being only a short distance away from Retford, Peppercorn chose to set up house there and commute daily to work. He moved into 29 Christchurch Road and employed Mary Creasor as his housekeeper. This arrangement carried on until 1924 when he moved along the road to number 11, where Ann and Emma Sherburn would look after his domestic needs. Both these small houses were probably leased from the GNR, which was normal practice at the time, a similar arrangement holding good in Thorne Road nearby. Here Gresley, Thompson and Bulleid lived in company houses for a time, so this area of the town became something of an enclave for the company's senior managers. It seems that each house was sufficiently large to accommodate occasional visitors which, according to some surviving cards and letters, included his mother and unmarried sisters. By this stage, Agnes Peppercorn, now in her late sixties, had moved from Lulham Court to Blenheim House on the edge of Hereford. She would remain here until her death in 1934.

Peppercorn's time at Retford proved to be brief, being brought to an end in 1920 when the Assistant in charge of the wagon works post at Doncaster fell vacant. However, this proved to be a small stepping stone only. A year later, he became Assistant to the Carriage and Wagon Superintendent, a post filled by Bulleid, who had just replaced the NER-bound Thompson. Undoubtedly,

Christchurch Road in Doncaster as it appeared when Peppercorn lived there in the years following the Great War. It was a world still dominated by the horse and cart but would soon see the first privately owned cars taking over this scene. Peppercorn was, by all accounts, an enthusiastic driver and car owner, though the types he acquired now seem lost to history. (*THG*)

the close relationship that had formed between Bulleid and Peppercorn over the years may have played a part in this promotion. Nevertheless, his professional skills would have been of greater significance when choosing someone to fill such a prominent position. Patronage of an up and coming talent was one thing, favouritism towards a friend, though possible, was most unlikely to have been sanctioned by Gresley or Bulleid for that matter. The industrial world they inhabited was far too cut and thrust for that to happen. Hard work and commitment in such a competitive industry were essential and were qualities valued by both men.

Peppercorn, by all accounts, was imbued with these virtues and expected those under him to work hard. However, he was not an unblinking authoritarian, although some photographs of him might suggest otherwise. Here was a man who appeared able to rule without rancour or unnecessary conflict. For the time this was unusual. Unquestioned autocracy and instant dismissal for those who fell out of favour or erred even in a minor way, were regularly practised. Peppercorn, who is often described as a kindly man, took a different approach. He laid down clear rules, allowed some room for error or mistakes and practised greater tolerance, if contemporary accounts are to be believed. Yet at the same time, he clearly understood that production targets had to be met and exerted pressure where necessary to achieve them. This is always a difficult balance to strike. Yet he seems to have managed it throughout his career with subtlety, good grace and firmness when required, negotiating settlements rather than seeking confrontation along the way. In this, if nothing else, he was a modern man fully able to combine inner steel with commercial sense and strong inter-personal skills.

In his approach to workshop management, Peppercorn was very much like Edward Thompson who, throughout his career, studied production line techniques closely and understood the need for a clear and efficient work flow on the shop floor. Gresley was probably less able in this field, perhaps reflecting his

With the war over, the railway companies tried to pick up where they left off in 1914. However, with the network suffering from over use, reduced maintenance and lack of investment, there would be no quick fix. Nevertheless, peace was greeted with some optimism for the future and pre-war express services were soonest restored; here pulled by a gleaming Ivatt Atlantic, in this case the 1904 built engine No. 279. (*RH*)

fascination with design. His skill lay in selecting men who could manage these areas confidently and well, so complementing his own skills in the process. Thompson and Peppercorn fitted this profile, as did many others. Between them, they seemed able to balance the occasionally conflicting needs of production and design engineering. But this isn't to say that conflict or disagreements did not arise at times. Some accounts suggest that Gresley and Thompson did not always see eye to eye on engineering matters. There seems to have been some mutual respect, but things did edge towards mutual antipathy at times; perhaps not surprising when two such strong ambitious men work together. The relationship between the CME and Peppercorn seems to have been a much more relaxed one. This was probably because Peppercorn didn't choose to challenge Gresley's authority and was imbued with a greater sense of diplomacy. If so, he was less likely to challenge his leader's position in a direct way.

By the time Peppercorn returned to Doncaster in 1920, Gresley's locomotive and rolling stock programme was developing rapidly, having been forced into a state of stasis by the war. Planning for the future had not ended during this period, of course, only the wherewithal to turn his ideas into a reality. If the changes made before the war by Gresley were significant, this was nothing compared to the explosion that followed, all of which Peppercorn witnessed from close quarters. However, his involvement was limited to rolling stock, there being no evidence to suggest he became involved in the design of locomotives, even though both Gresley and Bulleid were his supporters and probably keen to engage him in many matters. In truth, he probably had little to do with carriage design either at this stage, but he would, at least, share in their construction as assistant to the Carriage and Wagon Superintendent.

It was an area of work in which Peppercorn would become something of a specialist in the years that followed, first at Doncaster then becoming Works Manager at York in 1927. This period would see him become increasingly influential in the company's life, but only as far as carriage and wagon work was concerned. This would remain his lot until 1933, when posted to Stratford as Assistant Mechanical Engineer. Here he would finally take on responsibility for a large fleet of locomotives, their maintenance and development.

However, in the meantime, there was probably enough happening on the carriage side of business to stimulate and engage him. Even if these tasks were not creative in the design sense he could fully immerse himself in the organisation of the workshops. Before the Great War, assembly line technology and systems had begun to find favour. By 1914, this methodology, and the related issues of work study and measurement, had been adopted more widely in other fields of engineering. In many ways, it came into its own when war started and industry was forced to maximise its output of weapons, ammunition and all the other paraphernalia that total war demanded. Edward Thompson, who visited the States in 1911 to observe modern car plants in operation, became a disciple of these techniques and introduced them to the GNR and NER with Gresley and Raven's approval. This work proved highly successful and, by the time Peppercorn moved into the rolling stock side of business, the principles were well established and gradually finding wider application within both companies. However, it would be some years before all workshops adopted these production methods, aided in no small measure by Thompson and Peppercorn.

When addressing the progress Gresley had made since arriving at Doncaster in 1905 as Carriage and Wagon Superintendent, it is interesting to consider the evolution of carriage design. This is particularly important to Peppercorn's story because it was an important part of his development as an engineer. From the start it was an ambitious programme, reflecting Gresley's view of the future; the words higher capacity and greater comfort perhaps best describing his business mantra. In many ways, he predicted the way the market was changing, as Britain's middle class grew in size, affluence and ambition. This translated itself into a demand for more passenger trains and better quality carriages, even on city commuter lines where the need was rather different to the long distance routes. Gresley sought to place the GNR in the vanguard of this new world and began developing a fleet of new carriages to achieve it.

There was certainly scope for improvement. When he took over there was still a large number of carriages with four, six and eight fixed wheels mixed with the more flexible bogie stock. The fixed wheel configuration had, in modern terms, limited stretch potential so had reached the limit of its development. In addition, clerestory roofs were also much in evidence and, although providing ventilation and extra light, were outdated and ready to be replaced by more modern systems. In response to this challenge, and observing developments elsewhere, Gresley began experimenting with articulation, four and six wheeled bogie corridor stock, bow ends, elliptical roofs and dining facilities amongst other things.

When viewed in sequence, as shown in the following photographs, the gradual evolution of carriage design during the first part of Peppercorn's career is only too clear. Other companies followed a similar pattern of development and clearly learnt from each other, nevertheless the Gresley brand was distinctive and attempted to push back boundaries. He, and the GNR's Board members who approved this work, clearly understood the way the market was developing and sought to match supply to demand. He also had an eye for detail and an ability to apply new and occasionally novel ideas in doing so, whether it be the adoption of such things as articulation or the standard of furnishings and fittings to be used. Here was a man determined to improve the breed by careful analysis and experimentation. Later on, he would be criticised by some for the proliferation of types in service and an inability to achieve greater standardisation, with the cost penalties this can incur; the same would be said of the locomotive fleet during his years in office. But at the time, it doesn't seem to have been viewed this way. What was deemed more important was the ability to have sufficient rolling stock in the right place at the right time. As Locomotive Superintendent, with responsibility for the Running Department, this was within Gresley's ability to control, but in 1923, amalgamation changed all this, adding another level of management in the process.

A standard four-wheeler as inherited by Gresley. Despite their lack of capacity, the GNR continued to make use of four and six-wheeled close-coupled sets on some suburban services when their shortcomings were only too well known. Such were their number that some were still in service well into the 1930s. With limited resources, Gresley chose to adapt many in his articulation programme. (*ET/DN*)

1907 and a more modern non-corridor composite with two four-wheeled bogies emerges. This example was employed on Cambridge/Grimsby services. (*ET/DN*)

Comfort, meals on wheels and all round splendour in 1907. A new 1st class dining car emerges. The Gresley look and style, which built on some GNR traditions such as teak exterior panelling, is only too apparent and would continue to evolve. At this stage wood still featured large in construction (frames and panelling), despite its obvious weakness in a crash. Nevertheless, Gresley clung to this material when research was beginning to show that metal frames and bodies were much stronger. It was an issue that Edward Thompson raised with him in 1913 with little apparent effect. A teak finish held greater aesthetic value for him, it seems, and was much cheaper to use and maintain. He also preferred square cornered windows although they suffered from water ingress and rot so required more maintenance. (*ET/DN*)

It was impossible to deny that Gresley and his team had an eye for elegance and comfort, as displayed here in this publicity photograph taken in this 1st Class dining car during 1907 and kept by Edward Thompson as a souvenir. (*ET/DN*)

In 1907, the first of Gresley's articulated units appeared. It was an idea he patented then used throughout his career on both the GNR and LNER. Initially one of its key bonuses was that it allowed him to make use of six-wheeled redundant stock with two old carriages being joined together by a common central bogie. By eliminating rigid axles, greater flexibility was achieved and the units were noted to be good runners. Illustrated here is Gresley's 1909 twin composite articulated unit showing how he evolved the concept. In the 1930s this work would result in the ultra-sleek streamlined sets attached to A4 locomotives on the Golden Jubilee services. (*ET/DN*)

Carriage development continued with the appearance in 1911 of new four-wheeled bogie types, here represented by a 1st class brake. (*ET/DN*)

With the Great War absorbing so much effort and manpower carriage development was put on hold for some years. By the mid-1920s work had resumed and the results are best demonstrated by this 1926 3rd class carriage. (*ET/DN*)

Experiments in articulation continued with this 1928 triple composite unit in which first and third class carriages flank an all-electric kitchen car. (*ET/DN*)

By 1931, when this picture was taken, production of new carriages was reaching a peak and the style and design were well established. In this case it is an open third class coach consisting of two compartments, a single toilet and sixty-four seats. (*ET/DN*)

The final design to appear from York whilst Peppercorn was Works Manager there. The year is 1933 and he will soon be ensconced at Stratford in East London as Assistant Mechanical Engineer. However, before this happened he was responsible for producing five rather unusual sets of carriages, which were turned out in cream and green. Each set were made up of four twin-articulated open 3rd class carriages, two buffet cars and two open brake vehicles. They were built to meet a growing demand for cheap day excursion trips to the seaside and other popular destinations. (*ET/DN*)

During the war, all railway companies had been brought under government control to ensure that they served the war effort first and foremost. In 1919, this should have ended, but by then a view had formed that leaving the network in the hands of so many individual companies did not serve the country well. Following a central review of need led by Sir Eric Geddes, by now the Minister of Transport, the 1921 Railway Act became law and introduced rationalisation to the system. In these deliberations complete nationalisation was also considered, but the political will for this wasn't strong and awaited another war to encourage its introduction. From this seismic change, four large groups emerged, based on regions, although a few smaller companies serving specific communities did survive with their pre-war independence intact.

For the GNR, this meant an end to their long history and amalgamation with the North Eastern, Great Eastern, Great Central, North British, Great North of Scotland and the Hull and Barnsley Railways, plus a number of smaller subsidiary companies, such as the Colne Valley and Halstead Railway. Inevitably a scramble for posts and influence in the new company followed as the London and North Eastern came into being. Gresley came to the fore, but in the process of becoming Chief Mechanical Engineer lost authority over the running side of the business. It was a case of

When the LNER was launched in 1923 publicity remained key to selling this and all the other railway companies. This picture was a rough watercolour sketch prepared at the time to help create an advert, though not used. In many ways it captures the state of the newly created company. Engine No. 3061, an Ivatt Class D1 4-4-0 built in 1911, pulls a rake of articulated carriages created from obsolete GNR fixed wheel stock. (*THG*)

increased authority in one direction, but the inconvenient loss of power in another. He must have quickly realised the implications of this and the lack of control over deciding future needs it brought with it. Within the GNR, his authority as Locomotive Superintendent went largely unchallenged, the Board of Directors seemingly happy to acquiesce to his ideas for change. The only true limit was one of cash, but even here the state of their finances, which was rarely good, doesn't seem to have blocked these ambitions. Within the LNER this was no longer the case.

Now the CME sat alongside three Divisional General Managers – the Southern Area under Sidney Parnell, the North Eastern under Alexander Wilson and Scotland under James Calder. In a stovepipe hierarchy each had direct and equal responsibility to the company's first General Manager, Ralph Wedgwood. Whether Gresley found these changes onerous isn't recorded, but being considered by many to be a realist and an adept politician, he surely had the skills to persuade others of the strength and benefits of his ideas. Nevertheless, having three Divisional General Managers, each likely to present locomotive and rolling stock demands reflecting their individual areas, would add another, trickier layer of management to navigate. With this extra level of bureaucracy in place, progress might stall and the CME's life be made more difficult. Gresley seems to have had the wherewithal to deal effectively with these new demands, but Thompson and Peppercorn, when they became CME, would find their lives dogged by the Divisional Managers' interventions.

As the LNER settled into its new work patterns, Gresley looked at his organisation and decided how best to structure it. There would inevitably be problems in bringing teams from so many different companies together; feral loyalties, traditions and ways of working would be difficult to mould into one, with disruption likely. So it was hardly surprising that he looked to men who had proven their worth to him with the GNR to fill

A scene that would become only too familiar to Peppercorn over the six years he worked there. New 'Gresley' carriages being constructed at Doncaster in the post-war years. The standard of carpentry was always of the highest order and the teak finish a trademark of both the GNR and LNER. (*ET/DN*)

many important posts. He wasn't blind to the strengths of candidates from the other companies, but he would clearly need time to assess their strengths and levels of co-operation. Peppercorn, now proving himself as Assistant to the Carriage and Wagon Works Manager, would have been an obvious candidate for promotion. This proved to be the case and in 1923 he became Carriage Works Manager at Doncaster, succeeding Bulleid who moved to King's Cross with Gresley and Bert Spencer to man the CME's new London HQ.

Under Bulleid, he would have learnt much and participated in many important construction and maintenance programmes. He would also have watched with interest the way his manager worked and the way he engaged Gresley in any debate he thought relevant, revealing much about both men in the process. Henry Bulleid captured a flavour of this in his excellent biography of his father:

> 'Gresley's competence as Chief, his interest in the Carriage side and his growing rapport with Bulleid, all subscribed to an enjoyable and successful posting. Gresley always came when Bulleid phoned to say a new carriage was ready for him to inspect. Nor did they talk exclusively about carriages, Gresley typically confiding the bit of luck which came with a complaint by a director of late running in November 1921; the engine concerned was the Vulcan built compound No. 1300 and Gresley was able to point out that it had never been as satisfactory as the standard

simple Atlantics . . . the decision to buy it had been made (please note) not by Mr Ivatt but by the General Manager.'

He also described some of the experimental work undertaken by Bulleid, with Peppercorn's assistance, which did not always go well. In this case it involved the design of beds for sleeping cars:

'He mocked up a tapered bed as a space saver, but the Carriage Works verdict was sufficiently off putting; it was chalked neatly on the mock-up – 'the Coffin'. Mrs Bulleid, on one of her rare trips to the shops, had to test the beds for comfort, and voted them adequate. Then they rashly asked her if there was anything else of particular interest and she said yes, there was one thing she had always wanted, could she please pull the communications cord? [As Bulleid's wife and Henry Ivatt's daughter no one was likely to say no.] A.H. Peppercorn genial, and courteous as ever, was amongst those present. "Oh yes, of course", they all said, and watched with indulgent smiles as she grasped the chain and gave it a firm pull . . . in vain. Incredulous helping hands moved in to do it, also in vain. It wouldn't budge an inch. Even Peppercorn couldn't shift it. Laughter mixed with much embarrassment and everyone was suddenly too busy with the problem to find an alternative, pullable cord.'

With such an ebullient, energetic leader the days must have been full of interest and challenge. One can see that Peppercorn's character, which seems to have been more measured, probably acted as a counter-balance to Bulleid's more energetic, if not frantic behaviour. At one stage, Bert Spencer, who worked directly alongside him for a decade or more, was heard to exclaim to his assistant Eric Bannister, when hearing of another flight of Bulleid fancy 'what other mad idea has he got?' The word 'now', though not mentioned, was probably left hovering in the air.

With such clear differences between their personalities, it is safe to assume that Bulleid and Peppercorn would have approached work in different ways. One restless and constantly creative, seeking new solutions when established ideas might have proved more effective, achieving better value for money in the process. In other words, a true designer, but in this case one who needed his boundaries carefully policed by a strong manager if the development of impractical or unproductive ideas was to be avoided. Peppercorn was more methodical and pragmatic in his approach, allowing common sense and a better understanding of need and delivery to guide him. If this is the case, one can begin to see that Bulleid may have provided creativity and new ideas, but it was probably left to Peppercorn to bring order to the Carriage Workshops and ensure that production processes flowed smoothly and efficiently.

It seems that Bulleid was directly involved in the process of design not simply the construction and maintenance of rolling stock. Much is made of this in the two key biographies about him, by his son and by Sean Day-Lewis, which was written with Bulleid's co-operation. They both assert that he added his own ideas when handed a specification and designs prepared by the Drawing Office under the control of a Chief Draughtsman. This included such things as the styling, fixtures and fittings, types of cooking apparatus, when to use articulation and more. If this is so, it is interesting that he enjoyed such freedom and by implication, Gresley's trust. By all accounts, the CME was not one to stifle new ideas or independent thought and actions. However, he did seem to maintain very close control over what happened in his workshops and the way each design was developed. So to enjoy such freedom Bulleid must have been in a very privileged position.

One wonders whether Peppercorn experienced the same level of trust and was given equal freedom to influence design in the same way when taking the post over in 1923? Impossible to say without clear evidence, but it seems more likely that he saw his role in two ways. Firstly, having a voice in the conceptual process, bringing his undoubted experience to bear in any discussions with the draughtsman as they formulated their ideas and plans. Secondly, taking a design and producing it in line with the drawings presented to him. He would undoubtedly have sought some modification when and if a problem was found. But this is how workshops operate, then and now, and there is no reason to believe that he saw things differently or sought more control over the design process.

His primary purpose would have been production output, the quality of the work and meeting the operational needs of the railway as defined by the General Manager. It was a methodology he held to throughout

Peppercorn at about the time of his marriage in 1928. He has a calm, resolute and assured air reflecting his growing confidence and senior status within the LNER. (*THG*)

Too often the workshops clung to old ways of working and Sir Nigel authorised his managers to make changes to improve efficiency. At that time the theories of work and method study were coming into their own, encouraged in part by developments on the other side of the Atlantic. Most engineering companies were quick to seize on these ideas and implemented them with mixed results. Thanks to their efforts the GNR and then the LNER were well up with these changes. The savings made were, I believe, substantial and production certainly held up well especially when tested by the two World Wars when staff numbers dropped off.'

With so many challenging targets to meet at work, it might be assumed that Peppercorn had little time for a private life. Living quietly with a housekeeper to manage his domestic needs, some might have been forgiven for thinking he was slipping into a comfortable middle-aged bachelor's life. But in 1927, he announced his intention of marrying and his new wife then appeared in July of the next year. By this time, he had taken up the post of Carriage and Wagon Works Manager at York, succeeding Edward Thompson in the process, and was living locally.

The details of this important change in his life are sparse. At some point over the years he met Florence Marjory Furber who was brought up by her parents, John and Emma, at Brown's Hotel, Dover Street, Mayfair, London, of which her father was proprietor. At the time of the Peppercorns' wedding she was 32 years of age and still lived with her parents at the hotel.

How they met is unclear, but as the photograph at the beginning of this chapter records, Peppercorn visited Bulleid at his home on the outskirts of London post 1923 and was a family friend. In addition, with Gresley now running his HQ from King's Cross, meetings in London with key staff, such as Peppercorn, would have been essential. There seems a reasonable chance that the courtship developed during his regular visits to the City. Sadly, as events would soon reveal, the marriage proved to be a short lived one.

As the trauma of the Great War receded, Peppercorn found some personal happiness, although work on the carriage and wagon side of business would have absorbed most of his attention. Nevertheless, wider developments in the company would have featured

his career, even when CME and likely to have greater freedom to experiment. From this it could be assumed that he didn't possess Gresley or Bulleid's scientific curiosity when it came to design, but was more rooted in the practical application of engineering skills to workshop management. During this period, he would have seen the changes being made by Thompson in particular on the shop floor and probably brought his own ideas and experience to bear in these continuing programmes of change. As Bert Spencer later recalled:

'Thompson, Peppercorn and a few others saw very early on the need to make production more efficient.

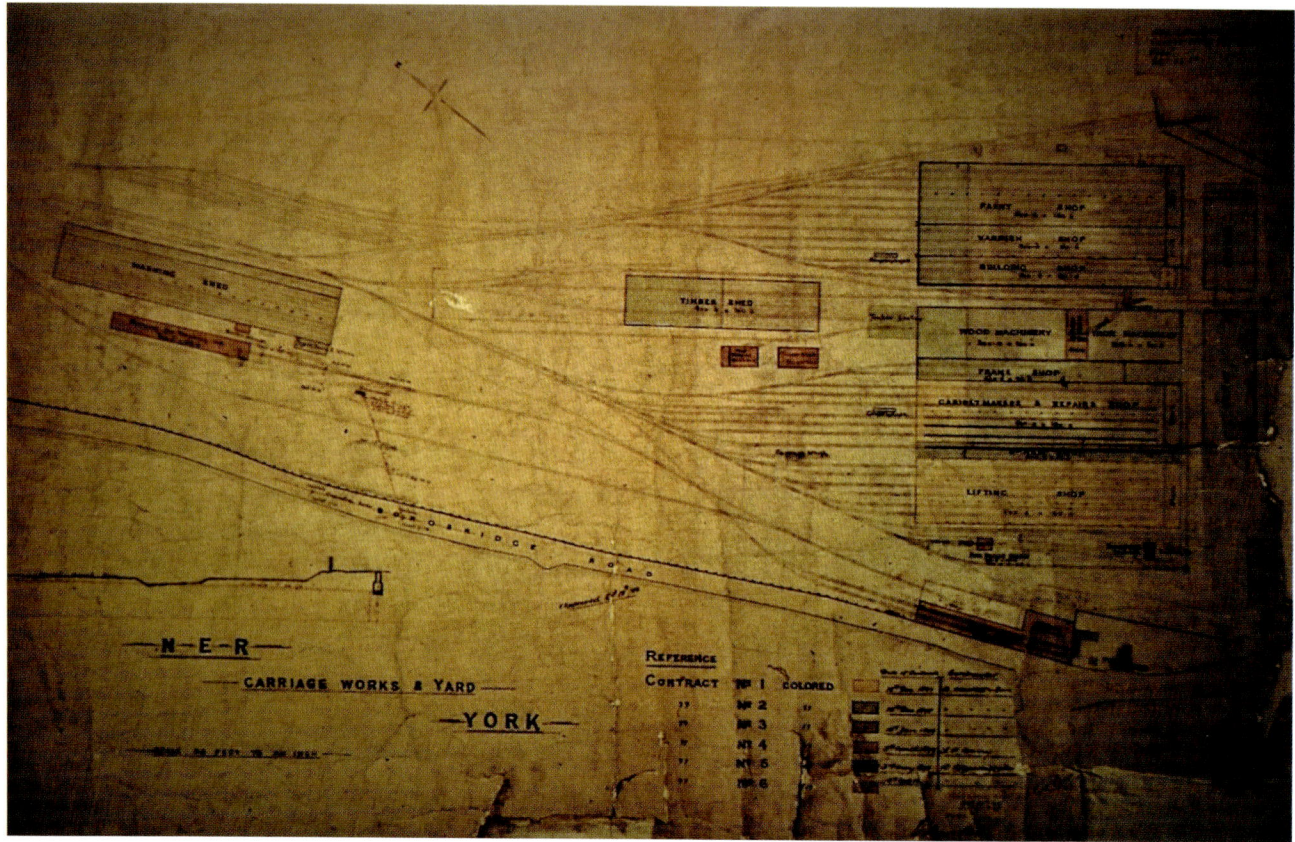

Above: York's Carriage and Wagon Works employed approximately 1,500 and 1,180 people respectively. Many of these people would have been carpenters, as portrayed here, much of the shops' work being in wood. It is interesting to note that Gresley, Thompson and Peppercorn are all noted as having been good, though amateur, carpenters by Spencer. As apprentices Gresley and Peppercorn would probably have honed these skills, though all three men seem to have discovered the pleasure of working with wood in childhood. (*ET/DN*)

Opposite above: Brown's Hotel as it appeared in the early years of the twentieth century when Peppercorn and his bride to be, Florence (who apparently preferred to be called Marjory), were courting. It seems that her father was owner and proprietor of the hotel. Its quality and prestigious address in Mayfair seem to have made it a frequent destination for royalty and members of Britain's upper class. (*THG*)

Opposite below: The layout of works at York, which Peppercorn managed from 1927 to 1933, was one of the North Eastern Railway's major centres of operation and remained so under the LNER when the company was formed in 1923. (*DN*)

large in his thoughts as well. In terms of policy and management of staff and resources in a rapidly changing business, there was much to consider. There were also intense social and economic forces at work in society bringing with them changed attitudes and changed priorities, each requiring careful management if the business were to adjust and succeed. And then there was the ever increasing expectations of customers to meet. Gresley had grasped this nettle and his rolling stock programme had sought to satisfy some of these needs, as far as it was possible within the company's limited budget. Nevertheless, much more was needed, especially in the field of locomotive design and capacity, if the company was to meet these growing demands.

Whilst Peppercorn re-established his career at Doncaster in the immediate aftermath of the war he would have been only too aware of Gresley's developing locomotive programme. Although working in the carriage and wagon side of business the arrival of the first ten H4 2-6-0s (Nos. 1000 to 1009) during 1920/21 would have been impossible to miss. Although not his first new engine with three cylinders and conjugated valve gear, they were the first to be mass produced and received a 'refined form of the valve gear'. In addition, they were fitted with a wide firebox and grate. In 1923 they would be re-designated K3 and by 1925 193 were in service. (*RH*)

In 1920 the first N2 0-6-2 passenger tank engines appeared, essentially an improved version of Ivatt's N1. Ten of the first batch were built under contract by North British in Glasgow, whilst Doncaster turned out another fifty at the same time. Construction ran on until 1929 by which time there were 107 of these two cylinder locomotives in service. Although not conforming to Gresley's three-cylinder dicta they still reflected his general design philosophy – larger diameter inside cylinders, 19in by 26in, with piston valves fitted, to improve the flow of steam and superheated. These engines were deemed to be a success and became the mainstay on many city commuter routes until the last were withdrawn in 1962. Here the class is represented by engine No. 2672 built by Hawthorn Leslie in 1929. This engine spent all but a few weeks of its life based at King's Cross (being scrapped in November 1959). (*THG*)

In many ways it wasn't a question of numbers. The GNR's fleet plus the vast array of locomotives he inherited from the constituent companies on amalgamation gave the running department plenty to play with. In fact, it was the variety that presented a significant problem – too many types, many well past their prime, a plethora of costly spares to provide and a maintenance programme of unnecessary size and complexity. Yet this was only part of the story. A more pressing concern, Gresley and the General Manager believed, was the lack of engines large enough to take on heavier loads without the recourse to double-heading and the extra cost this incurred. If anything, the over riding needs of war had reinforced this view. To prove this, if the strength of the argument wasn't already self-evident, the railway companies only had to look at government policy during the conflict. When seeking a solution to the problem of motive power at the Front, the Railway Executive Committee, during 1916, settled on heavy goods 2-8-0s as a standard design and then paid for the construction for five hundred and twenty-one. This number then added to the 2-8-0s already developed in Britain prior to 1914 by the Great Western and Great Central Railways, many of which had already been requisitioned by the War Office. And so, with the demands of the peacetime world growing stronger, coupled to the ever present need for economy, Gresley moved his big engine policy front and centre.

In the immediate aftermath of the war, his plans focussed on four designs – a 2-6-0 mixed traffic engine, a heavy goods 2-8-0, a development of the N1 0-6-2 passenger tank engine and, his pièce de résistance, a Pacific for express passenger work. Whilst the 0-6-2, which became the N2, continued the 2-cylinder theme, though with diameter increased in size to 19in by 26in, the others were developed with three cylinders. This decision resulted, in part, from his analysis of multi-cylinder designs over the years and the comparative benefits to be derived from each variant, whether they be two, three or four in nature. Three became his preferred option on the basis that coal consumption could be cut, the mileage between general repairs would be greater and the wear and tear on the track would be less due to a softer hammer-blow. But he enhanced this concept further by introducing his patented version of the conjugated valve gear. This was needed, or so the argument goes, to overcome the perceived disadvantage of having to have three separate sets of valve motion in such an arrangement. True or not, Gresley placed great faith in this idea, which Spencer later outlined in preparatory notes for his 1947 ILocoE paper entitled 'Development of LNER Locomotive Designs: 1923-1941':

'In the simple form the three valves are in the same horizontal plane, the middle valve being at the side of its cylinder. Two levers operate the same plane as the valves, a 2 to 1 lever pivoted to a bracket between the frames and attached at its outer end to one of the outside valves, and a short 'equal' lever connected at its centre to the forked inner end of the 2 to 1 lever. [In] the alternative form covered by Gresley's patent the Walschaerts gear on either side drives the outer arms of the rocking shafts which operate the middle valves. The 2 to 1 ratio is introduced by making the inner arm of one of the rocking shafts only half the length of the outer arms.'

Spencer then went on to describe how the 'alternative form' was first used with some success on Gresley's experimental 2-8-0 engine, No. 261, which appeared in 1918. He then touched on modifications then carried out with the assistance, grudging or otherwise, of fellow engineer Harold Holcroft, who had designed a similar system but allowed his patent to lapse during the Great War. There is a suspicion of plagiarism in this issue and the question of who did what has been long debated. In the first book in this trilogy, *Gresley and His Locomotives*, this issue is discussed in some detail so won't be repeated here. However, it is sufficient to say that the work of both men contributed greatly to the success of all the locomotives that followed, with Gresley remaining firmly wedded to the concept to the end of his days. Many, including Edward Thompson, harboured doubts about the effectiveness of the 2 to 1 gear, matched to three cylinders, and much debate would follow over the years. When Thompson became CME in 1941, with Peppercorn his deputy, considerable operational problems with the gear were reported to him. In due course, both men would be involved in finding a solution to this problem and in so doing giving rise to a controversy that continues to this day.

The conjugated valve gear wasn't the only significant idea adopted by Gresley in his development programme. There was much more to be considered as he sought to

In 1921, Gresley introduced the next phase of his 2-8-0 heavy goods engine programme with the first of his O2 Class (here demonstrated by the first of the class engine No. 477). Although only an initial batch of 10 were built construction continued in four more phases up to 1943, by which time sixty-six were in service. Peppercorn would oversee the construction of the last batch of 25 when Mechanical Engineer in charge of Doncaster. Building on the success of the prototype 2-8-0, No. 461, Gresley refined the conjugated valve gear along the lines of that used on his H4 (LNER K3) 2-6-0s, which came into service in 1920. In addition, he increased the boiler pressure from 170 to 180psi and raised the cylinder size to 18½in. Throughout any engine's life there were modifications and refinements. The O2s were no different though most changes were small in nature as demonstrated in the lower photograph. In this case a Silvertown Automatic Lubricator has been fitted to engine No. 3487 above the second set of coupled wheels. (*DN*)

make the engines more powerful and economic to run. Peppercorn was able to observe all this from close quarters, though not as close as Bulleid and Spencer or the plethora of draughtsmen the CME employed to do all the detailed design work. Nevertheless, even when sitting on the side-lines in the Carriage Works, the concepts being explored by them would have been of considerable interest to Peppercorn. Did he foresee a move into the

In the last two years before amalgamation both the GNR and NER developed Pacific locomotives. These two photos capture the end results. (Above) Gresley's A1 came first, portrayed here by the second engine built, No 1471 *Sir Frederick Banbury*. This huge leap forward in design, and its subsequent development until the A4 appeared in 1935, would have a profound effect on Peppercorn. In time he would see it as his responsibility to protect and extend this aspect of Gresley's legacy. (Below) The NER's version, portrayed here by the second of the five eventually built, No. 2402 *City of York*, which entered traffic in March 1924. Both types would become very familiar to Peppercorn particularly when working at York. (*DN*)

higher profile world of locomotive design and construction at some stage, as any man seeking to move upwards in their specialist field might? Undoubtedly they would, if aspiring to be a Chief Mechanical Engineer. And yet Peppercorn appears to have been ambivalent on this point, displaying no obvious sign that he harboured these ambitions. But common sense dictates that no one reaches the top without great ambition and will seek to

The Pacific development continues with the arrival of fifty more between 1923 and 1925. Here a close up of engine No. 1475 at Doncaster clearly demonstrates the elegance of line but, more importantly, the high standard of engineering and the quality of the finish. In time Gresley's frequent and 'some thought' dogged adherence to three cylinders and the conjugated valve gear was criticised in certain quarters. But as Bert Spencer recorded 'they did their jobs well and proved economical and effective in practice'. Peppercorn remained mute on this point, though would later assist Thompson in rebuilding the first of the class, No. 1470 *Great Northern*, and removing the conjugated valve gear as an experiment. (*ET/DN*)

Gresley's influence on the LNER is only too apparent in this photograph taken in the late 1920s. The locomotive appears to be A1 No. 4481, *St Simon*, (although the last number is unclear) which was built in 1923 at Doncaster. The tender, No.5232, is of the 1922 GNR type. The rake of carriages clearly demonstrates the way design had developed in the 20 years since Gresley moved to the GNR. (*RH*)

improve their credentials to encourage such an outcome. Peppercorn is unlikely to have been any different and so would have kept abreast of all that was happening in the locomotive field, as well as wider management issues embraced by the company, cultivating his leaders in doing so whenever he could press his case. However, he seems to have achieved this in a quiet measured way as befitted someone with his personality, causing few, if any recordable ripples in the process.

So what might he have observed in the years he spent in the carriage and wagon world up to 1933? Certainly the debates on cylinder numbers and valve gear, but also the size of boilers, use of superheating, booster engines to provide additional tractive effort, articulation of locomotives, the use of feed-water heaters and water tube high pressure boilers, corridor tenders, streamlining and much more. The array of experiments and developments was a stunning one, reflecting the dynamism of Gresley and his immediate advisors. But he would also have observed the way this perceptive and astute man operated in a highly politicised and competitive environment to realise his scientific ambitions. To have ideas is one thing, to persuade others in a hard-headed business world to allow you to develop them is quite another. Cases have to be made, influence and powers of persuasion brought to bear and any

As new express passenger services were introduced they received much PR attention. The press were eager for this news and the LNER were happy to feed this need. With the Pacific fleet growing ever larger and more effective the first non-stop runs from London to Edinburgh began. On 1 May 1928 the inaugural run took place with the third A1, No. 4472 *Flying Scotsman*, fitted with a corridor tender, in charge. Edward Thompson 'who kept a copy of this photograph in his album' recorded in his notes that the LNER's Chairman, William Whitelaw, 'is shaking the hands of Driver Albert Pibworth and Fireman Morris, whilst the relief crew, Blades and Morris, stand to one side'. He added that 'Thom and myself stand to the right of the Chairman, whilst Peppercorn is in the background. The CME and Bulleid are also in the crowd [it appears to be Gresley's tall bowler hatted figure to the right of the picture looking to his left and downwards as he talks to another guest]. They and Thom accompanied the train northwards'. (*ET/DN*)

opposition overcome. In any field this takes considerable political and business acumen. Gresley possessed this rare mixture of skills and made use of them with striking success. And, of course, he was able to deliver on his promises often with spectacular success, as witnessed in 1922 by the first of his Pacifics.

If one project came to epitomise Gresley's career it was his A1 Class Pacifics and the derivatives that followed over the next fourteen years. Such was the programme's power that it would also engage his successors until they also departed the scene, though for different reasons as we shall see. If anything, it was a design ambition that had its roots in pre-war years partially inspired by Churchward's work at Swindon and locomotives emanating from the USA. War checked progress, although planning continued, and in 1921 Gresley felt able to turn the nucleus of his ideas into reality. The result was the first two A1s, both constructed at Doncaster, which appeared in April and July 1922 on the eve of amalgamation. The timing couldn't have been better planned and they beat Vincent Raven and the North Eastern Railway's first two Pacific locomotives into service by eight and five months respectively. In so doing possibly affecting the choice of who would be the LNER's first Chief Mechanical Engineer.

Their impact was immediate and quickly drew the attention of the industry and the general public alike. Some commentators at the time suggested that Gresley's new locomotive caught a post-war spirit of optimism that some felt existed now that the conflict was fading

Gresley's first P1 2-8-2, No. 2393, heavy mineral locomotive pulling a load of 100 coal wagons on the East Coast Main Line near Sandy in Bedfordshire. They were designed to meet a requirement for an engine to pull coal trains with a 1,600 ton capacity. They proved more than capable of doing this, but such long loads proved to be difficult for day to day operations. In addition, the requirement changed with a preference being shown for shorter and faster trains. As a result, their role diminished and no more were built. They continued on in service, being modified along the way, until 1945 when Thompson and Peppercorn oversaw their withdrawal. In appearance they resembled the A1 Pacifics with boilers that were basically the same. But in the P1s' case Gresley experimented with a booster engine on the trailing wheels. This helped when starting with such heavy loads and provided another 4,180lb. of tractive effort, boosting its total to 47,000lb. (*RH*)

into the memory. High blown words indeed, and not borne out by events over the next ten years as recession and austerity nibbled at the public spirit. Nevertheless, one can understand how it may have come to embody aspiration and, perhaps, a sense of hope. Either way, it provided good copy for the PR team and helped sell the company and boost its coffers. For Gresley and his engineers it had a much deeper meaning though. Modernisation was essential and good headlines, plus well-constructed arguments, made the chance of taking further steps forward more likely.

The A1s embodied all the design elements that Gresley had been rehearsing with his H4/K3 and 2-8-0s, but this time brought together to produce an express engine of immense speed, power and endurance. The first two engines were prototypes and over the years would be refined until capable of serving the London to Edinburgh non-stop services, which began in May 1928, again to great fanfare. By this stage, the class numbered fifty-two and the next generation, the A3s, had begun to make their appearance. By 1935, twenty-seven of the new engines had been constructed, with fifty-one A1s eventually rebuilt to the same standard. But in the meantime, Gresley's fertile imagination had turned to other locomotive projects. These included the construction of two heavy mineral P1 Class 2-8-2 engines in 1925, a single U1 Class 2-8-0+0-8-2T banking engine bought from Beyer, Peacock the same year, two classes of 0-6-0 tender engines – the J38 and J39 – both of which began arriving in 1926, the D49 4-4-0 passenger engine and the B17 4-6-0. In addition, there were modifications made to many of the engines he had inherited from the constituent companies in 1923. Here, amongst other things, he was able to continue his experiments with articulation but this time using locomotives.

All this work was important because it tended to build on principles Gresley had established and practiced. Their science was interesting but such a creative man searched for new concepts to explore. He wasn't blind to other forms of motive power – diesel or

The single U1 2-8-0+0-8-2 banking engine constructed for the LNER by Beyer, Peacock at Gorton in 1925 for use on the Worsborough incline between Wath and Penistone in Yorkshire. This engine, which produced 72,940lb of tractive effort, conformed to Gresley's ideas as far as possible, with each segment of the engine having three cylinders and a valve motion matched to the Class O2 2-8-0 class. It continued in service on this line until electrification in 1949. Its demise coincided with Peppercorn's retirement, though in the engine's case it found employment for another six years on the Lickey incline south of Birmingham. (*DN*)

All 76 of the three cylinder D49 4-4-0 passenger engines were designed and built at Darlington in a programme that ran from 1927 to 1935. They employed the same boiler that was built for the 0-6-0 J39s which produced 180 psi of pressure, with a twenty-four element superheater. However, in this case the layout of the conjugated valve gear was modified. By arranging the three cylinders in line above the centre line of the bogie it was possible to place derived motion behind and not in front of the cylinders. It was believed that this would reduce maintenance needs; the effects of valve-spindle expansion on the middle valve being reduced and so retained their tightness. The engines came in three types reflecting Gresley's desire to experiment with different ideas. In this case 28 D49/1s were built with piston valves, 42 D49/2s with Lentz rotary cam poppet valves and 6 D49/3s which came with Lentz oscillating cam operated valves. The class is represented in this photograph by D49/1 No. 2753, *Cheshire*, built in 1929, and seen pulling away from Edinburgh with an express train to Glasgow. (*ET/DN*)

Above: Another programme to be noted by staff in the LNER in the late 1920s was the development of the Class B17 4-6-0. Due to lack of design and workshop capacity at Doncaster and Darlington the programme was contracted out to North British Locomotive Company. The specification Gresley issued to them, containing a maximum axle loading of 17 tons, proved impossible to meet. Faced with this dichotomy, Gresley agreed to revise the spec and raised the limit to 18 tons, which meant a revision to route availability. As a result, the initial order for twenty locomotives was reduced to ten. The concept drew heavily on the A1s' and K3s' designs, and included three in line cylinders with conjugated valve gear. However, there was one significant difference. The LNER requested that the valve gear levers be placed behind the cylinders. The only way that NBL could achieve this was to divide the drive. This meant that the outside cylinders drove the middle coupled wheels, whilst the inside cylinder, which had to be located well forward in the frames, drove the leading coupled wheels. In due course, another sixty-three locomotives were built, though no more by NBL. In the photograph above, engine No. 2813, *Woodbastwick Hall*, built at Darlington in 1930 and fitted with Westinghouse air brakes, undergoes a wash out. (*RH*)

Opposite below: The A3s make their appearance, here represented by engine No.2747, *Coronach*, built at Doncaster in 1928. This class was often referred to as 'Super Pacifics' to differentiate them from the A1s. Although both classes were very similar in appearance, there were two significant differences. The boiler produced 220 instead of 180psi of pressure and had a forty-three element superheater, as opposed to the A1's thirty-two. These changes lifted the tractive effort from 29,835lb to 32,909lb. In time, fifty-one A1s would be modified to this form, the first, No. 4480, *Enterprise*, being rebuilt in 1927. However, the majority of the A1s didn't become A3s during Gresley's lifetime. This photograph was taken at King's Cross on 8 July 1935 to advertise an accelerated timing for the popular 'Scarborough Flier' service. A begrimed Driver Jack Allen waves for the benefit of the photographer whilst Fireman Hazeldene just grins, both men aware of the hard work that lies ahead. These were tough men – to survive the rigours of footplate life you had to be – and often, when assigning credit to designers, their contribution is minimized or overlooked. Yet it was their hard work in very difficult conditions that made an engine, no matter how good or bad, a success. Gresley, Thompson and Peppercorn were aware of their huge contribution and each sought to improve their working conditions in any way they could. (*RH*)

(Top) The unique shape of W1, Gresley's great experiment. Peppercorn, according to Spencer, believed it to have been a worthwhile effort and, in different circumstances, worthy of further development. But he appears to have realised that there was sufficient life left in conventional steam designs to last until other forms of motive power could take over. This might have been sooner but for the bankrupting effects of two world wars, although the Southern Railway did still manage to take giant steps forward with its electrification programme. The lower photograph shows Gresley, and his daughters Marjorie and Violet, enjoying a moment of quiet satisfaction as his new locomotive enters service. (*THG/DN*)

electric – but the economic state of the nation, and his company, rendered their development virtually impossible. Until the recession lifted and capital investment, on a huge scale, became possible, forward movement would prove difficult. In the meantime, steam was the only realistic option and Gresley's next locomotive, the experimental W1 4-6-4, sought to tease more life from this rapidly aging but still essential technology.

This project had quite a long incubation period. For Gresley, its roots could be traced back some years to when he became aware of the water tube high pressure technology being explored by engineers in static and marine boiler designs. It was a constant search for greater efficiency and economy that drove these ideas forward and the CME came to believe that the concept could equally be applied to steam locomotion. As his thoughts gradually crystalized, he engaged Harold Yarrow, the industrialist and head of Yarrow Shipbuilders, in discussions over the practicability of these ideas. As a result, Yarrows were commissioned to design and then build such a boiler. By 1929 this was ready, as was a suitable Darlington built 4-6-4 chassis to carry it. To make best use of the high pressure steam produced by this unique boiler, it was decided to have a four-cylinder compound front end; two high pressure cylinders 12in by 26in driving the leading coupled wheels and two low pressure cylinders 20in by 26in driving the centre pair. In December it was ready for testing to begin. Sadly, it did not live up to expectations and was eventually rebuilt with a conventional boiler in 1937. Nevertheless, it was a brave attempt to extend the useful life of steam locomotion and this seems to have influenced Peppercorn. Bert Spencer when preparing his paper for the Institution of Locomotive Engineers in 1947 kept many notes, which his wife Elsie carefully stored after his death. In them he wrote:

'I talked through my ideas with the CME (Peppercorn) at Doncaster and in London. He was keen that I mention W1's development in some detail and emphasize

During the recession, the LNER continued to encourage social and sporting events to help bind the workforce more closely. Throughout each year, the diaries of most establishments were full of sponsored events, with senior managers closely involved in all that happened. Gresley, Thompson and Peppercorn appear to have been very active participants in these programmes, as witnessed here in 1933 with Peppercorn posing with his winning York based cricket team. By this stage his own sporting days were almost over, except when it came to golf and fishing or so it seems. (*LJ*)

its importance. He particularly wanted me to allay any criticisms there may have been about its purpose and success. He remembered talking at length with Sir Nigel about the programme and was firmly convinced that in different circumstances to those prevailing in the 1920s and '30s that more could have been achieved and more locomotives built. The CME felt that Stanier's Turbomotive suffered in the same way.'

By the time W1 was in service, and beginning her long programme of evaluation, Peppercorn was well into his stride at York. When taking over in 1927, he had inherited a set of workshops that had undergone modernisation in layout and working practices in Thompson's hands, as Works Manager, then Area Manager based in Darlington. Peppercorn, in turn, kept up the constant search for improvements and brought in a number of his own changes to enhance what had gone before. However, the strife that had resulted in the 1926 General Strike had barely subsided and in a tinder box environment careful but firm management was even more important. He was active in trade union related business and continued to seek improvements in terms, conditions and general safety; all areas which were likely to cause friction. However, the central issue of many disputes remained pay, over which individual managers had little control at a time of deep economic depression. In 1929, this became even worse with the Wall Street Crash. In its aftermath, a new, deeper recession set in across the world, damaging the slow and fragile recovery from the Great War. To live in those times was difficult by any standards, so to manage production and expectation must have been trying in the extreme. Seeking to appease senior managers and workers alike was a juggling act to test the skills of even the most talented and resolute leader. It says much for Peppercorn that he seems to have achieved this balance in a most skilful way.

He remained at York until 1933, overseeing the implementation of Gresley's carriage and wagon policy and meeting the running department's rolling stock needs.

Gresley's locomotive programme continued apace as the new decade began. In this case it resulted in the construction of 92 2-6-2 tank engines for suburban commuter services, principally in Scotland but later in the Newcastle area as well. The V1s, as they became known, adopted the Gresley standard of three cylinders and conjugated valve gear, plus a 22 element superheater and a boiler producing 180psi. Later on a boiler capable of 200lb was introduced and these were designated V3s, a modification that was then extended to 63 V1s. They proved to be excellent performers, with some remaining in service until the early 1960s. The photograph captures the first member of the class as it appeared in October 1930. The construction programme, at Doncaster, ran from 1930 to 1940. (*THG*)

After the V1s appeared there seems to have been a hiatus in the appearance of other new engines until 1934 when the first P2 2-8-2s arrived. Nevertheless, construction of more existing Gresley types, including B17s, A3s, D49s, J39s and O2s, continued each year. However, modifications to engines inherited at amalgamation pressed ahead. This photograph captures one such effort, which reflected Gresley's continuing interest in articulation and boosters. Consequently, two C7 Atlantic locomotives, Nos. 727 and 2171, (subsequently designated C9s) were modified in 1931 and then tested to gauge whether the engines could cope more effectively with express trains on steep gradients. But, with an ever growing number of Pacifics becoming available, the requirement for the C9s to haul these heavy loads ended. Subsequently, they were used mostly on secondary passenger services until withdrawn in 1942/43 by Thompson and Peppercorn. (*THG*)

Perhaps he spent too long there for a man of ambition, but, equally so, there may not have been a better or more suitable post for him to transfer to. Thompson had moved to Stratford in 1927 to become Assistant to the Mechanical Engineer, Charles Glaze, possibly taking a step down from his position at Darlington. However, it did take him into a post where he gained responsibility for locomotives, and within three years he did in fact replace Glaze as ME. In late 1933, Peppercorn followed his example and moved to Stratford to replace Thompson, who had transferred to Darlington to fill the vacancy created when Arthur Stamer retired. However, Peppercorn was given the title Assistant Mechanical Engineer, suggesting that the post had been downgraded. Did this reflect the diminishing importance of Stratford or was it simply part of a broader re-organisation of the CME's Department? The answer appears to be some of each. Peppercorn took on the full responsibilities of the old ME post, by then made subordinate to the Mechanical Engineer (Southern Area) at Doncaster,

Robert Thom, as part of a wider organisation undertaken in the wake of Stamer's departure

However, there may have been another reason for Peppercorn's transfer south. His wife suffered from chronic mitral disease of the heart, which is a degenerative illness in nature and, in the 1930s, virtually untreatable. In York she could only rely upon her husband and servants for help. In London, she had her parents and three siblings to support her, as well as being in close proximity to the country's small number of cardiologists; at that stage an embryonic field of medicine. The course of the illness was inevitably a downwards one, with sudden collapse a constant possibility. So being near her family, and the most expert care then available, may well have become a driving force in their lives as her condition gradually deteriorated.

Ultimately we shall never know if a mixture of reasons underpinned this transfer, but the end result was a disrupting move from the North East to London and a new life there. Rather than renting or buying a property in which to live, they appear to have settled into rooms at the Coburg Court Hotel in the Bayswater Road, which overlooks Hyde Park and was in close proximity to St Mary Abbot's Hospital and Harley Street. With her family in the hotel business, this may account for their choice of a home. Either way, they would remain there for the next two years, Peppercorn commuting daily to Stratford. It is hard to imagine, in circumstances coloured by ill-health, that their time in London was a happy or easy one. Nevertheless, it was an important move for him to make professionally, bringing him, as it did, into the world of locomotives again. It also continued his long association with the carriage and wagon side of business, which was still an important part of life at Stratford.

Ominously his arrival in East London coincided with the final stage of Hitler's rise to power and the slow unravelling of this peacetime world. In 1933 he became Chancellor and within months the Enabling Act had been passed by the Reichstag, ending democracy in Germany. Dictatorship, subjugation and suppression now became the rule of law and the countdown to war had begun, though few realised this at the time. Meanwhile life went on as usual and Peppercorn began his new life at Stratford, with ever present concerns over his wife's health constantly in mind.

The Coburg Court Hotel as it appeared in the 1930s when the Peppercorns were in residence there. (*THG*)

CHAPTER 4

PEPPERCORN IN HIS OWN WORDS

If Peppercorn's new post at Stratford had indeed been downgraded, and the establishment no longer had the central role it once enjoyed, the volume and diversity of work it undertook was still considerable. In the region of 6,000 people were employed there and the shops supported approximately 500 locomotives and a substantial rolling stock fleet. During Thompson's tenure much had changed. He had quickly reviewed working practices and implemented wide ranging changes in an effort to improve flow rates. Here, by all accounts, he had been successful and in 1933, Peppercorn inherited a modernised set of workshops, particularly those dealing with the higher density needs of wagons.

Assembly of new locomotives had ended in these works during the mid-1920s and so there was little or no chance of direct involvement in any Gresley-led new construction programme. There was an indirect route though. It seems that Stratford's drawing office remained in Thompson's domain and, occasionally, this team undertook some design tasks delegated by staff at King's Cross and Doncaster. This may have given Thompson the opening he needed to have a voice in design. Nevertheless, the scope for participation was muted by the nature of the engines based at Stratford, which, for the most part were those inherited from the Great Eastern Railway, and Gresley's wish to keep this work close to his chest. In essence, Thompson occasionally involved himself in modification programmes, but that was all, despite an obvious interest in design, possibly sparked by an ambition to become a CME somewhere within the industry. By the time Peppercorn arrived, even these limited opportunities were fast disappearing and he seems to have made no attempt to play a bigger role in the design process.

Perhaps he simply believed that he had nothing of value to contribute and recognised the CME's complete authority in this area of work. He was after all a most loyal lieutenant and so less likely to challenge Gresley's ideas directly, relying instead on quiet diplomacy if a point had to be made. If so, it was an approach that Gresley, who prized loyalty very highly, would

Peppercorn in the 1930s posing for an official photograph. Once again the look is an unflinching one as though assessing the photographer. One might be forgiven for thinking that here was a man not to be trifled with. This may well have been so, you don't reach the top in any profession without exercising authority in very difficult circumstances, displaying a determination to succeed and inner steel. This he did and much more beside. And yet he was described as possessing charm, modesty, good grace and an easy sense of humour. H.C.B. Rogers, in his book *Thompson and Peppercorn* wrote, 'Everybody liked him. Bad language he heartily disliked. He never swore at subordinates and told his assistant that if they did so they were out. He was extremely shy in unexpected ways.' (*LJ*)

Stratford Works as it appeared in BR days. It had changed very little from the time when Peppercorn was in charge. Many of the locomotives photographed here would have been in evidence in the 1930s. (*DN*)

have appreciated. Thompson possessed a more forthright character and when convinced of the strength of a case pursued it doggedly, much to the CME's recorded irritation. And yet he continued to approve Thompson's continued promotions. Perhaps he simply recognised that his deputy enjoyed exceptional skills as production engineer that he didn't possess himself. The saying 'horses for courses' may be apposite on this occasion? Together they made a dynamic team. Peppercorn appears never to have had such a relationship with Gresley and so provided no challenge to stir the creative juices. In fact, on the issue of locomotive design he seems to have little or no ambition or simply didn't record any thoughts or ideas he may have had.

Having let his membership of IMechE lapse in 1916, Peppercorn finally renewed it post-war, probably encouraged by Gresley and Bulleid who continued to be active members. However, he made no effort to present any papers that summarized his thoughts on any issue, design or otherwise, until very late in his career and then he only moved when under pressure to do so from Bulleid, who by then had reached the end of his period as President of the Institution and was eager for his fellow CMEs to outline the progress made in locomotive development. Gresley was a firm believer in the need to demonstrate and communicate one's ideas. He urged his staff, whether members of an institution or not, to follow his lead, pursue their studies, seek advances and write papers for others to consider. Bulleid and Spencer did so quite often, whilst Thompson and Peppercorn seemed loath to move in this direction.

Stratford Works in the mid-1930s with a freshly painted James Holden and Frederick Russell designed 'Claud Hamilton' 4-4-0 No. 8870 (ex-No. 1870 built in 1902), presumably having just passed through a period of overhaul or rebuilding. These locomotives, classed by the LNER as D14/D15/D16s, first appeared on the Great Eastern Railway network in 1900. Modifications were initiated by Alfred Hill, when he was the GER's CME; a programme continued by Gresley post amalgamation. The engine photographed, which first underwent modification in 1928, was one of a number subsequently rebuilt between 1933 and 1949. In this form they were designated D16/3s and had a distinctive Gresley look, accentuated by the round topped fireboxes. Both Thompson and Peppercorn were closely involved in this rebuilding programme. (THG)

Peppercorn did at times put pen to paper, most often when his job called for some general contribution on the role of locomotives or the introduction of a new service. The first time this happened was in 1929, when he wrote an article for the LNER's *Journal* describing new travelling Post Office vans then coming into service. However, he doesn't seem to have approached these tasks with ease as his limited output would seem to bear witness. Nevertheless, his published writings, which are few and far between, are well written and informative, but in them he describes established principles, not the formulation or outcome of new ideas and concepts as a true designer might have done. Modesty may have made him question his own abilities in this field, of course, but one is left with the impression that his creativity and curiosity may simply have been stimulated by production methods not the possibilities inherent in design.

For a man seemingly uncomfortable expressing his thoughts on locomotive design, or any other subject for that matter, 1937 contained a veritable flood of material. At the time, he was still at Stratford but combining his assistant mechanical engineer duties with those of Locomotive Running Superintendent Southern Area; a post based at Liverpool Street Station. This was an unusual arrangement in itself because he found himself serving two masters at the same time – Gresley and Charles Newton, Divisional General

Robert Thom maintained a personal record of all locomotives built or rebuilt by the LNER from 1923 until 1935. This page from 1934 describes one of the projects involving Stratford and its Mechanical Engineer. The LNER inherited seventy of these Stephen Holden designed 4-6-0s, which first appeared in 1911, then added ten new ones in the late 1920s. In 1932, rebuilding commenced with the most noticeable change being larger diameter boilers and round topped fireboxes. Thompson played an active part in the re-design process. One issue concerned the Lentz poppet valves that had been fitted and the problems these created. He advocated a change to piston valves and a design was produced and trialled at Stratford which gained Gresley's approval. Peppercorn would take on this rebuilding programme though it wouldn't be completed until 1944. (*RT/THG*)

Manager Southern Area. Newton would, in 1939, become the LNER's General Manager and, in time, be chiefly responsible for Thompson and Peppercorn's promotions to CME.

Newton and his fellow Divisional GMs, C.M. Jenkins Jones and George Mills, seem to have encouraged their senior managers to write articles for the company's monthly journal that had a strong educational element. Over the years, many appeared covering a range of subjects. The most notable were then printed in stand-alone booklets, witnessed by the production of George Musgrave's *The History, Evolution and Construction of the Steam Locomotive* and Peppercorn's *Use of Coal, Water and Steam in the Locomotive*. These were then given wide circulation amongst staff and trades unions then sold to the general public priced at 3d. In the foreword, Peppercorn wrote:

'The object is to describe in a straightforward manner the development and sequence of the energy of coal – the prime mover – in the steam locomotive, from the firegrate to the blast pipe.

'The modern stream of progress and efficiency of man and machine alike embraces the steam locomotive, and it is thought that a simple description of the efficient use of coal, water and steam in the locomotive would be of interest to readers in general and Locomotive Footplate Staff in particular.

'It is hoped that the chapters may be of special use to those whose job it is to manage a "reservoir of steam power", which, large or small, always remains faithful to the sensitive touch of man.'

Then, in forty-six compact pages, he gives an informative and clear analysis of all aspects of the steam locomotive engineering and operation. However, at no point does he attempt to introduce any original thought or describe how the technology might be improved or developed. Of course this isn't essential to such a work, but someone with design aspirations, such as Gresley or Bulleid, probably couldn't have resisted the temptation to expound their thoughts on many conceptual matters. Peppercorn stays strictly on the side of what there is and not what might be developed. Nevertheless, his fascination with steam locomotion is described in very affectionate, almost poetic terms, as the first few paragraphs bear witness:

'As the *Silver King* glides majestically to rest at King's Cross or Newcastle, having steamed through town and countryside from almost one end of England to the other, how many of the alighting passengers, still imbued with a sense of collaborated achievement, pause to realise that the source from which all the energy expended by the locomotive throughout its tremendous effort of power and speed is coal?

'The grimy features of the fireman bear eloquent testimony that he has not been idle, and he can tell of the several tons of "black diamonds" which, in all, have been shovel-fed into the firebox at regular intervals throughout the journey, to satisfy the insistent demands of the steady steam pressure.

'In order that the locomotive may perform its work well, it is essential that full steam pressure is maintained under all conditions of running, and to help satisfy this exacting requirement, combustion of coal on the firegrate must be efficient.

'Since the use of coal plays such an important part in the working of steam locomotives, the consideration of the constitution of this mineral, together with its natural requirement for proper burning and the means by which this is effected in the locomotive, are not without interest.

'Coal is an intense concentration of energy, which many thousands of years ago was absorbed from the sun by trees and vegetation. The actual amount of energy which is liberated from 1lb. of good quality locomotive coal by burning is sufficient to raise a weight of more than 13 tons from the ground to the top of St Paul's Cathedral; or if two "streamlined" Pacific locomotives and tenders, together with a third engine, all fully loaded with coal and water, were standing side by side, this energy would lift one engine and tender on top of the other and then the third engine on to the top of both (see Fig 1 above).'

As this series of articles were individually published in the *Journal*, Peppercorn, with Gresley's agreement, took on the Running Superintendent post on a full time basis. Why the CME agreed to this isn't clear, though. Pre-1923, when Gresley controlled both departments, it wouldn't have been unusual, especially with recently qualified apprentices who needed to widen their experience before being promoted. Hence time on footplates and wider exposure to the running side of business.

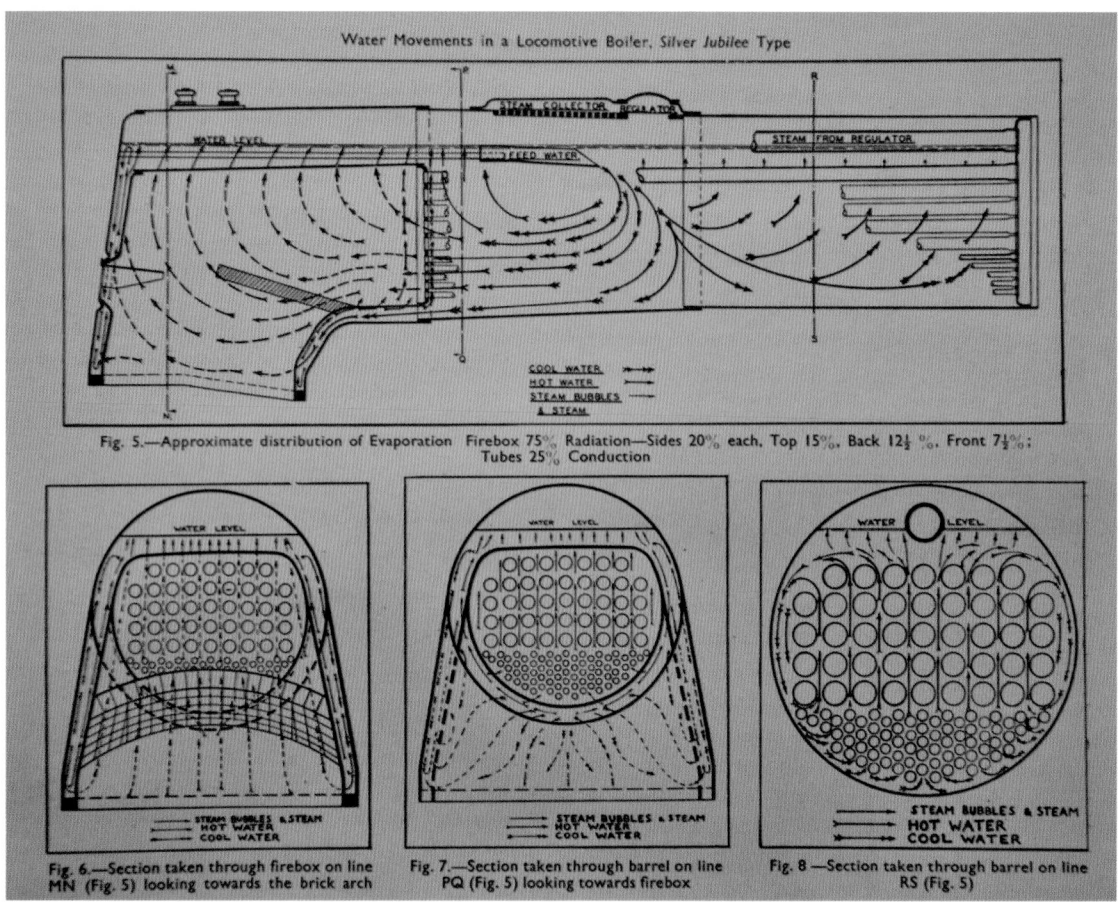

Fig. 5.—Approximate distribution of Evaporation Firebox 75%, Radiation—Sides 20% each, Top 15%, Back 12½%, Front 7½%; Tubes 25% Conduction

Fig. 6.—Section taken through firebox on line MN (Fig. 5) looking towards the brick arch

Fig. 7.—Section taken through barrel on line PQ (Fig. 5) looking towards firebox

Fig. 8.—Section taken through barrel on line RS (Fig. 5)

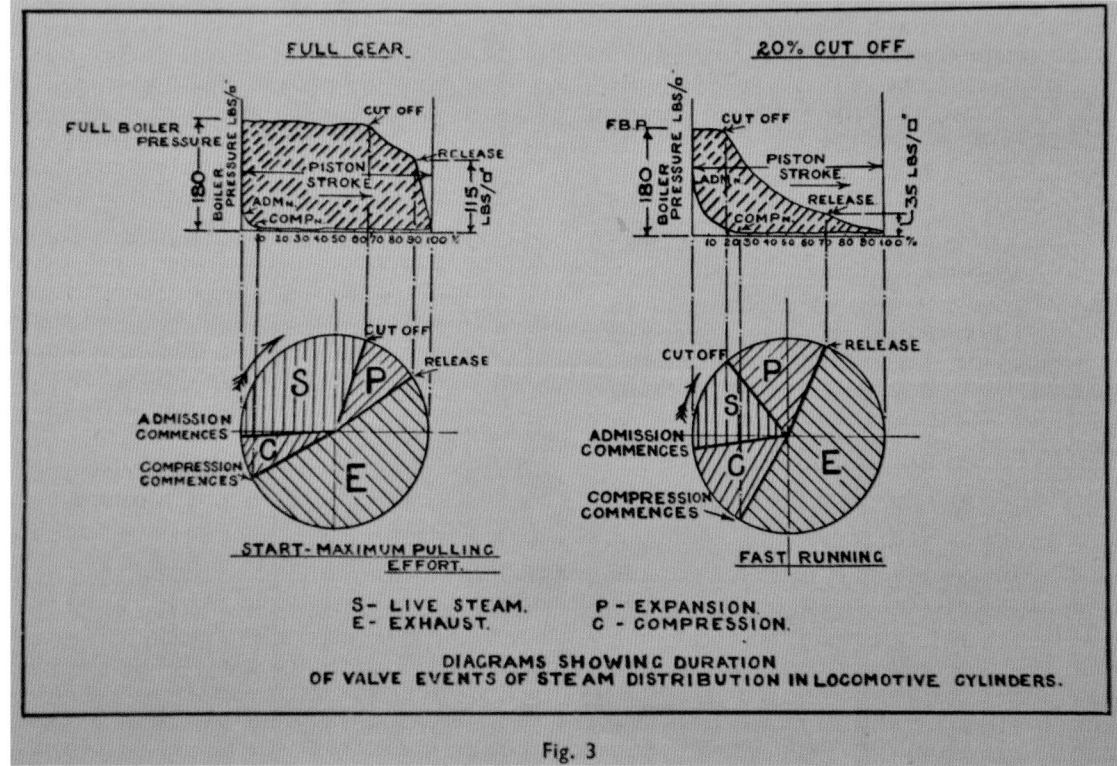

Fig. 3

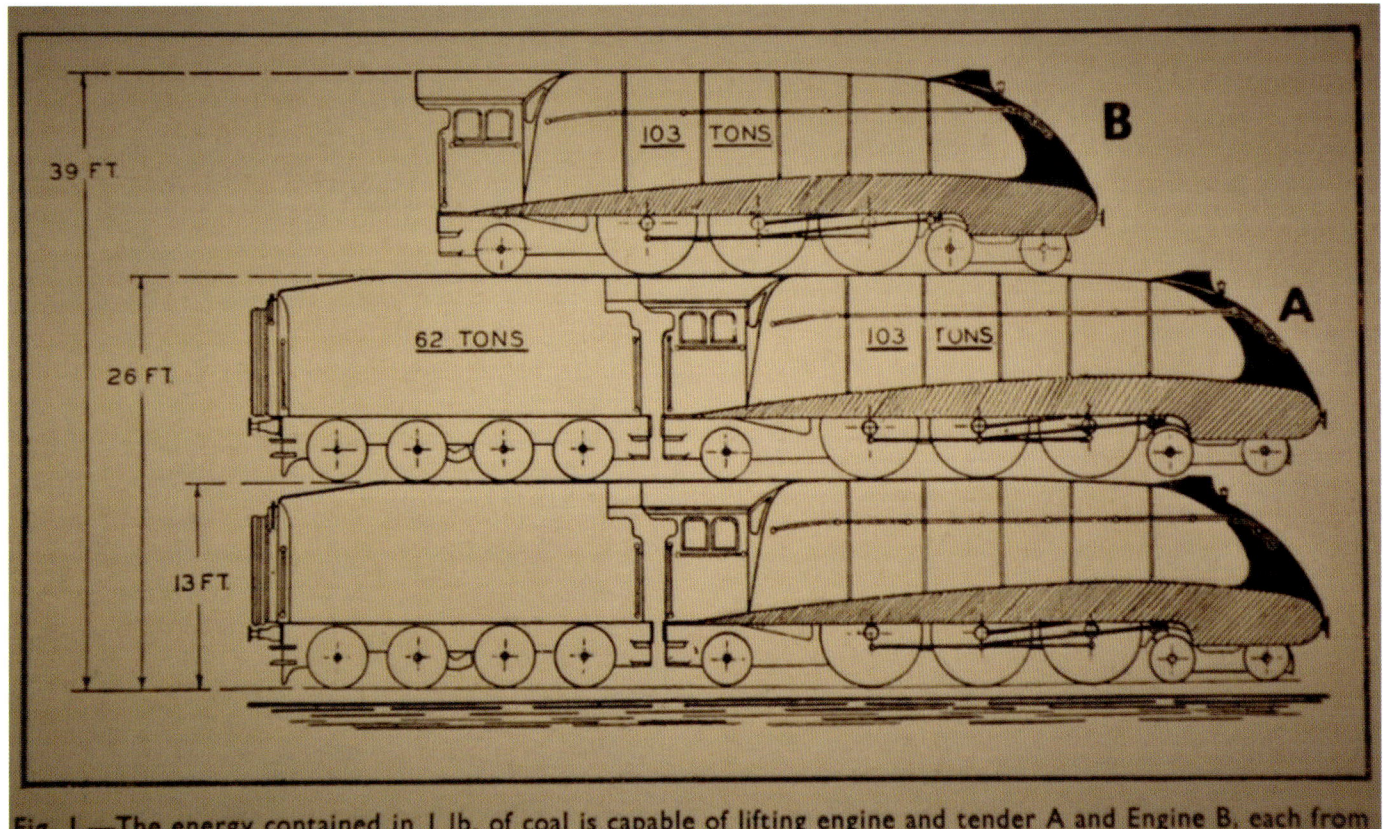

Fig. 1.—The energy contained in 1 lb. of coal is capable of lifting engine and tender A and Engine B, each from the ground to these positions

Above: Peppercorn used this wonderfully naive drawing to help illustrate his 1937 booklet to demonstrate the amount of energy created by burning 1lb of coal. He, by all accounts, prepared a series of illustrations, to take the reader, both professional and amateur, through all the processes that underpinned steam locomotion. Although not describing cutting edge science or the way this technology might evolve in the future, his fascination with steam engines is only too apparent. If anything, his writings capture the world of driver and fireman and not the engineer. (*THG*)

Opposite: Two illustrations prepared by Peppercorn describing aspects of steam locomotion. (Top) The probable movement of water currents in the boiler, in this case the A4 Pacifics. (Below) The comparative diagrams of steam distribution and pressure in a locomotive cylinder for 'full gear' cut off occurring when the piston has travelled 70 per cent of a stroke as when starting and for a fast running cut off of 20 per cent.

For someone in the 1930s, whose profession was intensely and centrally focussed on workshops at a senior level, such a move had become something of a rarity. Initially, it seems to have been a simple matter of expediency. The current Locomotive Superintendent, Isaac Groom, succumbed to serious illness early in 1937 and there appears to have been no suitable replacement available from the Divisional General Managers Department. Peppercorn, who seems to have developed a natural affinity with running matters early in his career, clearly felt able to combine both duties. However, Groom's illness proved so serious that he resigned from the service and a full time replacement was needed. Consequently, Gresley approved Peppercorn's release in July 1937 and he gave up the post at Stratford and moved to Liverpool Street. In his wake, F.W. Carr moved from Gorton to East London as his replacement.

Did the CME envisage his return at some stage? One assumes he did; men of Peppercorn's experience and skill are always highly prized. At the time, Gresley was due to lose two of his greatest assets; Robert Thom, his gifted and resolute Mechanical Engineer at Doncaster, was due to retire in May 1938, and Bulleid was due to become CME of the Southern

Railway in September 1937. So, in quite a short time, there was a need for a re-organisation in which someone of Peppercorn's experience might figure large. One assumes that Gresley bore all this in mind and may have negotiated a time limited appointment to ensure he could draw Peppercorn back into the fold when necessary, but this is only speculation. There is also a chance that he believed Peppercorn might have been better suited to the General Management side of business. A third possibility suggests that Gresley believed that the workshop and running departments be re-amalgamated under him, and campaigned for this to happen. With Peppercorn doing good work as a Locomotive Superintendent, the value of such a move could be demonstrated if such a case needed to be made.

Wherever the truth might lie, Peppercorn's time in London would have proved interesting and challenging in fairly even measures. It may have been a backwater in terms of locomotive development, but the demands placed on him were nonetheless significant. And yet he must have looked at the work being undertaken at Doncaster and Darlington during this dynamic period with mixed emotions. It seems to me that a good professional will always seek to test themselves in the most demanding way possible. For an engineer, this will invariably be at the cutting edge of the science they practice. Improving workshop systems and practices, and their effect on production and profitably, though challenging, are not in the same category as the development of new locomotives.

In the years Peppercorn spent in London, Gresley was bringing many of his long planned projects to fruition. In 1934, the P2 2-8-2 express locomotive, for use on the challenging Edinburgh to Aberdeen line, made its first appearance. This was followed by his ever increasing interest and exploration of streamlining and with it the development of the Pacific A4s in 1935, then modification of two B17s during 1937 and, finally, W1 the same year. At the same time, work on his new V2 2-6-2 Class of heavy mixed traffic engines reached fruition, the first of 184 being built at Doncaster before most production switched to Darlington. And to this was added the first of five K4 2-6-0s. This programme may not have been as active as that in the early years of Gresley's reign but the end result was nonetheless remarkable and headline grabbing. He may have continued to place too much emphasis on three cylinders to the exclusion of other ideas, but his engines still impressed.

At Stratford then Liverpool Street, Peppercorn sat on the sidelines of all this work, observing the results but, for the most part, unable to participate more directly. Undoubtedly, he would have seen Gresley and Bulleid regularly, being so close to King's Cross. Then there was also the sublimating influence of the IMechE. All three men regularly visited the institution's London headquarters in Birdcage Walk on the edge of St James' Park, according to the records that have survived. There were regular presentations to attend and the building was also a simple meeting place for people of like mind seeking to escape from the bustle of the city. In fact, it seems to have become something of a sanctuary for Peppercorn following the death of his wife.

Winter is always a hard time for anyone suffering long term health problems and this proved to be so for Florence in 1935. An infection took hold early in the New Year when she was already bedridden, bronchial pneumonia set in and, with her husband present, she died on 2 February in their rooms at the Coburg Court Hotel. It was the second death he had to bear in six months, his mother having passed away the previous August. At times such as this courage, patience, fortitude and a sense of duty may be all there is to get you through. Words of sympathy and false hope offer little comfort. Allowing the reassuring bonds of work to re-assert themselves is often the only way of coping. For Peppercorn, Gresley's presence and understanding may have been of great value at this time. In 1929, he too had been widowed and in the months and in the years that followed his work is said to have given him some relief from the contagion of mourning. If so, then Peppercorn may have found it so too.

It may have been the need for a distraction that encouraged him to write technical articles for the LNER's *Journal* and the booklet that followed. Although all appearing in 1937, they would have been some time in preparation, especially the drawings. But another piece appeared that year which revealed much more about Peppercorn and his sense of joy at being a railwayman. It is always interesting when a tough, committed professional looks beyond the nuts and bolts of their business to consider their trade in more prosaic terms.

The LNER rarely, if ever, missed a chance to publicise its operations. During Peppercorn's time in London this resulted in this interesting photograph which appears to have been taken on a busy day in August when these locomotives were lined up at Stratford preparing to pull trains carrying holidaymakers to the coast. By the 1930s the effects of the Great Depression caused by the crash in 1929 seemed to be easing and people felt able to enjoy summer breaks. (*THG*)

Some lacked the words to explore or describe their fascination with a subject or felt no need to try, preferring to submerge themselves in their work. Others, as Peppercorn did, allowed themselves to become a young man again and discover the words to explain something that was at the root of their lives. In this case, it was the arrival of two streamlined B17s that sparked his sudden outpouring of words.

During 1935, the eye-catching arrival of the A4s had gripped public imagination, though some engineers found little of true scientific value in their streamlined form, seeing them as simply a publicity stunt. The science was there, of course, but so was the PR appeal. When it came to the LNER's plan to convert two B17s to this form, publicity was probably a bigger driving force for change. The engines simply looked more modern and became the perfect vehicle to advertise a new fast service from London into East Anglia. As Locomotive Running Superintendent, Peppercorn travelled on the inaugural service with Charles Newton and went armed with his notebook. He recorded everything that happened with boyish enthusiasm, occasionally remembering to include some technical detail:

'Monday, September 27th 1937 is recorded in the history of railway development as the day which heralded the running of the first streamlined service in the Eastern Counties. The service is between Norwich and Liverpool Street, and the new East Anglian train makes the journey in each direction once every weekday, Saturdays excepted, in 2¼ hours.

'The introduction of the East Anglian marks a distinct advance in the service between Norwich, Ipswich and London. The facilities afforded allow the

The 'East Anglian' in idealistic form for publicity purposes and the reality. The two engines converted, Nos. 2859 and 2870, were as striking in looks as the bigger A4s, but the aim in streamlining, in this case, was probably more likely to have been sponsored by the needs of publicity. They looked glamorous and suggested the presence of a modern, fashionable world. (*THG*)

business man of Norfolk to devote two hours or so in the morning to current office duties, or his women folk to prepare for a West-End shopping expedition, or matinee, before departing from Norwich at 11.55, to travel luxuriously, have lunch on the way and arrive at Liverpool Street at 2.10pm. A long afternoon in London is thus assured before the East Anglian returns from Liverpool Street at 6.40 in the evening. Dinner is served on the down journey and at 8.55 the traveller alights at Norwich, in sufficient time to review the day's events at home.'

Having set the scene, Peppercorn then provides a striking eye-witness account of the day. There is a suggestion that he travelled some or all of the way on the footplate in both directions, which wasn't unusual at the time especially for someone so senior and experienced in footplate matters. Whilst doing so, he carefully monitored the locomotives' performance and recorded much detail, which then formed a substantial part of the article:

'The East Anglian was a great attraction at Norwich on the morning of the inaugural run. The station platform was crowded with enthusiastic well-wishers, anxious to witness the start of a new venture.

'Punctually at 11.55am, following the mellow resonance of its distinctive whistle at the chimney front, No. 2859 began to wind its way out of Norwich Thorpe station, round the curve, over the swing-bridge spanning the Wensum, through Trowse station and yard, and past the Upper Junction before the regulator was opened wide, and with gathering speed at 30 per cent cut off, the journey proper began.

'The top of Swainsthorpe Bank was reached at 60mph, the engine making light work of the exacting duty; the briefest descent past Florden saw the speed increase to 65mph, and at a reduced cut-off, the succeeding ascent and level through Tivetshall was covered at about the same speed. Beyond Tivetshall the speed increased to 78mph, approaching Diss, but fell to 60mph at Mellis – the effect of the bank. Approaching Finningham the engine was given a little more steam, and with ease reached 79mph, but a necessary check had to observe the 65mph restriction for curves through Haughley, which was passed at 12.31 – ½ minute early – after which the speed gradually increased down the "galloping ground" of Haughley Bank and beyond remaining practically constant at 70mph for nearly 7 miles until approaching East Suffolk Junction.

'Ipswich station was thronged with sightseers eager to see the latest development in East Anglian travel, but their enjoyment was short-lived, for at

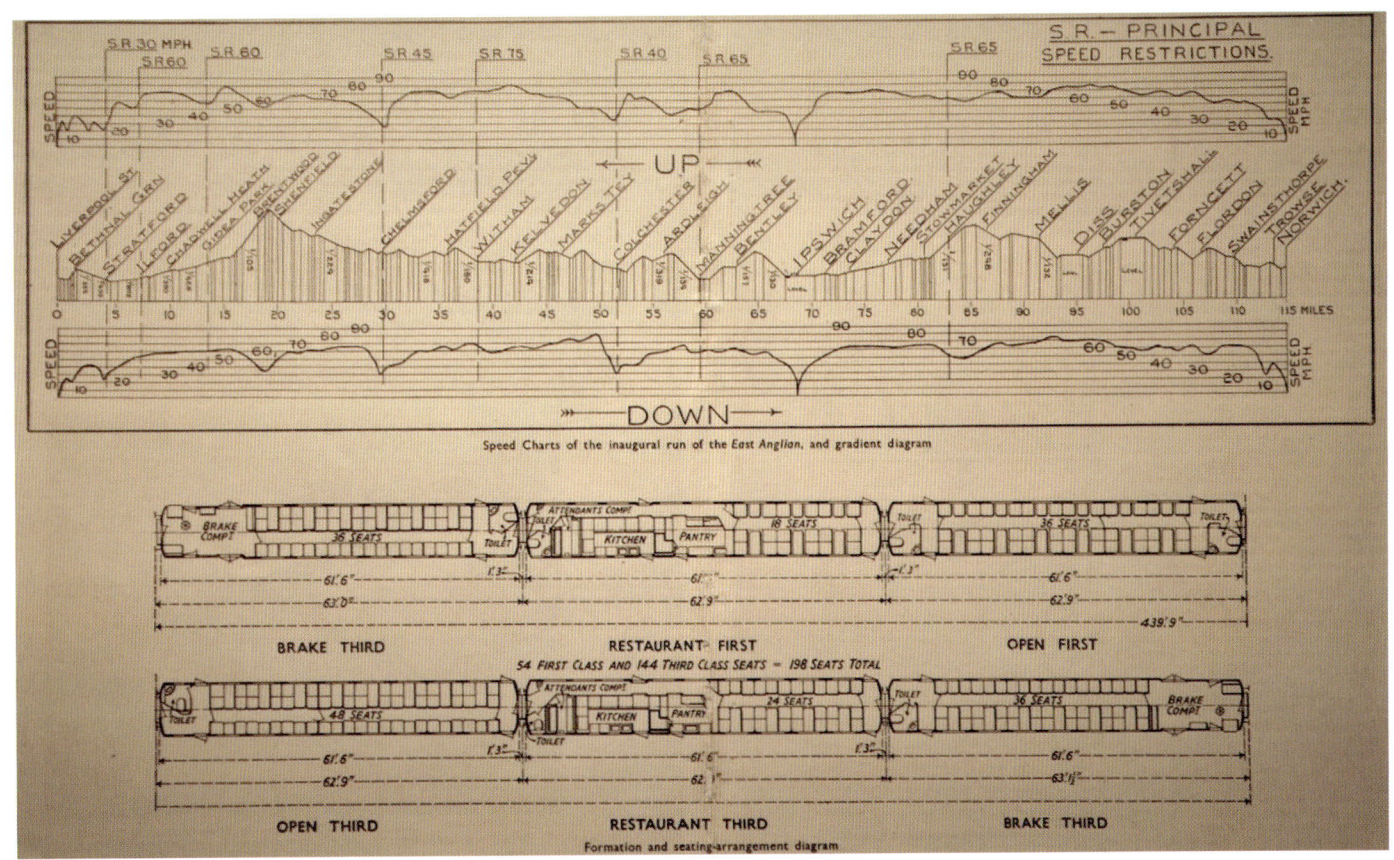

Peppercorn's record of the inaugural run on 27 September matched with the gradients the engine faced. He also included details of the train's layout. (*RH*)

12.50 – an exact four-minute stop – having entrained more travellers, East Anglian whistled melodiously and headed for the tunnel. Emerging therefrom, 1,500 gallons of water were scooped into the tender on passing through Halifax troughs and thence strong, constant acceleration up Belstead Bank – 2½ miles of 1 in 130 – carried the train over the summit at 45mph and down the other side at over 70, but checking for Manningtree was necessary, and 70mph was not reached again until just before Colchester, through which a speed of 40mph must not be exceeded.

'The undulating 22 miles from Colchester to Chelmsford offered little in the way of incident, with the exception that at practically every vantage point, men, women and children were gathered to cheer the progress of the train; a speed of 75 to 80mph was easily maintained between Kelvedon and Witham, but speed had to be reduced again through Chelmsford, which was passed one minute early.

'The arduous climb of 9½ miles from Chelmsford to Shenfield was easily accomplished in the allotted time of 11 minutes, Shenfield being passed at over 60mph, and the famous run down to Brentwood Bank showed 80mph on the speed recorder when passing Harold Wood (maximum permissible speed), but ended with the 60mph restriction through Gidea Park, and a final

Charles Newton congratulates Driver Fryer and Fireman Wright on arrival at Liverpool Street on 27 September. Newton and the Superintendent of the Eastern Section, H.H. Maudlin, had travelled to Norwich earlier that day, accompanied by Peppercorn, though only he made the return journey later in the day. (*RH*)

burst to 70mph through Chadwell Heath. Stratford was passed 1 minute early, but notwithstanding a signal check at Bethnal Green, East Anglian finally glided slowly, almost silently, and with majestic grace alongside No. 13 Platform at Liverpool Street – a significant number which to some may add to the value of a memorable achievement – to come to rest at 2.9, precisely one minute ahead of time.

'The first journey had been accomplished perfectly; the engine had satisfied all demands adequately; steam pressure had been easily maintained throughout; the firebox had consumed less than 1½ tons of coal, and the consistent rhythmic purr of the chimney top of the six exhaust beats per revolution, which blurred into a contented hum when the driving wheels were revolving practically six times per second – 80mph – had given ample manifestation of unstrained effort under every condition of running during the journey.

'East Anglian, her sleek green paint glistening, appeared well satisfied with herself, but Driver Fryer and Fireman Wright of Norwich, were unquestionably proud of their engine's performance and full of praise for its fine steady riding, good behaviour, and apparent "sense of understanding".

'The riding of the train had been so comfortable and steady, that many passengers were not always able to appreciate how fast they were travelling.

'Engine No. 2870, *City of London* in the charge of Driver Mace and Fireman Underhill, worked the first return of the East Anglian to Norwich in the evening, the train leaving Liverpool Street punctually at 6.40. The maximum speed of 80mph was attained when approaching Colchester, which was passed at 7.39 – 1 minute early – arriving with this advantage at Ipswich at 7.59, having 'scooped' at Halifax water troughs. Departing at 8.4, right time, the journey to Norwich was made with precision, and without incident, the highest speed – 75mph – being reached during the run down the bank from Mellis to Diss; Tivetshall was passed two minutes ahead of schedule and finally the train glided into Norwich Thorpe platform at 8.53.'

There is an almost breathless quality to this article hinting at the excitement the author felt at riding on the footplate that day. One is left with the impression that here

Distance from Norwich. M. Ch.		Station.		a.m.	Point to Point. Time. Mins.	Av. Speed m.p.h.
		Norwich	...dep.	11 55	—	—
14	33	Tivetshall	...pass	12 14	19	45·5
34	27	Stowmarket	... ,,	12 33½	19½	61·3
46	18	Ipswich	...arr.	12 46	12¼	57
,,			...dep.	12 50	—	—
55	42	Manningtree	...pass	1 3½	13½	41·3
63	24	Colchester	... ,,	1 12½	9	51·8
76	31	Witham	... ,,	1 26	13½	58·1
85	17	Chelmsford	... ,,	1 35	9	55·8
94	63	Shenfield	... ,,	1 46	11	52·2
105	0	Chadwell Heath	... ,,	1 56	10	61·2
110	74	Stratford	... ,,	2 2	6	59·25
114	77	Liverpool Street	...arr.	2 10	8	30·2

Distance from L'pool Street. M. Ch.		Station.		p.m.	Time. Mins.	Av. Speed m.p.h.
		Liverpool Street	...dep.	6 40	—	—
4	3	Stratford	...pass	6 48½	8½	28·5
9	77	Chadwell Heath	... ,,	6 56	7½	47·4
20	14	Shenfield	... ,,	7 9	13	47·2
29	60	Chelmsford	... ,,	7 18	9	63·8
38	46	Witham	... ,,	7 27	9	58·8
51	53	Colchester	... ,,	7 40	13	60·4
59	35	Manningtree	... ,,	7 49	9	51·8
68	59	Ipswich	...arr.	8 0	11	50·7
,,			...dep.	8 4	—	—
80	50	Stowmarket	...pass	8 19	15	47·5
100	46	Tivetshall	... ,,	8 39	20	59·5
114	77	Norwich	...arr.	8 55	16	53·5

Average Speeds.
Norwich to Ipswich = 46 miles 18 chains in 51 minutes = 54·4 mp..h.
Ipswich to London = 68 miles 59 chains in 80 minutes = 51·6 m.p.h.
Norwich to London = 114 miles 77 chains in 135 minutes = 51·0 m.p.h.
London to Ipswich = 68 miles 59 chains in 80 minutes = 51·6 m.p.h.
Ipswich to Norwich = 46 miles 18 chains in 51 minutes = 54·4 m.p.h.
London to Norwich = 114 miles 77 chains in 135 minutes = 51·0 m.p.h.
It will be observed that the average intermediate—London-Ipswich-Norwich—and overall speeds in both directions are identical.

The record of times Peppercorn kept on 27 September, which he later tabulated and included in his article. Although no other examples of similar work appear to have survived, this table suggests it may have been a regular habit of his when travelling. (RH)

was a man in his element and enthused by the world around him. It was clearly his vocation.

After this rush of material in 1937, Peppercorn's output seems to have dried up. More pressing matters to attend to may simply have been the reason for this,

The second streamlined B17, No. 2870, *City of London* plies its trade in the late 1930s. These locomotives carried this casing until 1951 when they were restored to their original condition. (*THG*)

exacerbated by his return to the CME's fold in 1938. In truth, and with the benefit of hindsight, it is easy to see that his literary efforts probably owed more to his position as Locomotive Running Superintendent than those of Mechanical Engineer at Stratford or Darlington, his next posting. In fact, all his writings seem to have been encouraged by Newton, ever eager to publicise the company's achievements and provide employees with an appreciation of technical and operational issues. By doing this, Peppercorn probably gained some kudos, which in Newton's case would prove useful in a career sense. He was, in the phraseology of the time, 'a coming man' and in March 1939 became Chief General Manager, succeeding Ralph Wedgwood. With this in mind, he was certainly someone to be cultivated by anyone eager for promotion.

One is then left to ponder why he doesn't appear to have published anything of note when working for Gresley, who, as we have seen, actively encouraged other men to do so. Here we fall back on the nature of Peppercorn's work as a production engineer under the CME and his own apparent lack of input to design at any level. If he had discovered something of note and wished to write about it, it is unlikely that Gresley would have discouraged him in this. Did this matter in the long term? Apparently not, as Peppercorn's promotion to CME after the war would reveal. Yet it may partially explain why he wasn't promoted to this post in the immediate wake of Gresley's death in 1941 instead. Was Thompson considered the better candidate because he had demonstrated a keener understanding of design as well as production needs in a variety of posts? He probably lacked the depth and breadth of Gresley's knowledge and skill in this area, but this was easily compensated for by his superior skills in production and workshop matters. Peppercorn, or so it seems, couldn't offer the same balance. When he did become CME in 1946, the LNER was facing nationalisation and the loss

Liverpool Street Station as it appeared in the 1930s when Peppercorn was based there as Locomotive Running Superintendent Southern Area. At one stage, this was considered to be one of Britain's busiest stations, with daily numbers of travellers moving close to 250,000. (*ET/DN*)

of all independence and he was fast approaching retirement. In this situation, design issues would soon pass out of his control into the hands of a new central body eager to standardise and rationalise

During his remaining years there were three other occasions when Peppercorn felt able to describe his views on an industry he had graced for more than forty years. Coming so late in his career they are particularly interesting, because they are the product of a mature and intelligent man in the twilight of his career who had thought deeply about his role and his profession.

In 1947, just before the railway industry was consumed by nationalisation, Bulleid encouraged his three fellow CMEs – George Ivatt for the LMS, Frederick Hawksworth from the GWR and Peppercorn – to summarize their views on 'Railway Power Plant in Great Britain'. On 12 June that year, all four men presented their thoughts at a centenary lecture in London to an audience of fellow engineers as well as those from other scientific and management fields and politics.

Ivatt spoke first and was followed by Peppercorn. He began with a very revealing statement about the state of play within the LNER before moving on to a detailed description of the work undertaken by his department:

'Policy respecting locomotive developments has been largely influenced by the factors governing production in the immediate post-war period, and investigation into advanced designs with a view to production of such units has not formed any part of the LNER's policy. The company's resources of finance, manpower, and facilities, are being concentrated on

The LNER's London running sheds were responsible for providing engines to meet a wide variety of tasks. As a result the fleet was a mixed one, as confirmed by this photograph taken in the late 1930s. It contains mostly goods and shunting locomotives, plus an N1 tank engine possibly still used for commuter services. The task facing Peppercorn would have been a daunting one even without his duties at Stratford Works. (*RH*)

restoring the basic locomotive stock to its previous level of mechanical reliability, and to building up a fleet of modern locomotives of improved performance and greater availability to replace many of the now obsolete classes.

'Steam. The same broad principles of design, which have proved so successful in the past, are being maintained in the eight new standard designs selected as representative of the traction needs of the company [a programme set in motion by Thompson, who was in the audience].

'Altogether some 150 of these engines are already in traffic, and larger orders are now in hand both in the company's workshops and in workshops of contractors.

'It is not expected that within the limited territorial boundaries of the LNER anything approaching the monthly mileages of 25,000, and the mileages between overhauls of 200,000 miles, so common in America today, can hope to be realised. Nevertheless, the fact that steam locomotive mileages of the high order attained in America are possible, undoubtedly points to considerable possibilities in our own case in the future.

'One of the essential requirements, in order that a wider range of operation such as this may be approached, is a controlled system of boiler-water treatment throughout the whole line.

'Research into valve events points to future development in one or two directions. If the piston valve is retained its diameter can with advantage be increased. On the other hand, poppet valves seem a logical field for study provided that, with the speeds visualised on the large poppet valves, adequate means are provided to close the valves positively and rapidly after emission of steam. From the point of view of simplification of motion details, especially to the middle cylinder of three-cylinder designs, poppet valves have marked advantages.

'Much consideration has been given to the question of the steel firebox and its many advantages are not overlooked – in particular the elimination of objectionable overlap of plates at rivet joints which, by welding fireboxes complete, are avoided. Galvanic action is removed by eliminating dissimilar metals, and weight is lessened, enabling higher evaporation per unit of weight to be obtained. Nevertheless, steel fireboxes require the best of waters for their use, and water softening to the pitch required to achieve immunity from scale has not yet been reached in this country.

'Whilst the foregoing represents the general trend of development for steam locomotives, it should not be assumed that the LNER is without interest in advances which have been made in the practical application of alternative forms of traction for main line service. The gas turbine, for example, is meriting

During Peppercorn's time in London Gresley's locomotive programme continued apace. During 1934 the first two of his majestic P2 2-8-2 express locomotives appeared, with four more added in 1936 in streamlined form (which the first two engines assumed in 1936 and 1938). During the war years, they were rebuilt as Pacifics, a programme for which both Thompson and Peppercorn would bear responsibility as CME and Deputy CME. (*THG*)

considerable thought but as yet is insufficiently developed to enable future policy to be determined.

'Diesel. In the field of traction employing internal-combustion power the LNER has now formulated schedules for the introduction of a not inconsiderable number of diesel rail-cars over a wide range of secondary services. The rail-cars proposed are of the diesel-mechanical type, each car having two power units, each of 105 bhp. The basic seating capacity is to be forty-eight passengers, and the cars are to work either singly, in multiple units with or without trailers, or, alternatively, two units with a standard type coach in between them. The cars employ pre-selective electro-pneumatic gear change, and maximum designed speeds in high and low ratio are 65mph and 46mph respectively, this giving a fast, secondary line, limited passenger service for which steam traction is neither economical nor sufficiently adaptable.

'The introduction of diesel-electric units for shunting purposes has been made; engines of this type are undergoing trial. The units are 350 bhp, and six-coupled, with nose-suspended traction-motors on two outside pairs of coupled wheels. Double-reduction gearing is provided between the motors and the driving wheels in order that motors may have a reasonable speed of rotation when the locomotive is operating at very low speeds of 'hump' shunting work.

'A further shunting locomotive is expected to be delivered for trial shortly; this engine, of 200 bhp, employs a mechanical drive.

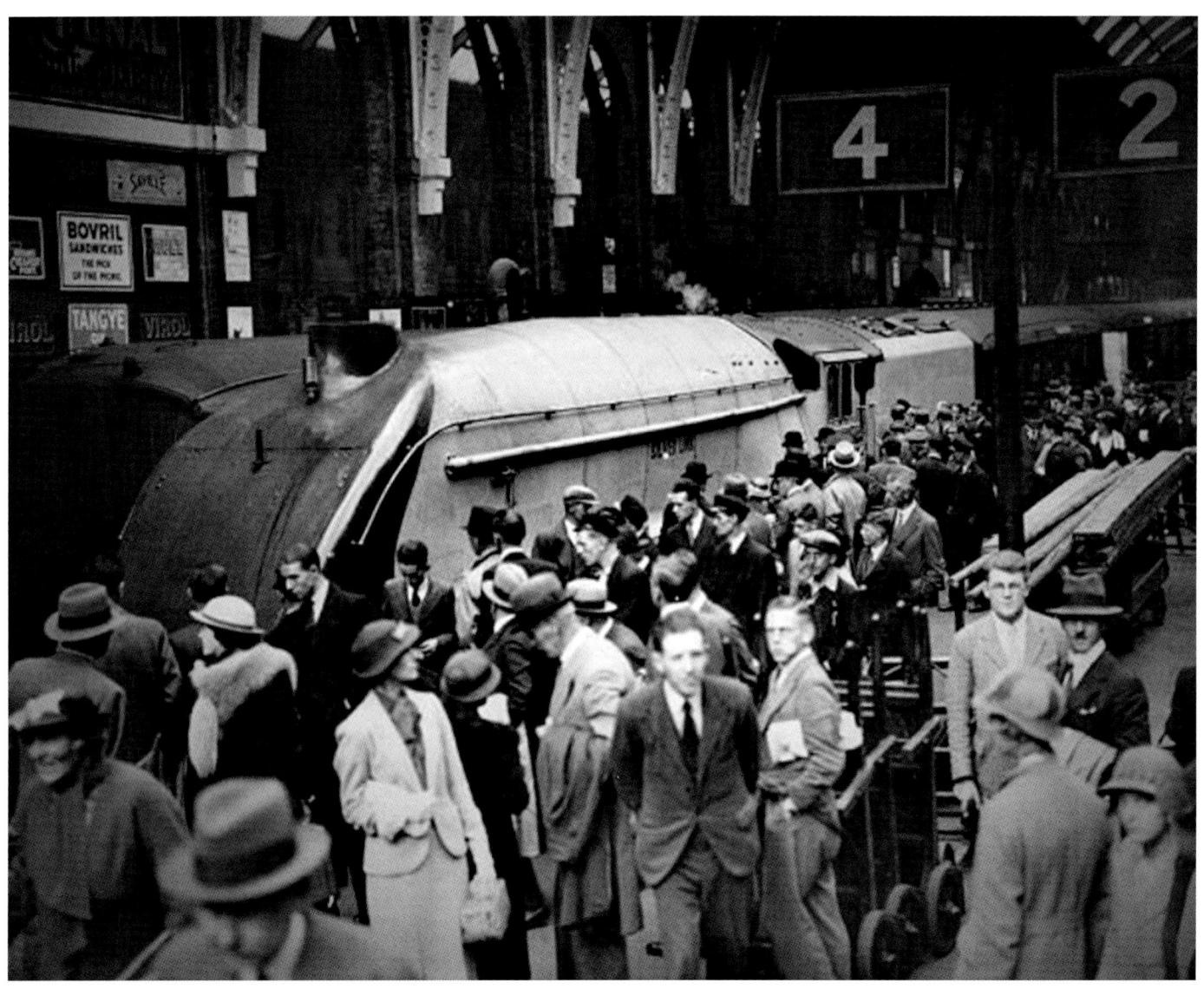

PEPPERCORN IN HIS OWN WORDS • 131

Opposite and this page: Although playing no obvious part in the development and construction of the new A4 Pacifics, Peppercorn attended several naming ceremonies and the launch of the two new services these locomotives pulled, according to notes left by Bert Spencer. (Opposite page) Engine No. 2509, *Silver Link* draws an admiring crowd in 1935 as it introduces the 'Silver Jubilee' service. (Top) A little later this premier service is captured as it passes Durham. Two years later, on 5 July, No. 4489, *Dominion of Canada*, pulled the first 'Coronation' service which was a top hat and tails affair. It was attended by the LNER's chairman William Whitelaw (photo to the right in centre). (Above) A month earlier, on 15 June, the engine had been named by the Canadian High Commissioner, Vincent Massey, who can be seen on the engine's footplate with Gresley. (*DN*)

'Electric. The Doncaster locomotive works has built the prototype 0-4-4-0 all electric, mixed traffic locomotive of 1,868 bhp, for the Manchester-Sheffield electrification scheme [design work being overseen by the Chief Electrical Engineer Henry Richards and his Chief Draughtsman Tom Street, the CME only providing workshop capacity to meet construction needs].

'Conclusion. The LNER has concentrated its design policy on the orthodox steam locomotive rather than on other forms of traction, because of the greater maintenance advantages which accrue from operating a large fleet of straightforward, simple and similar machines.

'For adequate power, three-cylinder propulsion has been favoured in preference to four, and often where the same power could have been produced by two-cylinders. Fundamentally, the more nearly the variable crank-effort of a reciprocating engine can be made to approach uniformity, the greater will be the advantage derived for traction from a given adhesive weight.'

His views on the industry for which he worked, as expressed here, seem strangely at odds with a modern and rapidly changing world. To be fair, though, they may have been driven by a sense of caution induced by overpowering financial constraints. Basically, carry on with what you can afford and don't wish for the stars. This approach is both pragmatic, non-speculative and realistic, but can stifle imagination and experimentation. Gresley, one feels, always looked more broadly and searched for new and better solutions. He wouldn't, or so it seems, have been deterred by current problems or restraints, but looked beyond them in to the future. Perhaps Gresley was simply a more optimistic person, whereas Peppercorn allowed pessimism, dressed up as judicious prudence, to be his guiding light.

It is interesting to compare his presentation to those of his fellow CMEs. Did they share his views in any way? Ivatt gave a detailed assessment that looked in depth at steam, diesel and electric programmes underlining, in no uncertain terms, his ambitions for the future in each area. In particular, he highlighted the new diesel engines under construction for main line and secondary duties and their advances in the field of multiple-unit electric stock. He ended with a view of the not too distant future. 'The LMSR authorities hold that a complete break away from steam towards the internal combustion engine is the logical step to take.'

Hawksworth, in contrast, expressed the view that all that could be done had been done with steam and the company was simply pressing ahead on well-established principles apparently without deviation:

'The present position of steam locomotives is directly the outcome of a consistent policy initiated by Churchward in the early years of the present century and followed throughout the intervening years in the design of the company's stock … He set the seal on locomotive design for the GWR.'

When it came to the future, he touched on plans for both diesel and gas turbine engines, but saw neither as realistic alternatives to steam for main line use yet.

The Southern Railway were in a quite different position. The company had a long established electrification programme and had converted one third of its network, with much more to follow as financial constraints gradually eased. There was still a role for steam, but it was a diminishing one, which Bulleid clearly regretted. He touched on his work with diesel, electric and gas turbine engines for main line use, but one feels that his heart still lay in steam. As a result, he talked with great enthusiasm about his Merchant Navy and West Country Class Pacifics, which were still being produced, and his development work on a coal fired heavy, mixed traffic tank engine being built on two six-wheeled bogies (the ill-fated 'Leader' project).

As one might expect, each CME's views reflected their personalities, ambitions and level of scientific curiosity. Ivatt and Bulleid seemed to display a more expansive approach to design and were eager to explore alternative forms of locomotion. They may have been wedded to steam, but they saw it working in conjunction with newer systems until eventually replaced. In contrast, Peppercorn and Hawksworth reflect the attitudes of good managers not scientists. For the most part, they describe policies and constraints, whilst making best use of what they have in their respective inventories. When they touch on new developments it seems that they do so from the side-lines as though observing others at work.

A cartoon that appeared when the A4s made their appearance, a copy of which Peppercorn kept amongst his papers. He left no record of his thoughts on the 'craze' for streamlining, as some called it, unless the archiving of a copy of the cartoon contained a subtle subliminal message. The passenger is saying to the porter 'I would like a seat with my back to the engine . . . if it is an engine!'. (*DN*)

The streamlining programme continued with W1's reconstruction and re-appearance in November 1937. Apart from the 4-6-4 wheel configuration and longer cab the engine bore a strong resemblance to the A4s as the photo above taken at King's Cross bears witness. The A4 is No. 4466, *Herring Gull* which appeared in January 1938. (*THG*)

In 1947, Peppercorn was asked to write the foreword to a book written by George Dow, one of the LNER's press officers. There is a sense that it could easily have been written when he was still a child, such is the passion for steam locomotion that he expresses:

'There is something about the alliance of man and steam horse – of human skill with huge mechanical strength – that never fails to capture the imagination of those who admire an intricate piece of machinery, brilliantly designed, skilfully put together, and beautifully handled.

'It is this alliance of man and one of his most powerful and influential inventions – one of the few, that as Roger Lloyd has said "has not been prostituted to purposes of lying, hatred, and slaughter' and still possesses 'a queer innocence and decency" – that is the theme of this book. Mr Dow describes the sort of men who serve the locomotive, from her designers to those who feed, groom, and water her and under whose hands she often performs prodigious feats of speed, strength, and endurance. Any footplate man or loco engineer will tell you that no steam horse ever behaves exactly like any other steam horse, whatever stable she comes from.

'The details of day-to-day maintenance that turns a locomotive out on to the iron road at the highest pitch of efficiency are only less spectacular and not less fascinating than the stories of the famous record-breakers and how they won their laurels.

'I venture to think that this book will be enjoyed no less by locomotive and other engineers than by youthful collectors of engine-numbers and the passenger who likes to stroll up the platform to see what breed of steam horse it is that stands snorting with apparent impatience to be off.'

From the few written words that have survived, it is possible to glimpse Arthur Peppercorn and the sort of man and engineer he was. He was clearly enthused by all aspects of railway life and seems to have been consumed by this passion. Every element of his personality seems to have found a voice in his work, so it is little wonder that from the earliest he was drawn to this world and was consumed by all its wonders.

Words can be used to confirm or hide one's thoughts, so must be treated with circumspection especially at senior level in any organisation. Politics and the art of diplomacy have to be exercised at all times if a business or an idea is to gain favour and succeed. But when Peppercorn described his run on the East Anglian during 1937 and when he wrote a foreword for George Dow's book there was no need to apply constraint or spin. The result is an open expression of his feelings about something he held dear. As a result, we see him more clearly and I, for one, liked what I found. Intelligence, enthusiasm, kindness, an innocent delight in the world around him, an engaging power of self-expression, professionalism and much more. In photographs he may well have looked stern but it seems to have been a protective layer which hid a man of warmth, honesty and honour, as well as a manager of great authority and skill.

During 1938 Robert Thom, Mechanical Engineer Southern Area at Doncaster (pictured above – the portly figure in the foreground looking carefully at the activity surrounding engine No. 4495, *Golden Fleece*), was reaching the end of his long career. The loss of this gifted man, who had been a central figure in the development of Gresley's locomotives since taking on this key post in 1927, would leave a huge gap in the organisation. Consequently, finding an effective replacement would be difficult. Edward Thompson, who had been Mechanical Engineer North Eastern Area since 1933, was chosen and moved from Darlington to Doncaster in June 1938; a transfer delayed for a short time by the sudden death of his wife. Peppercorn was selected to fill the vacancy left by Thompson's. His return to this important position in the CME's Department came at an auspicious moment in time with Germany's occupation of Austria fresh in the mind, soon to be followed by the ill-fated Munich Agreement and the annexation of Czechoslovakia. (*ET/DN*)

There is one last piece of Peppercorn's literary work to consider. It was an article written at the end of 1947 on the eve of nationalisation when his future was uncertain and he felt the need to express his thoughts on locomotive development over the previous twenty-five years. As a witness of all that happened, his thoughts and opinions would have been eagerly anticipated and again he was probably encouraged in this by Charles Newton.

In preparing his article, Peppercorn had the good fortune to have Bert Spencer beside him as technical assistant. He had recently spent many months researching and writing about Gresley's achievements, which he then presented to the IMechE. This material would have provided Peppercorn with a sound base for his own review. Of the three CMEs, only he attempted such an evaluation, so for this reason alone its importance cannot be over-emphasized. However, he wasn't someone to court controversy and so there is no critical element hovering over this assessment. Others may have attempted to do otherwise, but he understood the pressures of the CME post and knew only too well the stresses and strains under which they all operated. He also appears to have liked and admired his predecessors and clearly wished to recall their work sympathetically and with understanding. So there are no words of criticism, though, as always when an intelligent person expresses their thoughts, there are moments when 'reading between the lines' is possible. What emerges is a work of importance, albeit a brief one, in which this modest man plays down his own contribution, highlighting the work of Gresley and Thompson instead. Some excerpts from Peppercorn's 1947 paper are quoted later in this book, but below are some of the other key points he made, suggesting his own thoughts and opinions on some of the key issues concerning locomotive design during his career:

"The first Pacific, No.1470, *Great Northern*, went into service in 1922 and was the forerunner of one of the most successful types of express locomotive ever built in this country. This type classified A1 was later developed into the more powerful A3 class and then finally into the A4 class streamlined Pacifics. The form of streamlining adopted not only contributed to the efficient working of the engine by reducing the air resistance but also proved highly effective in lifting the exhaust from the chimney clear of the cab windows.

A policy of rigid standardisation was not adopted during the Gresley regime and several types of engines were built for special duties, the most notable being the P2 class 2-8-2 designed for hauling trains of up to 550 tons unassisted over the heavily graded route from Edinburgh and Aberdeen. These engines were the first British eight coupled express locomotives.

Sir Nigel Gresley's great career came to an end on 5th April 1941, but his designs largely anticipated traffic requirements and are today adequately meeting the heaviest demands. His successor, Mr Edward Thompson, faced a formidable task. Prior to 1941 LNER policy had been to relegate to secondary duties the engines which had been displaced by heavier types of modern design. The question of replacing large numbers of second-line engines was consequently coming to the fore and, at the same time, the existing locomotive stock had to be kept fit to handling the rapidly increasing war-time traffic. Whilst Sir Nigel favoured the three-cylinder single expansion engine, the new classes designed by Mr Thompson were evolved on the principle that two-cylinders should be adopted, unless the power required was greater than two cylinders could provide satisfactorily.

In the provision of new three-cylinder engines for heavy main-line express work, Mr Thompson perpetuated much of Sir Nigel's practice, but a major alteration was the adoption of three independent sets of Walschaerts valve gear and divided drive."

All this was far in the future when Peppercorn's time in London drew to a close in 1938. A transfer northwards beckoned in the wake of Robert Thom's retirement. This move would herald the beginning of the most important stage of his career, one made significantly more difficult by the coming of war. All the long years of training and labour had equipped him well for the trials that lay ahead, but even he couldn't have predicted the size of the task that awaited him. Sadly, he didn't have time or the energy to record his thoughts and impressions in the way he had in 1937. If given the chance, there is no doubt that the result would have been illuminating and thrown much needed light on his greatest challenge and greatest triumph.

CHAPTER 5

RISING TO THE CHALLENGE

No matter how challenging he found being Locomotive Running Superintendent in London, taking over the works at Darlington, with all its historic associations, must have stirred his interest. Once again he followed Thompson, though the occasion must have been tinged with some sadness for both of them. Thompson was widowed only days after his departure to Doncaster. In these circumstances, the recently widowed Peppercorn was given a stark reminder of his own situation. His note to Thompson, which the older man kept, although containing a traditional message of sympathy was clearly influenced by his own loss. Nevertheless, life goes on and soon Peppercorn had found a house in which to live, most probably rented, and a new housekeeper, Isobel Wilkinson, to organise his domestic life.

The house he chose, called the Grove, was on the outskirts of Darlington in the village of Middleton-St-George with views south over the River Tees and an area called Over Dinsdale. It was an affluent district and his neighbours reflected this – doctors, businessmen of some standing and so on. Darlington Works was only a short drive away and the village sat just to the south of the historic railway line to Stockton. After the rigours of life in London, this new world must have seemed much calmer, with golf providing an occasional distraction again. But it was the lull before the storm and in the months ahead, with Britain belatedly beginning to re-arm in the face of German aggression, the pace would begin to hot up.

After nearly five years of Thompson being in charge, the works at Darlington had undergone a number of reforms to improve efficiency and the flow of work. Change is rarely welcomed, with many preferring a continuation of old, familiar methods. To soften the blow, new working practices are often accompanied by bonus schemes related to productivity. Thompson was known to be a strong advocate of such arrangements, having been introduced to the concept, the brainchild of the industrial engineer Frank Gilbreth, during a visit to the USA before the Great War. He was keen to develop these schemes here, but the LNER's Board were less enthusiastic. Keeping a weather eye on profitability in the face of an economy still barely out of recession had become second nature.

A photograph of Peppercorn published in 1938 when he was posted to Darlington. As is often the case, the picture may have been taken before then and held on file by the PR Department. As always, or so it seems, he doesn't allow any expression to escape, but assumes a bland yet authoritative look. (*DN*)

So change without incentives had faced strong opposition at times. By the time Peppercorn arrived, the position had stabilized somewhat. Nevertheless, friction and disputes were not unknown, adding a layer of difficulty to an already challenging post.

The works at Darlington covered a number of sites employing 3,000 plus men and women, but this wasn't the limit of the task Peppercorn managed. As Mechanical Engineer North East Area, his responsibilities also extended to workshops at York, Gateshead and Shildon. Unlike Stratford, where locomotives were no longer built, Darlington still managed a construction programme, though Doncaster and Gresley's small headquarters team at King's Cross remained the main centres of design activity.

The peaceful world of Middleton-St-George as it would have appeared when Peppercorn moved there in 1938. (*THG*)

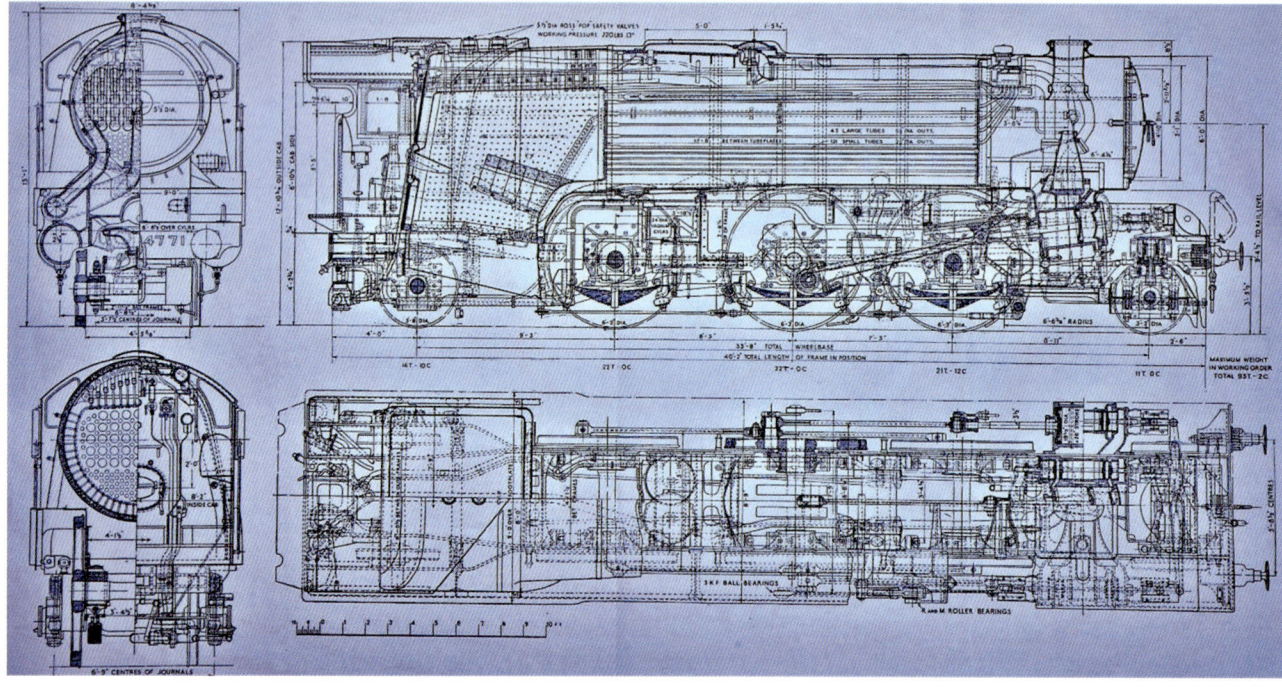

When Peppercorn arrived at Darlington in 1938 the V2 2-6-2 programme was well into its stride. The first five engines appeared in 1936 and by the time he became Mechanical Engineer Southern Area in 1941 the number had increased to 100 plus, with another 20 being built at Doncaster. The V2 drawings above, which were given wide circulation amongst journalists at the time, reflect these engines' clear genetic links back to Gresley's A1/A3 Pacifics. As usual they combined three cylinders – built in a single monobloc casting which incorporated the smokebox saddle, outside steampipes and steamchests - with 2 to 1 conjugated valve gear. The boiler was a cut down version of those built for the A3s but still produced 220psi. However, there was one small departure from the Pacific design – the conventional dome was replaced with a 'banjo' steam collector. (*THG*)

Nevertheless, by 1938 a hiatus seems to have settled on the company. It may merely have been a pause for breath after a long period of intense design work in which Gresley's fertile imagination had roamed free. Or, perhaps, the LNER had built sufficient engines of all types to meet its present and future needs. However, a third possibility is suggested by Gresley's declining health, which by 1938/39 was giving some cause for concern. No one can work at such a great pace as he did for ever and if suffering from arteriosclerosis, with the linked condition of vascular dementia, maintaining such an output would become virtually impossible. Gresley's medical records suggest this was the case.

So, the momentum he had established may simply have run on, but no longer in the same inspired way. The coming of war in 1939 may have disguised his reducing activity, much of Britain's industrial might being absorbed by armaments production, but Gresley's decline was already self-evident to a number of his close associates. Much later Bert Spencer referred to his CME's 'increasing confusion and the need for I, and a few others, to regularly work from his home in Watton-at-Stone from 1938 onwards', whilst Dr Patrick Ransome-Wallis, a noted observer of railway matters, remembered Gresley, late in his life walking along the platforms at King's Cross 'insisting that all drivers of all Pacifics blow their whistles for him'.

There is little doubt that the men with whom he had worked closely would have found the decline of their greatly admired leader a bitter blow. Yet the programmes he had set in motion continued and now two of the last of these would fall to Peppercorn to manage. No longer would he sit on the side-line of these great achievements but begin to move centre stage and take on their management. The continuing production of the V2 2-6-2 heavy mixed traffic locomotive, followed by the K4 2-6-0 mixed traffic engines at Darlington would soon absorb his attention. In the V2's case, construction continued on, year by year, until 1944 by which time all but 20 of the 184 built would have rolled off the production line at Darlington and Doncaster.

The second V2, No. 4772, shows off its classic Gresley lines to good effect. Although showing clear similarities to the A1/A3 Pacifics, they did have their own distinctive look, helped by the 2-6-2 wheel configuration, the 'banjo' dome and the different, wider spacing of the coupled wheels. (*PR*)

As Peppercorn settled into his new job, he oversaw the completion of the second batch of V2s built – 28 in all. No. 4801, the third to last of these, received particular attention and was photographed from many angles. The cabs that Gresley and his team designed were deemed sound from an ergonomic point of view and appeared to be well liked by the men who crewed them. (*PR*)

The first V2, No. 4771 *Green Arrow*, undertaking its primary duty as a heavy mixed traffic engine pulling a fast goods train. With war gradually becoming a reality, these engines would soon find these duties increasing in scale. They also became a worthy stand in for Pacifics on fast expresses. (*PR*)

The first K4 class 2-6-0 mogul was a prototype designed and built at Darlington in 1937 for the West Highland line, where conditions were particularly harsh. It was a requirement set in motion by General Manager Scotland's office, headed by George Mills, a year earlier. Gresley and his team initially considered using an eight-coupled design but went back to the drawing board when the Civil Engineer's Department ruled that it would be too long and too heavy for the track. With 193 K3 2-6-0s in service it should have been a straight-forward decision to detach a small number to the Highlands. But here again, their use was rejected by the CE. So, a suitably modified mogul was suggested as a solution and the K4 began its evolution. As one might expect, it drew heavily on Gresley's tried and tested ideas. To get the right balance, a cut down version of the B17's boiler was constructed initially set to produce 180psi of pressure and a tractive effort of 32,940lb, nearly 7,400lb. greater than the B17. However, this was later uprated to 200psi which advanced tractive effort to 36,598lb., greater than the A4s, A3s or V2s; quite a remarkable achievement in an engine of this size. This boiler was matched to cylinders and motion of the type fitted to the K3s, plus 5ft 2in driving wheels and a 24 element superheater.

A successful period of trial running followed. This led to the construction of four more K4s in 1938/39 under Peppercorn's guiding hand. How he viewed these developments isn't known, but he would no doubt have followed their progress with interest.

Gresley's first K4 2-6-0, No. 3441, *Loch Long*, appearing to pass through a loop on the Highland line (date not recorded). These powerful locomotives did sterling service, but lower maintenance standards during the war are said to have resulted in problems with their three-cylinders and conjugated valve gear, so reducing their efficiency and availability. The same problem is said to have afflicted Gresley's other three-cylinder designs. In due course, Thompson, with Peppercorn as his deputy, advocated change and sought to institute a programme of modification to two cylinders. Some work was undertaken, but nationalisation then intervened. (*RH*)

K4 No. 3445, *MacCailin Mor*, operating under wartime conditions – a long heavy load and unkempt condition. During 1945, this engine was rebuilt with two cylinders and in this form was re-designated K1 and reappeared in December that year. No other members of the class were converted. (*RH*)

Although the construction of new locomotives was only one part of an ME's life, and took its place in a very complex and varied work schedule, new schemes such as this would have stood out and been worthy of close scrutiny. Likewise, he would also have been aware of Gresley's interest in these projects and been ready to brief him on progress at all stages. Bert Spencer later described the level of involvement Gresley had when he wrote:

'The CME rarely if ever let a day pass when he was not personally involved in all aspects of construction of a new class of locomotive or modification to existing types. He made it known that frequent briefings were necessary. He also phoned regularly and sent many memorandum and minutes to his senior managers to ensure the work was proceeding as he wished. There were regular debates with both Mr Thompson and Mr Peppercorn, from Doncaster and Darlington respectively, about any new work. Nothing passed him by, even when in decline, although it slowed the pace of his work quite considerably. One frequent debate centred on the need for more standardisation in locomotive types which both MEs pursued when the occasion allowed. They were concerned over the number of types and extent of spares necessary to maintain such a varied fleet of engines. The CME tended to take a non-committal position on this question, seeing in it many practical difficulties.'

It is said that Gresley did little to foster a standardisation programme during his time as CME, preferring to build locomotives for particular needs. If this is true, the construction of only five K4s for the Highlands and six P2s to traverse the Edinburgh to Aberdeen line does provide some support for this view. Yet, when looking elsewhere in his building programme, the assumption becomes less clear. 184 V2s, 76 D49s, 324 J38/39s, 107 N2s and 110 plus Pacifics for example, with many common features speaks of some thought on the subject. Could he have gone further faced with all the myriad designs he inherited in 1923? Possibly, but the financial constraints the LNER faced in the years between the two world wars were severe. This would inevitably have stifled many things, including a large rationalisation and standardisation programme. Gresley was probably taking a pragmatic position on the issue and not wishing for the stars. Thompson and Peppercorn were less constrained and felt able to pursue this issue more vigorously when their time came to be CME.

For the moment, though, there were more pressing matters to occupy their minds. By the summer of 1939, Britain was on the point of declaring war against Germany, but this extreme action awaited a final spark, which came on 1 September when the Nazis invaded Poland. The die was cast and twenty-one years of a difficult peace came to an end. If anyone believed that this war would follow the pattern of the last, with stalemate followed by a campaign of little movement and huge casualties, they would be surprised. Within nine months, France was lost and Britain faced invasion. In this dire situation, the railways became central to the country's survival and were exhorted by the government to greater effort. In a repeat of 1914, the network quickly came under central control and all businesses were soon subject to a high degree of scrutiny by ministers and the Railway Executive Committee. This body, which had first come into being during the Great War, was reconstituted in 1938 under the chairmanship of Ralph Wedgwood, until 1941, and then Sir Alan Anderson, who combined these duties with that of Controller of the Railways having relinquished his directorship with the LMS. In this situation, independent action was discouraged, especially when it came to new construction, and much workshop capacity was turned over to armaments production. This wasn't always well planned and failed to take account of the railways' primary function; to keep the network running in the face of growing demand and enemy action.

In the LNER's workshops and sheds, the many operational problems they faced were soon exacerbated by the loss of many trained staff to the Army, Royal Navy and RAF. Equally, there was a problem at the top. Gresley's health continued to be of concern throughout 1940 with this once robust, dominating figure, as Bert Spencer later put it, 'becoming a shadow of his former self, and rarely able to venture from his home in Hertfordshire even before the bombing started'. To this he added, 'In these circumstances he couldn't exert the level of authority he had once done so easily, though never gave up trying.' He was still a giant presence, but in his declining state, the huge added burden of war could have proved to be a crushing one. Younger, fitter men had to step into the breach and take greater control and here Thompson and Peppercorn came into their own.

Very soon the many holiday posters that had covered billboards across the country were replaced by adverts urging greater effort in the conflict. During the Great War the railways were in danger of reaching breaking point when meeting the demands of industry and the military. They suffered from lack of funding, loss of trained staff and inadequate maintenance. The same was to happen in the Second World War. This advert, which found its way into workshops and sheds across the country, reminded all staff of the importance of the work they were doing and the need to keep all equipment in working order. In the circumstances this would become near impossible at times. It fell to Thompson and Peppercorn to shoulder much of this giant burden. (*RH*)

Although workshop duties dominated their daily lives members of staff took on other tasks during the war, so time to rest diminished rapidly. Here, the many Air Raid Wardens from Darlington's North Road Railway Works muster before another night's duty in the area. Peppercorn, by all accounts, took on his share of these extra night time duties. (*DN*)

Although there was great sorrow when Gresley died in May 1941, one gets the impression that some of his powers had already passed into the hands of his assistants by then. Nevertheless, the impact of his loss would still have been immense. He was a giant figure who had exercised authority with a sure touch for a very long time and guided his department to many successes. Such people are not easily replaced and their departure can leave a huge gap which can take years to fill. Thompson, who was selected to replace him, didn't have the luxury of time to bed himself in before the crushing pressures of wartime service descended. Luckily, he had experienced staff to help him shoulder this overwhelming burden and very quickly pushed to have Peppercorn posted to Doncaster as Mechanical Engineer and Assistant CME, being replaced by Luther Reeves at Darlington. It proved to be a wise and astute move, especially in the light of Gresley's apparent inability to select someone to fill such a role. Arthur Stamer had been Assistant CME until his retirement in 1933, but Gresley hadn't felt it necessary to replace him except as ME Darlington. Perhaps it didn't matter but one is left wondering whether, as his health declined, the department may have lost some direction at a critical moment in time which an active and appointed deputy might have corrected. If so, it was a mistake Thompson didn't repeat.

(Left) The new team at the top. The newly promoted Thompson and Peppercorn side by side during 1941 at Doncaster during a royal visit. (Above) Peppercorn looks on with interest as Queen Elizabeth talks to one of the hundreds of young women drafted into the workshops to replace men joining the services. Although there was a huge skills gap during the war, by applying great effort and enthusiasm, and supported by the trained men who remained, these women learnt new trades and played a significant part in keeping the railways running. (PR)

The only area of Gresley's work which didn't pass to Thompson and Peppercorn concerned electrification projects. Henry Richards, who had led on these issues under Gresley, was promoted to Chief Electrical Engineer and worked directly to Charles Newton, taking with him Tom Street as his Chief Draughtsman. Neither Newton or Thompson commented on this change and one can only assume that it arose from an assessment of the vast workload that would fall to the CME. Bearing in mind the costs involved, electrification was probably seen as a peacetime luxury to be considered but not pursued until the war ended. Neither Thompson or Peppercorn would have any significant involvement in this programme, although some of the development work was undertaken in their workshops. So steam remained their primary focus for the rest of their careers.

The relationship between the new CME and his deputy always seems to have been a cordial one, although their personalities differed in many ways. Whilst Thompson could be direct to the point of rudeness at times, Peppercorn remained the diplomat, managing people and resources in a measured way. Strangely enough, both approaches seem to have worked fairly well and at times even complemented each other, especially when it came to negotiations with trades unions. Despite Britain's critical position in the first three years of the war, disputes were commonplace across the railway industry and threatened to become seriously distracting at times. As CME, Thompson could afford to take a hard line, be tough and, apparently, uncompromising when seeking to resolve a dispute. He could then stand back as Peppercorn and others negotiated a solution in the face of 'his intransigence', arguing that he had to be placated if a fair settlement was to be reached. This is a common feature of any negotiation, particularly with trades unions, but takes great skill and understanding to achieve success. Between them they seemed to have managed it effectively and kept disruption in the workshops to a minimum throughout the war.

The two men, of course, shared a long mutual history, whether in the posts they occupied or their love of golf and fishing. They also shared a keen understanding of production engineering and workshop processes, which in war were essential skills to cultivate if they were to meet or exceed very demanding targets. This also meant that they could introduce other, military specific, tasks into schedules and still maintain overall production rates. But it would prove to be a case of diminishing returns as the conflict went on and placed even heavier demands on an increasingly weary work force. In these circumstances, absenteeism due to illness increased, presenting yet another problem for already hard-pressed managers to resolve. Inevitably, this issue fell most heavily on Thompson and Peppercorn's shoulders, both of whom were soon sleeping at the office regularly in a bid to cover all the tasks that fell to them.

In part, widowerhood allowed both men to ignore their home lives and focus almost exclusively on work. Isobel Wilkinson moved with Peppercorn from Darlington to Doncaster and continued as his housekeeper. But while Thompson remained a bachelor for the rest of his life, the more gregarious Peppercorn moved on. During 1942, when living in 80 Cantley Lane, Doncaster, he met the twenty-six-year-old Dorothy Louch, who worked as an Assistant Surveyor in a local branch of the Yorkshire Division of the Coal Commission. Shortly afterwards, she joined the LNER's drawing office, where she worked in close proximity to the CME. From this a friendship blossomed and marriage followed in September 1948, a year or so before his retirement.

With some happiness in his private life providing compensation for the long hours and stress of work, Peppercorn immersed himself in wartime production at Doncaster. But as Thompson's deputy, he had wider duties which at times could be quite onerous. On occasion, he acted on the CME's behalf, which meant attending some of the many meetings led by external bodies in government, as well as the normal LNER management groups. In peacetime, accountability was simply an internal company matter. In war, it had three additional masters in the Minister of War Transport, Frederick Leathers, the Minister of War Production, Oliver Lyttelton, and the Minister of Labour, Ernest Bevin, and the committees they set up. There was also the Railway Executive Committee, which continued to exert considerable influence on day to day operations directly and through a number of sub-groups. All these bodies set standards and measured performance, often independent of each other. The difficulties Thompson and Peppercorn faced in meeting these conflicting demands is easily imagined. Without a doubt, their reserves of energy and their patience must have severely tested.

In terms of new production of locomotives and rolling stock, the company was limited in what they could do by directives from central government. In essence, any work of this nature had to be war related and approved in London. This policy didn't always hold true, though, as witnessed by Oliver Bulleid's Merchant Navy Class. They received Bevin's support and approval in 1941, although clearly locomotives more suited to the glamorous pre-war express traffic than the grind of wartime work. But for the most part, the railway companies didn't enjoy such freedom, although this did not stop their senior managers and design engineers giving thought to post-war needs. Equally, they had to ensure that existing equipment was fit for purpose and capable of meeting increased daily demands both efficiently and cost effectively. By their very nature, high performance locomotives were liable to stress their component parts more severely than more modest engines. They were essentially racehorses and so required more maintenance. War demanded more of these machines and, at the same time, its exigencies led to less frequent and less effective servicing. In these circumstances, they were likely to deteriorate more quickly and suffer breakdown. As this began to happen, the running department came to believe that engines with three cylinders and Gresley's conjugated valve gear were suffering more than other types and sought action to correct the defects.

Robert Inglis, who replaced George Mills as General Manager Scotland in 1941, was particularly concerned about the deteriorating condition of the six P2s under his control and made his feelings known to the CME. Thus he set in motion a controversy for which Thompson is still blamed and often condemned. Received wisdom has come to suggest that he deliberately took these Gresley masterpieces and had them rebuilt as Pacifics purely out of spite. Putting to one side the obvious 'pantomime villain' element of such an argument, the facts do not bear out such a conclusion. Maintenance records

On 29 April 1942 York came under heavy attack by the Luftwaffe. (Above) A4 No. 4469 *Sir Ralph Wedgwood*, was in the wrong place at the wrong time and suffered catastrophic damage. This engine, originally named *Gadwall*, was re-railed and made sufficiently safe to be moved 40 miles to Doncaster where the photograph below was taken on 18 May. The tender, No. 8954, was eventually repaired post-war and attached to the 1944 built A2/1 Pacific No. 3696, *Highland Chieftain*, a product of the Thompson/Peppercorn era. (*ET/DN*)

Under wartime conditions even the A4s were soon allowed to deteriorate as the photo above of engine No. 4486, *Merlin*, bears witness. At this stage the locomotive still carries side valances over the wheels. Under Thompson's guiding hand these were soon discarded in an effort to make servicing easier, including 4486 during a general overhaul in late 1941. (*RH*)

add much needed detail as did the reports submitted by footplate crew and maintenance staff working in the sheds. These reveal the extent of the problem and the rising amount of downtime as servicing standards slipped. There was also a number of incident reports to consider. On 18 July 1939, engine No. 2005 suffered a severe failure in its crank axle assembly. Luckily this didn't result in a major accident or casualties, but raised concerns over a potential weakness in the design, exacerbated by the tight curves over which the engines operated in Scotland. Repairs were made and the loco returned to traffic at the end of August. But in 1942 No. 2004, *Mons Meg*, suffered a similar breakdown and in 1944 this was followed by No. 2003, *Lord President*. There are also some indications that there were similar problems of wear in the other members of the class.

The P2s were not the only Gresley three-cylinder locomotives suffering problems with their 2 to 1 valve gear as demand increased and maintenance standards slipped. But they became the focus of most attention because of the crank axle failures. Charles Newton and his General Managers could have alleviated this problem to a certain extent by sanctioning their move south of the border, where the curves were probably more forgiving. However, this wasn't to be and the engines soldiered on with the CME trying to find a solution to these long term problems. In seeking an answer, he moved with some caution, undoubtedly due to the many other important issues he and Peppercorn had to manage. And the list was a long and complex one indeed.

War production is a very broad term and, at times, almost impossible to pin down so varied were the needs it describes. Far more certain were the requirements of the railway itself. Quite simply the CME and his organisation had to produce and maintain sufficient engines and rolling stock to meet the daily requirements of the running department. A simple answer but a very complex delivery process with many variables to heighten the degree of difficulty. The most pressing of these was lack of trained staff, but lack of workshop capacity also proved of significance as the war went on. Restrictions on independent action and funding also created many problems. External oversight of day to day activities and production rates then added another layer of scrutiny, often making a challenging job even more demanding; Government and the REC could be hard, often unsympathetic, task masters. Yet all this had to be managed in the face of many, often loosely specified, war related production activities that could vary considerably and be dropped on the company at short notice.

The list of extra tasks was a long one and included such things as the manufacture of various calibre ammunition and weapons of all types and sizes. There was also the construction of landing craft and small boats to meet a variety of purposes, marine spare parts, aircraft repairs and the production of their component. To manage all these things, Thompson soon set up a special team, led by Cyril Elwell, to oversee and manage all these diverse needs, with both he and Peppercorn directly involved in their work. Without such a team of progress chasers and planners it is possible that the production process would have spiralled out of control to the embarrassment of the company.

In peacetime, the successful transport of passengers and goods is essential if a company is to remain in business, but in war, the consequences of breakdown have wider implications. Failure to deliver weapons and service personnel to front line units was essential, and for most of the war the front line was on the company's doorstep. On one hand, the LNER frequently came under enemy attack and faced severe disruption. On the other hand, they became the major supplier of men and material to the RAF and USAAF during the long and critical bombing war and, on top of this, the Army and Royal Navy required constant support too. The pressure all these demands placed on a creaking system were immense.

No. 2004, *Mons Meg* looking particularly shabby in June 1943 south of Aberdeen. In appearance all the LNER's pre-war express locomotives suffered due to staff reductions and pressure of other work brought on by the conflict. But with the P2s the problem was more than skin deep. Like other Gresley engines there were concerns over the increasingly dilapidated condition of their three cylinders and conjugated valve gear. A view was growing amongst some that the deterioration, whilst having its roots in running conditions and the poor standard of maintenance, was, in reality, a result of poor design. It fell to Thompson and Peppercorn to seek a remedy. The P2s, being deemed in worst condition, became the primary focus of their attention. (*DN*)

By 1942 women made up a high percentage of the CME's workforce and very quickly began to fill the skills gap left by those men volunteering or being conscripted for military service. Despite this, the number the LNER were allowed to recruit fell short of demand as the Ministry of Labour tried to fill vacancies across many industries. This photo was one of a number taken at Doncaster to encourage more recruits to come forward. (ET/DN)

A photo taken at Doncaster during the war years that helps illustrate the variety of work the LNER's workshops were obliged to undertake. In this case the manufacture of a four inch naval gun sits alongside locomotive frames and what appears to be gun mountings soon to be bolted to ships' decks. (ET/DN)

The construction of specialist military rolling stock became one of Thompson and Peppercorn's occasional tasks during the war. In the photo on the left the two men pose with the US Army's liaison officer, Colonel Bingham, during the handover of a specially designed accommodation carriage for General Eisenhower to use post-D Day as the Allies drove across France towards Germany. The photo below highlights the LNER's work in building hospital trains for use in this country and in Europe. It is said that the Deputy CME took the lead in these tasks, though this is difficult to verify so long after the event. (*ET/DN*)

For much of the time, they could only apply 'sticking plaster' methods using their ability to think on their feet to improvise solutions, at which both men seem to have been adept. They would also regularly tour the workshops under their control to encourage and cajole where necessary and help solve many pressing problems. According to Thompson's few surviving papers, both men also visited their customers regularly to see for themselves the problems they faced. On one occasion, this was prompted by an incident at Barnham freight sidings in Suffolk. Due to the number of air bases locally, it had expanded rapidly. In 1938, it handled approximately 2,000 trucks holding 7,000 tons of freight. Between 1939 and 1945, this increased to 139,729 trucks containing 721,000 tons of mostly ordnance of all types. One part of this task involved the transport of mustard gas canisters manufactured at a nearby Imperial Chemical Industries factory. Although never used in action, by either Bomber Command or the USAAF, they were stockpiled at nearby air bases and would often spend time in the sidings at Barnham. It is here that some canisters leaked and heavily contaminated the local area. During the 'clean up' work that followed, Peppercorn is recorded as having visited the site, presumably to ensure that rolling stock design had not contributed to the accident. If it did, no papers have survived to confirm any action taken in this most secretive of wartime activities.

Above and overleaf: The requirement to support military activities throughout the war was a constant and demanding feature of life on the LNER. As witnessed by these two photographs, the loads moved covered ordnance in vast quantities, in this case thought to be mustard gas canisters (in sidings at Barnham), which were stockpiled but never used by the RAF or USAAF, to the deployment of these Sherman tanks in vast numbers and other Army equipment. Locomotive and rolling stock availability had to be on the 'top line' to ensure all moved swiftly and efficiently. For most of the time the CME's Department worked three shifts to ensure this happened. (*RH*)

The mess and clutter of a typical locomotive workshop during the war, in this case Crimpsall Locomotive Repair Shop, Doncaster, when Peppercorn was in charge. In reality it differed little in appearance between peace and war. The only real change was the continuous pattern shift working and the strict adherence to blackout regulations. (BS)

When the war was over, the LNER's senior managers released a book entitled *By Rail to Victory – The Story of the LNER in Wartime*. With some pride, it depicts the huge volume of work the company undertook in these troubled years. In one chapter, the author, Norman Crump, describes in detail the extent of the task the CME and his team managed. He concluded, for example, that nearly a third of staff were almost exclusively involved in the production of munitions to the exclusion of everything else. This number wasn't in addition to pre-war staffing levels, but simply a redirection. It is little wonder that maintenance standards slipped so alarmingly, even with long hours and twenty-four-hour shift working. Crump concluded that many staff worked sixty or seventy hours per week and rarely took leave of any sort. He added an interesting caveat to this:

'The trouble was that both men and machines had originally been put there [in this case at Darlington's North Road Locomotive Works] to build and repair locomotives, and not to make fittings for guns and tanks. So the men had to be taught to work to much finer limits than those needed for locomotives. Here much ingenuity and improvisation was needed.

'The women were described [by a chargeman at Darlington] as "if good, they were very good". They were very useful on repetition work. The introduction of untrained men as dilutees occasionally delayed production, but with all these qualifications, the record of the shops speaks for itself.

'Through all this Chargeman Watson was one of those engaged on the more humdrum task of repairing locomotives. Fifteen gangs were on this job, and they repaired 300 locomotives during the war. These were all heavy repairs. So Darlington, with all its war work, did not neglect its proper job.'

Nevertheless, despite these expressions of pride and descriptions of some of the difficulties faced, it is clear that such a titanic effort could not be sustained indefinitely. Cracks would and did appear, no matter how good the

Luther Reeves who replaced Peppercorn as Mechanical Engineer at Darlington in 1941 then followed him to Doncaster in 1945, when he relinquished the ME post there to become Assistant CME on a full-time basis. He remained with him until Peppercorn retired in 1949. Reeves is little remembered today and yet in the 1930s and 1940s he held key positions at very difficult times. He bore a primary responsibility for the construction of Thompson's A2/1 Pacifics at Darlington, then his A2/3s at Doncaster, followed by Peppercorn's A2s and a share of his A1s. In between times he also oversaw the rebuilding of Gresley's first Pacific, engine No.4470, *Great Northern*. Reeves was a Londoner by birth (Leytonstone in 1892) and possibly served an apprenticeship with the Great Eastern Railway at Stratford. By 1941 he had progressed rapidly and when selected to become ME at Darlington was already serving in the same capacity in Scotland. He went on to serve BR until his retirement and death in 1958. (*RH*)

work force and management. In such situations, the law of diminishing returns tends to apply and collapse become a real possibility. By 1945, the long conflict had drained most reserves leaving a huge residue of unfinished tasks and poorly maintained equipment. Peppercorn, or so it seems, coped with the strain fairly well, but Thompson suffered bouts of ill-health due to the colossal effort he made. Despite this, his absences were not excessive, but it seems likely that Peppercorn took on extra duties as a result. In 1945, this led to him relinquishing the ME Doncaster post in favour of becoming Deputy CME on a full time basis. He was again replaced by Luther Reeves. Did Peppercorn's move reveal good successor management in anticipation of the CME's retirement or did it simply reflect increasing concerns over his health? Either way, it was a sensible move especially in the light of Gresley's recent demise when signs of failing health seemed to have been ignored. A good deputy might have relieved him of some of the pressure and allowed his successor to take up the reins in a measured way and not through the disorganised scramble that followed Gresley's sudden death. The Chairman and General Manager may have delayed taking action in respect of Gresley's feelings, but by 1941 the war and increasing problems of production demanded much firmer action. With Thompson they did not repeat this mistake and Peppercorn stepped up to the plate to provide cover should the CME be overtaxed by these heavy burdens.

At such a difficult time, few would have had the capacity or the energy to look beyond the war, but during 1943 the tide was turning and a time beyond the conflict began to be glimpsed. Sir Ronald Matthews, who had succeeded Ralph Wedgwood as chairman in 1938, caught a flavour of this in a speech to the LNER's shareholders at their Annual General Meeting early in 1943. He detailed the problems the company faced and their response in almost impossible circumstances. He then moved on to outline his view of the future and what needed to be done:

'Still greater demands in the coming months will be made on the endurance of man and metal and I have no doubt that in this supreme test the railways of Britain will play their part. But I would take this opportunity to remind all those who use the railways that there is a limit to their capacity.

'This war has proved the essential part that railways must play in the life of all civilized nations. It has proved too that our railways are able to carry efficiently a much greater volume of traffic than,

As the war progressed engines undergoing overhaul took on a wartime guise. Here A4 No. 4901, *Capercaillie*, begins a period of General Repair in mid-July 1942. A first step in this process was to remove her side valances and, as the gauges demonstrate, begin pressure testing. (To the right) The engine re-emerged, painted in wartime black without lining, on 22 August to be re-named *Sir Charles Newton* after the General Manager, who is seen on the footplate. Naming locomotives after such senior figures was a common feature of each CME's period in office. A noble idea, but also a useful way of encouraging support for their plans and, perhaps, discouraging dissent. (*ET/DN*)

as a result of the archaic restrictions and regulations by which they were fettered, they were able to acquire in pre-war years. However, the transport services may be recast to meet post-war requirements, the significance of that aspect will, you may be sure, not be allowed to pass unnoticed.

'Volume and efficiency of production are what are required. The first can only be achieved by the provision of a prosperous home market – in which we must trade freely and on a greater scale than before, the second by the fullest encouragement of individual enterprise and initiative.'

This speech, which was given wide circulation within the LNER, contained a clear message to the company's senior managers – now is the time to think and plan for the future. Thompson for one, ably assisted by Peppercorn, was eager to begin this process, particularly on the question of standardisation and rationalisation, two issues he felt had been ignored for too long. But there was also the question of the Gresley engines and their perceived problems to be resolved and here the outstanding issue of the P2s moved centre stage. By 1942, pressure from Robert Inglis to do something about their apparent deficiencies could not be ignored. In response, Thompson tackled the wider issue of Gresley's conjugated valve gear in a bid to understand the depth of any problem. To do this, he invited William Stanier and his assistant Ernest Cox of the LMS to review performance. Their autonomous report was submitted in June. It pulled few punches in its criticism of the valve gear and recommended, amongst other things, its replacement with an independent set of valve gear for the inside cylinder.

Armed with this assessment, the CME looked more closely at the P2s. He concluded that, apart from the valve gear issue, problems associated with crank axle failures, excessive tyre wear and poor availability made action unavoidable. This in turn fed into his ideas about standardisation and the need to reduce the types of engine in the fleet and, in so doing, achieve more commonality of parts. But in deciding which way to move, he and Peppercorn, neither of whom were designers of any note, had to rely on the Drawing Office team led by Edward Windle to provide original thought on the many questions involved in locomotive design. In this case, they would be ably supported by Bert Spencer, who, since Gresley's death, had been working for Cyril Elwell on the production planning side of business. It is thought that Peppercorn may have been responsible for his resurrection as a designer, but wherever the truth may lie, Thompson moved quickly to re-establish him in his old role. He even occupied a desk close to the CME where he stayed for the remainder of Thompson's career. He doesn't seem to have enjoyed the same relationship with this CME that he'd experienced with Gresley, but, at least, he was now better placed to advise on policy and design. In fact, when leaving London for Doncaster in 1941, he was encouraged by the new CME and Peppercorn to bring Gresley's archive of work with him, as he reported later. 'Mr Thompson suggested I maintain Sir Nigel's papers and work on the ideas he had pursued regarding steam locomotives, but with an emphasis on alternative cylinder arrangements.'

In reality Spencer took this a little further before moving across to assist the CME in 1943:

'Thompson and Peppercorn, who were regular visitors to the planning office managed by Elwell, would often stop for a chat. Peppercorn in particular would talk about olden times and look over some of the drawings of locomotives that had been designed and, in some cases, not built. He was particularly interested in Gresley's ideas on 4-8-2 and 4-8-4 type engines, which, in my spare time, I had continued to work on and would again be considered by Peppercorn before nationalisation. Thompson was much more interested in the more traditional engines particularly the 4-6-2, 4-6-0, 2-6-0, 0-6-0 and 2-8-0s and talked about standardisation from the first. He gave no hint of criticism of Gresley three-cylinder engines to me and praised the A4s particularly. But he did express his concerns over their rapidly deteriorating condition and the growing need for change, which I took to mean three sets of independent valve gear or reduction to two cylinders. These were issues Windle was considering from 1942 onwards and I did become involved in these discussions in due course.'

In this slowly changing climate, brought on by better news from the many battlefronts on which the Allies were fighting, the CME could consider long term development programmes again, though constraints would still restrict progress until the hostilities ended.

Even late in their lives as streamliners the P2s presented a picture of strength and durability, as demonstrated here in this picture of *Lord President* passing over the Firth of Forth rail bridge on her regular stamping ground. Nevertheless, the problems were mounting. Even before the war they were giving the Divisional General Manager (Scotland), George Mills, up to 1941, cause for concern. His successors, Robert Inglis and then Tom Cameron, seem to have chanted the same message. (*ET/DN*)

The war could make strange bedfellows. In a drive to provide engines for wider use in war LMS 8Fs were adopted as a standard design before being superseded by specifically built 'Austerity' 2-8-0 and 2-10-0 locomotives. A number of the 8Fs were built at Doncaster and Darlington between 1944 and 1945 for use on LNER lines. They were passed to the LMS after the war. Tom Coleman, the LMS's Chief Draughtsman, was attached to the LNER for a brief period to advise on their construction. This is a photo he retained with the words 'L&NER loco with Progress Staff' written on the back. (*TC/ML*)

The V2 construction programme continued late into the war at Darlington and Doncaster. Engine No. 3645 appeared in March 1942 painted in black livery. In due course the LNER on the tender would be cut down to NE. (*ET/DN*)

In some ways, he was only allowed to nibble around the edge of some major issues, but in so doing he attracted the ire of many who considered that his subsequent actions were unnecessary and even smacked of cultural vandalism. Remarkably, it is a debate still played out to this day, with the P2 story at its core.

In taking a design, considered by the running department to be something of a liability, and overseeing their reconstruction, after a period of assessment and as part of his wider Pacific development programme, Thompson stands accused of destroying a Gresley masterpiece.

In *Thompson, His Life and Locomotives,* the case of the 'mutilated' P2s is covered in some detail, so won't be repeated here. However, it is probably true to say that it is a debate that only came to the fore much later when the main characters were long gone. At the time, there seems to have been little said in opposition or strong views expressed except by the Divisional General Managers who had to live with the P2s' perceived shortcomings. For the purposes of this book, a more interesting aspect is Peppercorn's reaction to the changes made, particularly as he was fully involved in the task at all stages as Assistant CME. Did he voice any concerns or seek to turn Thompson away from this course of action? From the limited information available, it seems not. His only apparent words on the subject were written in 1947 as part of his locomotive review. Although confirming that Thompson perpetuated many aspects of Gresley's design work he added that one major alteration saw the adoption of three independent sets of Walschaerts valve gear and divided drive. He added that:

'The new cylinder and valve gear arrangement was first tried out when the P2 Class engines were rebuilt as 4-6-2 type engines and also on the last four engines of an order for twenty-five V2 Class engines which were built as 'Pacifics'. Both types, classified A2/2 and A2/1 respectively, had 6ft 2in driving wheels.

'In order to obtain information regarding the performance of the modified front end arrangement when used in conjunction with 6ft 8in diameter coupled wheels, the original Gresley Pacific, No. 1470, *Great Northern*, was also rebuilt on similar lines to the A2/2 and A2/1 engines. These conversions provided the data upon which two standard Pacific designs having 6ft 2in diameter and 6ft 8in diameter coupled wheels have been based. Fifteen engines of the former type have now been constructed.'

Peppercorn presents a simple, balanced picture which diplomatically avoids anything that might be termed a criticism. He portrays the programme as a progression of Gresley's ideas. He doesn't make clear whether the programme was right or wrong, a success or a failure, even in an oblique, implied way. Some were good at damning with faint praise and others might adopt the principle 'if you can't say anything good, say nothing'. Peppercorn takes neither route but simply emphasizes the evolutionary nature of the work. To me this implies that he had been closely involved in the programme and understood the reasons for the changes proposed and made. By implication, this suggests that he had been party to all the reports gathered about the deteriorating condition of both the P2s and other three-cylinder Gresley engines. And he would have seen for himself their condition, and gathered information directly from his staff, as the engines passed through the workshops he controlled. So he didn't need to rely on Thompson's interpretation or any bias he might have fostered, but could make up his own mind. As a man of strength and resourcefulness, and having been selected by Thompson to be his deputy so clearly enjoying the CME's complete trust, it is unlikely that he would have kept quiet if he thought something was wrong or ill-considered.

In the world of locomotive engineering, it has become accepted practice to label any development with the name of the CME. As leader he must bear ultimate responsibility for all that happens, both good and bad, but this doesn't reflect the reality of the design process which is far more complex than this simple epithet suggests. In this case, Thompson alone is deemed to be the main arbiter of all ideas relating to engines produced under his watch. Yet neither he nor Peppercorn had the time or, possibly, the technical skill to do more than oversee the process, relying on Drawing Office staff to consider options and fill in the considerable amount of detail needed to complete a development. To the leaders in this field goes the true credit for this work and, perhaps, any criticism due.

Between 1941 and 1949, the chief designers were Edward Windle and David Dickson Gray, two figures who have remained resolutely in the shadows, despite the importance of their positions. During these key years, Windle was Chief Draughtsman and Gray his deputy with the title Chief Locomotive Draughtsman. In these capacities they would lead on the redesign or design of all Thompson and Peppercorn's locomotive projects, including the reconstruction of the P2s and then the Pacifics. As such they are both worthy of closer scrutiny.

Windle's presence had been a constant feature of life within the Great Northern Railway and LNER from the beginning of his apprenticeship at Doncaster.

Gresley's P2 before and after the Thompson, Peppercorn, Windle and Gray partnership oversaw their conversion when hoping to salve concerns expressed by the Running Department over their deteriorating condition. It is a controversy that seems likely to get a second wind when the new P2, No. 2007, *Prince of Wales* appears. There is no denying, as the picture of No. 2003, *Lord President*, reveals the streamlined version was an elegant engine. It might have been better served if it had been allowed to run south of Edinburgh, rather than north, where its wheel configuration and power may have inflicted less wear and tear on them mechanically. But this wasn't to be and a new Pacific (Class A2/2) rose from the ashes, in this case engine No. 2006, *Wolf of Badenoch* photographed in April 1944 shortly after being rebuilt in the workshops at Doncaster. 2006 was the second P2 reconstructed, the first, in January 1943, was No. 2005, *Thane of Fife*. (PR)

The youngest child of a GNR railway clerk, with two brothers also employed by the company, it seemed a natural step for him to follow them into the Works, which he did in about 1908, remaining there until the end of his career. In due course, he became a fitter, gained footplate experience then specialised as a draughtsman, reaching a senior position in the Drawing Office under Gresley. Undoubtedly, he was then involved to some degree in all the CME's most important projects. However, he doesn't seem to have left any written account of his career so it is difficult to establish how far his own ideas came into play and whether he agreed wholeheartedly with the direction in which Gresley took the department. In this situation, it is probably safest to assume concurrence, but recognise that the CME didn't readily accept advice or criticism even from respected colleagues.

Bert Spencer caught a flavour of this when he wrote, 'He ran a tight ship and woe betide anyone who stepped out of line . . . there was a tendency to put people too firmly in their place when it wasn't strictly necessary.'

Windle was encouraged by Gresley to join the ILocoE and contribute papers for members' consideration. This produced three items between 1929 and 1933 on such subjects as locomotive smokebox design, cylinder performance and valve and valve gear. It was in the last of these that he revealed something of his own views of Gresley's work with three-cylinders and his conjugated valve gear. He wrote:

'The valve gear question on the three cylinders can be solved by one of the forms of two-to-one motion, while the improved torque, shown already in many previous articles and papers, is a decided factor in favour of the three-cylinder arrangement. It is also true that three large cylinders in place of four smaller ones throws a greater load on crank pins and axlebox bearings, and in the case of the inside cylinder, where the drive is in the centre of the crank axle, throws a much greater bending moment upon this detail, and if all three drive on to one axle there is difficulty in keeping the stress down to a reasonable limit.'

The Chairman, T.H. Sanders, sensing a debate or even some disagreement within LNER circles, about the number of cylinders to be used, wryly observed, as Windle ended his presentation in Leeds, 'I am left with the impression that the Author prefers a four-cylinder engine to a three-cylinder engine.' The author made no reply, perhaps believing that discretion was the better part of valour.

During the war it became common to see once bright and gleaming Gresley Pacifics in this unkempt condition. Despite concerns over the deteriorating condition of their three cylinders and conjugated valve gear these engines still did sterling service. Here engine No. 2580, *Shotover* shows how far standards had slipped by the war's end. The engine, originally built as an A1 in 1924, and upgraded to A3 standard in 1928, was finally restored to peacetime condition towards the end of 1946. (*THG*)

Windle was an active participant in the design of the P2s, and accompanied the prototype, No. 2001, when sent to France in December 1934 to be put through her paces in the new Test Centre at Vitry-sur-Seine, in the South-Eastern suburbs of Paris. He and Bulleid were in constant attendance in the weeks that followed, but Windle's part in the process tends to be forgotten in the light of Bulleid's dominating presence. However, correspondence emanating from his time at Vitry suggests that Windle played a significant role. Bearing this in mind, he was then well placed to consider and evaluate any apparent shortcomings in the P2's performance when actioned to do so by Thompson when Chief Draughtsman. One wonders whether he harboured any doubts about their effectiveness from the first and are these reflected in his correspondence from France in 1934/35.

For the most part, he simply records the results of each day's work and then sends brief reports to Robert Thom and Tom Street at Doncaster. But the programme was soon plagued by a series of mechanical failures which necessitated the engine's frequent return to the workshops for repair. This caused a great deal of frustration, which he soon found hard to disguise in his reports, of which these are just a few examples:

'After suffering from a right-sided hot box the engine was taken from the Testing Station to the Paris-Orleans wheel drop. With the help of the P.O. men the wheels were stripped down and axleboxes dismantled yet again. Both the right and left boxes had badly pounded the horn checks on the side away from the wedge. The left hand box, the one that showed no

The control room of the Vitry-sur-Seine Test Centre, in early 1935. With a locomotive in the background, possibly No. 2001, this group of four closely examine recordings being made by the Amsler pendulum dynamometer. Windle is second from the left and Bulleid second from the right. The other two gentlemen may be two principal French engineers, possibly from the centre itself. (*HB*)

signs of heating showed rather more of this than the hot box. As a result a new box was fitted onto both R & L hand journals of the driving wheels.'

'As you know we are not having the best of luck, but the whole trouble is concentrated in the axleboxes. The metal is gone before you can realise they are warm. Of course all sorts of theories are advanced by all sorts of people, but a lot is moving around in circles: the oil is too thin, the brass bars are the cause and all the old yarns fought out time and time again.'

'The engine maintained the conditions for some 20 minutes when the boiler pressure began to fall back and as is characteristic of this engine once the pressure falls with only a low steam chest it is almost impossible to regain.'

'The A.C.F.I. installation was not working . . . losing too much water – difficulty in maintaining boiler pressure above 150 lbs – engine never rode well in the plant – the engine has gone into the works again.'

'I made the suggestion [to Gresley during one of his visits to Vitry] that the two gear boxes and cam boxes for the centre cylinder be entirely dispensed with and the inside valve be driven in a different way.'

'For the most part I am all alone here . . . The various questions which have arisen have entailed my moving from one Works to another and my day at present is one from 0700 to 2230 hrs or even later. We are exploring every avenue where we think the trouble might originate.'

His time in France proved to be very difficult, with mechanical failures constantly in danger of rendering all his best endeavours worthless. Nevertheless, it was a prototype and many of its problems were ironed out in time, with later members of the class benefitting from all this work. But first impressions are often hard to overcome and in Windle's mind the influence of those frustrating weeks at Vitry may have lastingly affected his view of Gresley's P2s. As Chief Draughtsman, tasked with leading a review of their performance and condition, did this shape his thoughts and the course of their reconstruction, especially in the light of reports from the Running Department and Stanier's independent assessment? It is hard to escape the view that it did.

David Gray, as Chief Locomotive Draughtsman, approached the project from a different viewpoint. He was born in Gateshead during 1889 the only son of George Gray, a Foreman Erector with the North Eastern Railway. Gray junior served an apprenticeship with the company and by 1911 was a Mechanical Draughtsman working in the Locomotive Department for Vincent Raven. On amalgamation it seems he transferred to Doncaster to work for the LNER's first Chief Draughtsman William Elwess. Here he remained for the rest of his career becoming Chief in 1941, having been personally selected by Thompson for the task. It seems likely that it was a relationship cemented when both men were serving with the NER at Darlington, though this is hard to verify so long after the event. Wherever the truth might lie, Gray's connection to the NER would have been a strong one. According to the records that remain, in public and private hands, it seems that he was closely involved in many of Raven's key projects, especially his Pacifics and Atlantics. He would also have been aware of Raven's preference for three cylinders in his designs, with motion usually of the Stephenson link actuating piston valve variety. In such circumstances, it is likely that Gray's own thoughts on design would be shaped by his experiences at Darlington. And here he would have seen, and possibly been involved in, Raven's cutting edge work on electrified motive power. Before amalgamation this had moved forward rapidly and it proved of some frustration to ex- NER designers that work was bought to a virtual stop when the company was absorbed by the LNER in 1923.

So we have five men – Thompson, Peppercorn, Windle and Gray, with Spencer restored as an advisor – responsible for the future of Gresley's deteriorating three-cylinder engines, each in their own way affected by history and driven to seek solutions by a Running Department increasingly concerned with their condition. Of the five, it was probably only Peppercorn and Spencer who brought a completely neutral view to these deliberations, although their wide experience and management abilities would have told them that something was wrong and needed to be fixed.

As the P2 development programme became a reality, it coincided with Thompson being allowed to develop a mixed traffic Pacific concept still

Windle, now thinner on top, (centre) with, it is believed, deputies David Gray (Locomotives) and F. Day (Carriages and Wagons) in 1945 four years before Gray retired. (*ET/DN*)

further as part of his standardisation plans. With a view to a future beyond the war, he obtained approval to take four of the last batch of V2 2-6-2s on order and build them as 4-6-2s instead. With the V2s having been derived from Gresley's A1/A3s, it was an interesting experiment insofar as it sought to upgrade the master's work to reflect changing ideas. Ultimately, they were still Gresley engines, though. But first came the P2 conversion to test these theories and engine No. 2005, *Thane of Fife* became the first of the class to be rebuilt, emerging from the works in January 1943 as an A2/2.

There were, of course, huge changes in the look of these engines. Gone was the streamlining as was the fourth set of 6ft 2in driving wheels; their loss seeming to restore a more traditional Gresley look to the locomotives. What lay underneath had also changed considerably. The three cylinders had independent sets of Walschaerts valve gear. But in using as many existing parts as possible meant that the P2's short outside connecting rods, which drove the middle coupled wheels, were retained. In wartime, such economy is commendable, but on this occasion meant that the outside cylinders had to be moved back to make sure there was a sound connection. However, to ensure the middle cylinder had sufficient clearance meant that it had to drive to the leading driving axle.

These changes gave the engines a stretched look, rather like the LMS's Princess Royals, with the outside cylinders located to the rear of the new four-wheel pony truck. Despite some reservations, it seemed to work, but the design appears to have caused some flexing and stress damage to the frames requiring modification later, just as the Princess Royals did. Later on, when in retirement, Thompson came to believe that placing the cylinders in this way hadn't been ideal and the solution adopted by Peppercorn and team on the later Pacifics was better. The established view is that Thompson had pushed through this solution without due consideration of other ideas from his Assistant CME or Windle. It may be true but the evidence is very slight either way.

However, there may have been an interesting debate on the subject that is now lost to time.

The 'new' locomotives remained fitted to their eight wheeled tenders and were also fitted with a Kylchap exhaust system and because the cylinders were so far back the P2s' boilers were shortened to ensure that the steam pipes had sufficient clearance. And with this the pressure was increased from 220 to 225psi, which helped produce a tractive effort of 40,318lb, down from the P2's 43,462lb.

Once released from the workshops, No. 2005 underwent a period of trial running which allowed some of the snags to be ironed out. It was then sent back to Scotland for the Divisional Manager and his staff to evaluate the changes and agree that the other five members of the class undergo the same treatment. It seems that Inglis was eager for this to happen, but the next engine, No. 2006, didn't pass into the CME's hands until early in 1944, returning to Scotland in April. The other four engines slowly reappeared in June, September, November and December the same year.

The slow production rate was due to the more pressing demand to manufacture munitions to support the invasion of Europe as the war moved to its bloody climax. The same problem afflicted the development of Thompson's four new Pacifics.

The A2/1s began making their appearance at Darlington in May 1944, but here again the development work proceeded at a painfully slow pace. It took until January the following year for this short programme to unfold, with an end result strikingly similar to the P2 conversions. They both had leading, coupled and trailing wheels of the same size, a maximum axle loading of 22 tons, 'banjo' dome steam collectors and wing type smoke deflectors initially; though the A2/1s received a larger, more traditional version in 1946. The cylinder, motion, valve gear assembly and piston valves were also the same, as was their 6ft 5in diameter boilers, both producing 225psi. However, the A2/1s' boilers were taken from the V2s, so had a total heating surface 20sqft less than the A2/2s and a tractive effort of 36,387lb, nearly 4,000lb. lower. There were other differences too.

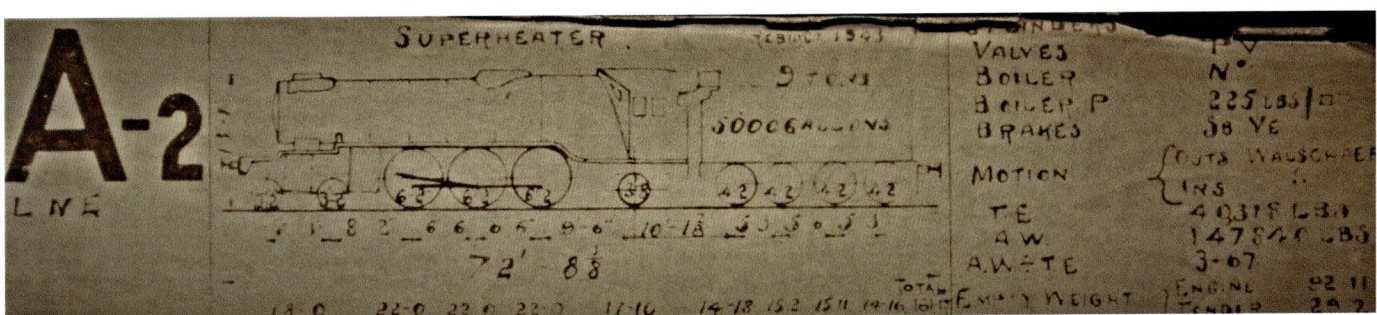

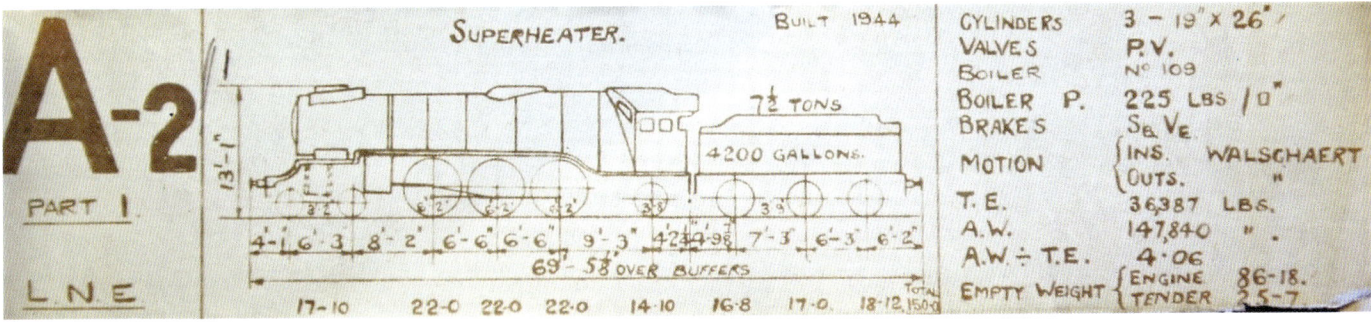

Bert Spencer kept many records of his time at King's Cross and Doncaster. A small book of hand sketched diagrams is perhaps one of the most interesting. He, according to his wife Elsie, kept this with him in his pocket whenever at work and regularly added new detail. The book contained all the classes on which he worked including all those developed during the Thompson and Peppercorn administrations, as demonstrated by these very basic drawings of the converted P2s (top) and A2/1s built during 1944/45. Even in these crude sketches the family connection is only too apparent. (BS/RH)

The A2/1's overall length was 3ft less than the A2/2s, they were 3 tons lighter and the grate area was smaller by 9.75sqft. In addition, the new Pacifics received six-wheeled tenders, firebox rocking grates and hopper ashpans. There were also some other refinements such as electric lighting, a small thing perhaps, but adopted on these four engines as an experiment by the CME.

All four members of the class were in regular service as the war finally came to an end, based at King's Cross and Haymarket for service on the East Coast main line. As they settled into their stride, Thompson was already into the next stage of his standardisation programme, the controversial reconstruction of Gresley A1, No. 4470 *Great Northern*, as a potential development or replacement of the A4s. Once again, Peppercorn and Windle were active participants in this work.

If the modification of the P2s has become a cause celebre, then Thompson's focus on *Great Northern* has probably proved more damning. In truth, it wasn't the work undertaken as much as the locomotive chosen to be modified that later caused eyebrows to be raised. But as Richard Hardy, who was a draughtsman at the time, later wrote:

'The Drawing Office team were a hard bitten group of engineers and never a word did I hear regarding the selection of No. 4470 for rebuilding. Most of them including Windle were steeped in the Gresley tradition but the choice of this engine meant nothing to them at the time [with the war daily killing or maiming tens of thousands this was hardly surprising] . . . she wasn't one of the best anyway.'

Later he added in a letter:

. . . 'she was just another engine and simply next in line for a general repair. If Thompson was involved in the decision to rebuild No. 4470 he may have thought that it acted as a memorial to Gresley's work. The first of a new standard breed of Pacific, to last for another thirty years or more, arising from his predecessor's first Pacific engine.'

Poetic symmetry from a hard-nosed engineer? It's not beyond the bounds of possibility, he was, after all, a keen student of history.

Planning for the project took some time to complete and could have involved any of the A1s still in the fleet. Based on experience gained from the A2/1 and A2/2s' programmes, various drawings were prepared and even streamlined solutions considered in the process, but the aim always remained standardisation and, as Peppercorn recorded, was simply necessary 'to obtain information regarding the performance of the modified front end arrangement when used in conjunction with 6ft 8in diameter coupled wheels'. So, it was evolutionary process that relied upon trial and error to underpin progress, undertaken with open, enquiring minds in judging results and seeking new solutions. It wasn't, as some believe, a slash and burn programme undertaken without true scientific purpose and due consideration.

Finally, *Great Northern* entered the works at Doncaster during May 1945 as though timed to celebrate Germany's surrender and the return of a peacetime world. Reconstruction took four months and 4470 returned to traffic on 25 September, still recognisably a Gresley engine, but now with the stretched look made familiar by the A2/1 and A2/2s. It followed the same pattern in other ways too. Gone was the conjugated valve gear to be replaced by an inside set of Walschaerts, 10in piston valves, the same grate area of 41.25sqft, a maximum axle loading of 22 tons, a 6ft 5in diameter boiler and, due to space considerations, the outside cylinders were again set between the front truck and the first set of the retained 6ft 8in driving wheels. However, a new A4 style boiler, producing 250psi, was fitted and new frames, similar to those used on the A4s, but longer by nearly three feet, were cut. Under test the engine was found to produce a tractive effort of 37,397lb., an increase of nearly 2,000lb over the A4.

During May and June 1945, a set of comparison tests were undertaken, with 4470's performance being measured against an A4 on express duties over the same routes. But at virtually the same time, as part of the standardisation programme, another A4 was being compared to an A2/1 and an A2/2 on passenger and freight duties. These were trials organised by Thompson, but attended by Peppercorn and Spencer, with George Musgrave, Locomotive Running Superintendent Western Section Southern Area, acting as facilitator throughout the process. It would be he

Thompson obviously saw engineering or publicity value in streamlining and commissioned a study in 1945 to evaluate encasing the new Pacifics in a way similar to the A4s. This work got no further than drawings and models for wind tunnel testing (two versions pictured here), but the CME seemed keen to pursue the work until he retired in 1946. Peppercorn seems to be less enthused and let these proposals quietly drop in 1947 as he and his team prepared newer versions of the Pacific. It is interesting that both versions in this photograph had outside cylinders over the front truck, not as happened in the final design to their rear, suggesting that Thompson and Windle didn't have closed minds on the subject. Another point of interest is that Thompson, who is now seen as being the antithesis of all things Gresley, should pursue his passion for streamlining, whilst Peppercorn, deemed to be a Gresley disciple, should let it drop or have been convinced by others that it had no place in the LNER's post-war plans. Perhaps a streamlined 'Thompson' conversion or new Pacific might have gone down better with the Gresley traditionalists than the engines eventually built. (ET/DN)

who analysed the results and wrote the report, apparently independently of the CME and his staff. This suggests that his boss, the newly appointed Divisional General Manager, Victor Barrington-Ward, wanted a hand in the process. He would soon be appointed to the Railway Executive Committee team overseeing nationalisation, would gather a knighthood, and be instrumental in much that would happen in BR over the next decade. So there is little doubt that such a man would wish to consider the way the LNER set its locomotive programme and conducted business. The two sets of trials were combined into a single report which was published in December 1945, one copy countersigned by Peppercorn. Its findings would not have displeased Thompson or Barrington-Ward.

Between the A4 and 4470 there was parity, but Musgrave added separate notes concerning the A1/1's performance:

'The steaming properties of No. 4470 are considered to be good. During this series of trials it was considered by the Locomotive Inspector that this engine was not worked to its full capacity. The Inspector reported that acceleration was good on rising gradients, but the engine had a tendency to slip if it was not handled carefully. Difficulty is experienced with drifting smoke rolling along the boiler which prevents a driver having a clear view of the signals and the road when the engine is being worked on a short cut-off. With regard to maintenance, it is considered too early to make any concrete comments.'

Initially engine No. 4470 ran with winged deflectors but like the A2/1s soon relinquished them for larger versions. However, the type attached to *Great Northern* were cut more rakishly and had a swept back look that seemed to match the engine's new shape. (*ET/DN*)

Date	Engine No.	Class	lbs. per train ton mile.	lbs. per engine mile.
5.11.45	4466	A.4	.087	39.8
6.11.45	"	"	.085	39.2
7.11.45	"	"	.086	39.5
8.11.45	"	"	.081	38.4
9.11.45	"	"	.093	42.6
13.11.45	4470	A.1	.081	38.1
14.11.45	"	"	.085	39.4
16.11.45	"	"	.087	40.9
19.11.45	"	"	.089	41.9
20.11.45	"	"	.063	38.5

The results of the November 1945 trials between the new *Great Northern* and A4 No. 4466, *Sir Ralph Wedgwood* (up to 1944 called *Herring Gull*). This one measure of performance was interesting because the two engines turned in virtually the same average consumption over 5 runs, with only slight variations in each test as one would expect. The A4 averaged slightly over 39.8lbs of coal per engine mile, 4470 averaged a little over 39.7lbs.

On the trials between A4 No. 2512, *Silver Fox*, A2/1 No. 3697, *Duke of Rothesay* and A2/2 No. 2003, *Lord President*, a different approach was taken to test out the mixed traffic nature of the three Pacifics. Between April and June, they were all tested pulling express passenger trains, then identical freight duties, with the same driver and fireman being used throughout. On the first set of trials the A4 was marginally better than the A2/1, with 2003 well behind in third place. However, on freight turns the A2/1 delivered much lower figures than the A4 on each run, with the A2/2 in third place again. Musgrave commented:

'On express services the A4 benefited from its 6ft 8in. diameter wheels, against the 6ft 2in of the other two engines. During the trials the A2/1 and A2/2 Class engines did not have to be worked to their full capacity. It was considered by the Locomotive Inspector that they both worked the freight easier than the A4.'

All this is far from providing irrefutable evidence of success, but it was a hopeful start nonetheless and in terms of the standardisation programme, some more information was added to the A1/1-A4 debate.

Basically, there was little to choose between them and more testing was needed to prove the superiority of one design over the other. There was also the question of reliability and maintenance costs to be considered and this needed a period of day to day running before any clear conclusions could be drawn. Nevertheless, Thompson seems to have seen something in these trials that set in train another phase of his Pacific programme. This may have arisen because 4470's conversion didn't offer sufficient advantage over the A3 and A4s to warrant such a rebuilding programme, though this didn't preclude modification to their Gresley valve gear, as time and funds allowed. Instead, he settled on a further refinement to his A2/1 concept and, in 1946, as he reached the end of his career, the first A2/3s appeared.

During 1944, with the P2 and A2/1 projects in full swing, Thompson sought approval to build thirty more new Pacfics incorporating all elements suggested by the evolving LNER standardisation plans. With the end of wartime restrictions in sight, this was agreed by their political masters and the company's Locomotive Committee alike. A further thirteen engines were added a year later signifying confidence returning to the business.

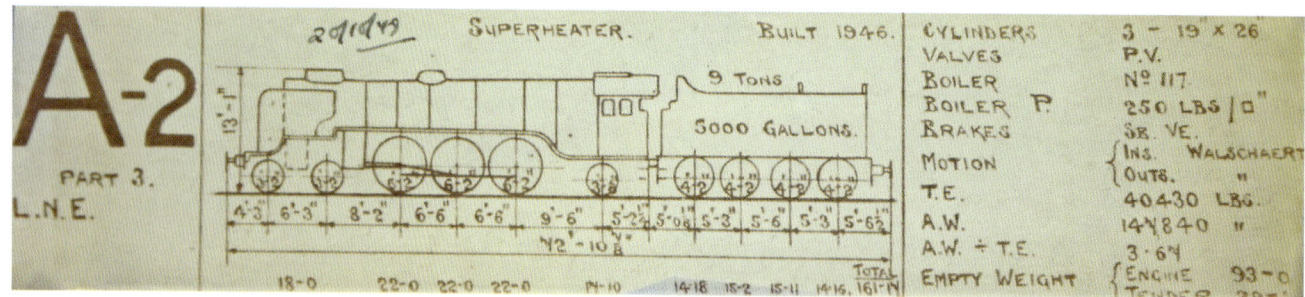

Bert Spencer captures the new A2/3 Class Pacific in his pocket book apparently amended to show the engines in 1949 shortly after Peppercorn's retirement.

(Above) The reality of the A2/3 design with No. 500, soon to be named *Edward Thompson* at Doncaster on 24 May 1946. Fifteen months later No. 523 *Sun Castle* appeared and is captured below when pulling an 'up' express at Potters Bar in April 1948. Fifteen of these engines were built during 1946/47, fourteen of them with Peppercorn as CME. He would develop the concept further with his A2s and A1s. Opinion on their looks differs and seems as polarised as reactions to Thompson himself. For myself, I think they possess the same sleek, racy look of a ship with a long clipper bow; they have a certain grace and style all of their own. Performance is, of course, quite another thing. (*DN*)

Their design incorporated much that had been rehearsed when constructing the A2/1s and rebuilding the P2s and *Great Northern*, so reflected an evolutionary process that sought improvement. But whilst these efforts were admirable, peace didn't witness the sudden return of the craftsmen who had gone to war, many having been lost in combat or were now too damaged to work in heavy industry. There was an inevitable skills gap that had only been papered over by the temporary expedient of women entering the industry. This had many knock on effects and meant that any construction programme could only be managed by drawing on a limited supply of truly competent staff, aided by semi-trained workers, many of whom left the industry when the war came to an end. Tasks could be completed at a push, but there was no guarantee over quality and many of the faults emerging in locomotives at this time could probably be traced to this deficiency. As Bert Spencer later observed:

'The depth of skill was just not apparent; it had been denuded by the war. Before 1940 the average machinists would work to very fine tolerances indeed and consistently produced work of the highest quality. Post-war, and for some years after, this level of skill was just not apparent and quality slipped badly. By the 1950s it had picked up somewhat as a new generation came forward, but there were fewer numbers wishing to enter into such a long apprenticeship, especially when other forms of non-manual, better paid work were opening up to them.'

It was a problem that would affect all aspects of railway engineering for many years, exacerbated by the poor state of the country's finances and the possibility of nationalisation under the new Labour government elected in 1945. It was against this background that the A2/3s first emerged in May 1946, at the same time as the LNER sought to reverse the effects of overuse, particularly in the condition of its locomotives. Thompson would soon retire from this fray, but it was Peppercorn's misfortune to inherit so many very trying problems, with so little time to resolve them.

The A2/3s followed a very similar pattern to Thompson's earlier Pacifics. There were three cylinders but no place for Gresley's conjugated valve assembly, three sets of Walschaerts gear being used instead, plus a double blastpipe and chimney, 10in diameter piston valves and cylinders measuring 19in by 26in. But he also uprated the boiler from 225 to 250psi, in line with *Great Northern* and the A4s, boosted the total heating surface to 3,141sqft, an increase of 31sqft, and achieved a larger, 50sqft grate area in the firebox. These changes took the tractive effort to a substantial 40,430lb, well ahead of either the A2/1s or A4s and slightly more than the A2/2s. In addition, they contained a number of refinements which had become typical of Thompson and Windle's recent work. These included a self-cleaning smokebox, steam brakes, electric lighting and a hopper ashpan. All these changes meant that these engines were longer and weighed nearly three tons more than the A2/1s.

With the arrival of the first of these engines, Thompson retired to be replaced by his faithful deputy. There are indications that the break was not a sudden one. Over the previous six months there had been a gradual shift of power from one to the other, a practice which the outgoing CME seems to have accepted without objection. There were clear signs that the stress and strain of the war had taken a heavy toll of his health and in the last year or so the adverse effects of this had become only too apparent. Having stepped into the breach five years earlier in difficult circumstances, he had held the department together in a way few others could have done, but now his time had come to an end and he could rest.

His legacy had many interesting aspects, but Peppercorn, Windle and to a lesser extent the Mechanical Engineers, had played a significant part in its development. Thompson recognised this and sought some official recognition and in due course Peppercorn was awarded an OBE. It is said that he had dissuaded the CME from taking this action twice before, out of modesty and shyness. But Thompson, who clearly felt strongly on this issue, eventually prevailed and the award was confirmed in 1945. Peppercorn's second wife later reported that he declined to attend any ceremony and the decoration had to be sent to him by post.

Development of the Pacific concept was most probably the highest profile design task that Thompson and his team undertook during his term of office, but planning for standardisation might be deemed more important in the longer term. Yet all this pales into insignificance when compared to their supreme effort in supporting the war and his work in rationalising the workshops to increase efficiency and flow rates over many years.

Part of Thompson's legacy at work in the years before nationalisation swept away the Big Four companies' independence. Very quickly BR instilled a culture of collective responsibility, brought in central control and added another layer of bureaucracy. (Top) *Great Northern* in her new guise with the LNER's peacetime colour scheme bringing some glamour back to the premier passenger services. Meanwhile A2/3 No. 512, *Steady Aim*, as she looked when beginning life in 1946. (*DN*)

Meanwhile the A4s continued to ply their trade under Thompson's guiding hand – virtually unaltered apart from the removal of the side valancing to aid access during servicing. It is interesting to consider why, if Thompson had genuinely set out to trash Gresley's legacy, the highest profile engines of them all, the A4s, didn't end up being rebuilt. The truth would seem to be that he saw their great merits, admired and protected them. He even sought to extend the nature of Gresley's streamlining ideas with his own Pacifics. Here, engine No. 25, *Falcon* displayed the new LNER numbering scheme that was introduced post-war, but only lasted until BR was formed in 1948. (*RH*)

Without these improvements there seems little doubt that the LNER would have struggled to meet many pressing demands at a time of national crisis. But history has dictated that Thompson has been remembered and judged on his contribution to locomotive design and the apparent damage he did to Gresley's legacy.

In time, this would be promoted by several authors, most notably H.C.B. Rogers, in his rather caustic work *Thompson and Peppercorn*, into a cause celebre, with Peppercorn appearing to ride to the rescue like some latter-day knight errant. The reality, of course, lies elsewhere and rests in the sure knowledge that Thompson could not have worked in isolation, but was directed and led effectively by Charles Newton and was supported by a strong, experienced and skilled team of engineers, with a talented deputy who wasn't a 'yes' man or a weak willed flunky doing as he was bid. Peppercorn and Windle would have played an active part in each project and argued strongly for or against each element of the design, offering practical alternatives where necessary. But it would have been in the Drawing Office where the real work was undertaken, led on a daily basis by David Gray. Here the minutiae of each project would be considered and developed, with each draughtsman bringing their own thoughts to bear on the final product. However, it has to be remembered that they were a team constrained by a far wider concern than the supposed peccadilloes of its leader and this was simply the war.

By rights, extreme shortages should have dictated little new locomotive development work over these years, but this proved not to be the case simply because Thompson had the vision to see beyond the conflict. In this he gained the full support of his General Manager and Chairman and slowly moved these plans forward. I think it safe to say that he may have been a difficult man at times, but he was certainly no fool and didn't have the time or the freedom to act in any way except a very reasoned one.

All this resulted in some development work taking place, but with progress largely determined by wartime shortages of men and material. Yet by early 1946, Thompson had gathered sufficient information and experimented with a number of options to finally be able to put forward a plan for the future. It was published in March 1946 over Newton's signature. Judging by the records that remain, all this was achieved with Peppercorn's full support and agreement. Just as well, because it would be a bequest that would become central to his work as CME until BR took over. While modernisation and rationalisation of the locomotive fleet sat at its core, one of the primary questions it addressed was the future of Gresley's engines. It was a debate that crystallised around the reconstruction of the P2s and then *Great Northern*.

When considering the validity of the argument that Gresley's three-cylinder engines lacked resilience and required more maintenance to keep them going, especially in wartime conditions, the historian really has little to go on. Most records have not survived and few if any of the main characters involved recorded their memories. In the absence of such detail, Thompson has been painted as the villain of the peace. The story peddled

3696 *Highland Chieftain* during 1945, making profuse amounts of smoke and justifying the decision to fit larger, more conventional smoke deflector plates to improve the footplate crew's view ahead. Part of the problem may have been the quality of the coal used. Alfred Ewer, who became Locomotive Superintendent at Doncaster, having served the LMS in the same capacity at Camden/Willesden sheds in London, recorded that 'during the war more often than not the fireman might have nothing but a pile of coal dust as the locomotive neared its destination and this soon disappeared up the chimney as a cloud of black smoke'. The converted P2s retained their winged deflectors until scrapped, suggesting that they didn't suffer in the same way. (*THG*)

widely is that he took action to rebuild Gresley's engines without justification or by making claims of poor performance that couldn't be sustained. If so, Peppercorn, as a trusted and fully involved Assistant CME, would have been party to these actions, as would the Chief Draughtsman and the Divisional General Managers. The truth would seem to be that their concerns were genuine and had to be addressed by Thompson and his team, which they did in a measured way. If he had been truly out to destroy Gresley's legacy, as some suspect, he would surely have gone further than the P2s and struck out for his predecessor's high profile A3s and A4s as well. In reality, his and Peppercorn's main concern was to keep them operating as best they could and in this they succeeded, despite the difficulties involved. Both men undoubtedly realised that once the war was over there would be a catching up process on maintenance and this proved to be the case.

So, in the time available to them, Thompson and Peppercorn did what they could to improve the breeds they'd inherited from Gresley, but no more. Their primary aim was to ensure that all these engines were kept running at minimum cost, try as best they could to meet the demands of the Running Department and plan for a future beyond the war when normal trading resumed. It is here that the March 1946 standardisation paper is so important. It pulled no punches, is well argued, explained the rationale behind the programme and set out a realistic plan of action that Peppercorn seems happy to have endorsed and then develop when his time came.

Of course, the P2s and the Pacifics were only part of Thompson, Peppercorn, Windle and Gray's locomotive programme. Much more went on, even with wartime restrictions in place, and all this became part of the broader development plan. Standardisation and common sense demanded a limited number of engines to cover all needs. Some of these had to be specific to a task for such things as shunting, stop/start city commuter traffic and high speed long distance expresses, whilst others could be met by mixed traffic locomotives. The CME and his team saw these diverse needs eventually being met by upwards of nine or ten basic steam designs, though in the meantime, a more diverse fleet had to be managed to best effect. Beyond mentioning the development of diesel shunting engines, no reference to other forms of motive power is made. In 1946, its absence was probably an admission that capital simply didn't exist to fund this work, so it was best to focus on well-established solutions that relied on coal; a home produced, cheap and plentiful fuel. In any case, all work on electrification rested with the Chief Electrical Engineer, whose sole aim was to breathe new life into two projects the coming of war had caused to be placed on hold – the Shenfield line and the Sheffield to Manchester development.

Thompson's standardisation plans envisaged two types of Pacifics, which in a 1945 booklet published by the General Manager and CME were simply listed as an A1 and A2. However, the photographs used in the first version were the A1/1, *Great Northern*, with its 6ft 8in driving wheels, and the A2/1. A second version produced in 1946 replaced the A2/1 with the A2/3, showing the evolving nature of Thompson and Peppercorn's work. But beyond that, the engines were a mixture of their work and a number of designs they had inherited and, in some cases, modified. The pre-1941 locomotives included the 0-6-0T J50s, the 2-6-0 K1s, the Robinson designed J11 0-6-0 tender engines, the Q1 0-8-0T which evolved from Robinson's 1902 0-8-0 tender engines, and the type O1 2-8-0s. To this list was added two classes of engine designed and built by Thompson and team during the war - the B1 4-6-0 mixed traffic locomotives and the L1 2-6-4 tank engines for commuter services. It is noticeable that apart from the Pacifics, all the models he and his team espoused were all two-cylinder designs.

Thompson didn't envisage the end of all Gresley's engines as part of this plan, as he made clear in his paper, and saw them running on, possibly with modified valve gear, for many more years until rendered obsolete. In addition, as he again makes clear, the standard engines he suggested were in most cases representative examples only. In essence, the strategy he and Peppercorn promoted, and which the General Manager supported, was more a statement of intent that recognised many practical difficulties and financial constraints that would come into play to impede progress. By 1946, it was becoming ever more clear that nationalisation would soon be upon them and any company plans would soon be overturned by a new management team with many new ideas. Looking back, with the benefit of hindsight, the LNER's plans have the look of a wish list or paper exercise to test the minds of its senior engineers, with little real hope that it might ever be implemented, which proved to be the case. However, BR's standardisation

Record 1

No. ~~[crossed out]~~ (Pretty Polly) **Maker** [illegible]   6708 6 24 60061

Dept.	Class	Type	Built	Rebuilt	Brake	H.A.	Pick-up	Valves	Lubricator
Gorton 18 4 25	A 3	4-6-2 Four Cylinder	11-4-25		Vacuum	Fitted (Lever)	Yes	Piston	Mechanical Detroit 4 feed sight
Kingsbross 23 5 25									
Grantham 25 11 28									
NEW ENGLAND 10 10 42									
Leicester 6 2 49									
Dover 4 6 50									

ROBINSON SUPERHEATER. R.H. DRIVE

Heavy Repairs.

Date in	At	Booked out	Back in Traffic	Remarks	Special Fittings
25 4 25	Doncaster	—		Light	Ball & Roller Bearings on Rev'g Valve Gear
15 3 24	"	24 5 24			Fitted with Knorr Piston Valves (See A3 6468)
15 9 28	"	6 12 28		*	
25 11 29	"	28 1 30			* N.E. Gr. for signalling apparatus - Oct. 1923
17 11 30	"	29 1 31			
21 10 31	"	12 12 31			
18 11 32	"	21 1 33		68,030	
23 11 33	"	25 1 34		64,355	Ring control piston valves 25 1 34
30 8 34	"	10 10 34		44,402	Narrow piston rings. 10.10 34
26 10 34	"	6 11 34		LIGHT	
24 1 35	"	31 1 35		LIGHT	
6 9 35	"	7 11 35		57.494	
3 12 35	"	10 12 35		LIGHT	
20 6 36	"	1. 8. 36		45 973	

Record 2

No. ~~[crossed out]~~ 61 18.11.46 A3.   **Maker** LNER DONCASTER   6708 6 24

Dept.	Class	Type	Built	Rebuilt	Brake	H.A.	Pick-up	Valves	Lubricator
N. ENGLAND 10 10 42	A.3	4-6-2	4 25						
Leicester 6 2 49									

Heavy Repairs.

Date in	At	Booked out	Back in Traffic	Remarks	Special Fittings
28 5 37	Doncaster	3 7 37		66191	
21 5 38	"	25 6 38		69585	
1 6 39	"	15 4 39		71869	
1 12 39	"	20 12 39		Light	
7 3 40	"	13 4 40		Light	
22 11 40	"	28 12 40		74.800	
16 7 42	"	21 8 42		79951	
20 4 43	"	19 8 43		Light - fractured frame	
25 3 44	"	6 5 44		81,995	
1 7 45	"	3 8 45			
15 10 45	"	27 10 45		Light	
10 12 45	"	22 12 45		Light	
29 12 45	"	30 12 45			
17 3 46	"	23 3 46		Light	

Above and opposite: In the absence of archive material, the only source of information that remains concerning the day to day performance of any locomotive are the Engine Record Cards of which those illustrated here are just a few examples. This group relates to Engine No. 2560, *Pretty Polly*, which started life as an A1 in 1925, then became an A3 in 1944. The information recorded is limited to the time the engine spent undergoing maintenance at Doncaster and does not include the time spent being repaired in the sheds to which they were attached. On face value the periods under maintenance do not seem excessive. However, by this stage Thompson ensured that the sheds kept sets of Gresley's conjugated valve gear and other spares so fitters could replace parts more rapidly when breakdowns occurred, which they seem to have done frequently. This removed the need for trips to the already heavily engaged workshops and reduced downtime in the process – an essential need for any company, particularly one caught up in a total war. (*THG*)

Much of the Thompson team's locomotive work has been roundly criticised, often unfairly. The one exception seems to be the B1 4-6-0 mixed traffic engines which first began appearing in 1942, with 410 being constructed over ten years. By any standards they were a successful design and earned many compliments. Perhaps the most important of these were uttered by Robert 'Robin' Riddles, ex-LMS Vice-President and BR's future CME, to his biographer, H.C.B. Rogers: 'Thompson, who succeeded Gresley, produced his excellent B1 with two cylinders, which was probably the most useful engine ever built for that line.' The engine pictured, No. 8301, *Springbok*, is the prototype that appeared in December 1942 and survived in service until 1962. (*THG*)

Thompson's L1s were less well received than the B1s, some considering that they fell a little short of expectations, nevertheless 100 were manufactured and saw service into the early 1960s. The prototype appeared in May 1945 but another ninety-nine didn't emerge until BR had come into existence. These engines were built between 1948 and 1950 at Darlington and, under contract, by North British and Robert Stephenson and Hawthorns. The engine pictured above, No. 67715, was constructed at Darlington during 1948 and is seen here the following year at Marylebone in London. Between September and November 1945, the prototype engine No. 9000, underwent extensive testing across the network, but not in Scotland. The summary, written by George Musgrave and endorsed by Peppercorn, who seems to have attended some of the trials, contained the words 'the enginemen commented favourably upon its performance and considered the arrangement of the cab provided good vision of the road in either direction . . . The boiler is considered to steam well and its high pressure (225psi) assists enginemen to work the engine economically . . . Accessibility for maintenance is good . . . Worked these trains with plenty of reserve and the acceleration from stations was most marked, the station to station timing being easily maintained. The acceleration on inclines was pronounced . . . The engine steamed and ran freely . . . It is considered that this engine could be improved so far as passenger work is concerned if the diameter of the coupled wheels were increased from 5ft 2in. to 5ft 8in.' (*DN*)

plans would have two-cylinder engines at its core, so endorsed much of Thompson's thinking on this issue.

With the war over, and despite the looming threat of nationalisation, the LNER's senior management encouraged its managers to look to the future. Earlier in the century, it had become common practice to look overseas and observe how change was being managed in other countries. With railway systems in most European countries virtually destroyed, the USA shone like a beacon. In 1945, the LNER and LMS decided to send a joint team, including Peppercorn and Henry Richards, to the States to study all forms of locomotion there. This was followed by other groups who looked at different aspects of railroad operation. E.S. Cox, then with the LMS and soon to rise to senior rank in BR, recalled that:

'The party of six [Peppercorn, Richards, Bramworth from the LNER and Cox, Pugson and Harper from the LMS] set sail on the *Queen Elizabeth* in October 1945 in company with 11,000 Canadian soldiers returning home on a ship still in wartime guise. The normally luxurious cabins were gutted, and each now held eight makeshift bunks in two tier pairs. Only two meals a day were served, and the ship was dry. Groups of hard bitten officers in the lounge looked distinctly thoughtful over their nightly intake of Coca Cola!

'Landing in Halifax, we took the train to New York, and spent 52 days in the New World, visiting 9 of the leading railroads, as well as the principal rolling stock builders. We travelled as far west as Nebraska, and south to Virginia, 5,000 miles in all.'

After nearly six years of war filled high intensity work, Peppercorn must have found the trip to North America something of an eye-opener. The voyage over the Atlantic, with all its military overtones, must have contained many reminders of his own military service. Messing together in cramped and spartan cabins would only have added to this impression, with Halifax presenting a dismal picture on arrival. It's always a gloomy place in October, but with the pall of war still present there was little to improve its welcome. But once on board a train heading to the bright lights of New York, and travelling through the most beautiful countryside in 'the Fall', would have lifted their spirits considerably. After Britain's austere, battle damaged dreariness, where rationing still cast a heavy shadow over everything despite the ending of the nightly blackout, New York would have presented a vision of plenty. Wherever they went, this impression would remain unchanged and the six men must have thoroughly enjoyed their weeks away considerably.

Peppercorn by this stage must have been aware that he was CME heir apparent and would within months be promoted. It is more than likely that Thompson fully supported the elevation of his long term and much trusted associate. All his actions, since becoming CME in 1941, had focussed on establishing Peppercorn in the hierarchy of the LNER and his department and now he could release the reins to his greatly respected deputy. So it must have been with this in the forefront of his mind that he journeyed across the Atlantic to see what may be gleaned from the railroad industry there to influence his own work at home.

The tour to the USA gets underway with the joint LMS/LNER team enjoying the early morning sunshine on *Queen Elizabeth*'s deck (L to R they are Ernest Cox, Bramworth, Pugson, Richards, Peppercorn and Harper). (*EC*)

A postcard that Peppercorn acquired and sent to Thompson from New York during his expedition. In a short note he mentions following parts of Gresley's 1929 tour and being impressed by the 'Niagara 4-8-4 Class and the 'Selkirks' 2-10-4s on the Canadian Pacific'. (*ET/DN*)

A Canadian Pacific Selkirk 2-10-4 No. 5907 on its home ground leaving Banff with a westbound express in the post-war period. Peppercorn, according to surviving papers, made the trip across to Alberta by himself in 1945 to travel on one of these locomotives just as Gresley did in 1929 when these engines were first introduced. It is unlikely that he would have learnt anything new from this aging design, so one suspects it may have been a pilgrimage of sorts or simply a brief holiday away from the rest of the tour party and their focus on east coast to central railways. (*DN*)

A Union Pacific articulated 'Big Boy' 4-8-8-4 engine, in this case No. 4002 built in 1941, one of 25 constructed by the American Locomotive Company (ALCO) of Schenectady, New York. The British party visited the works and saw several of them undergoing maintenance though didn't have the opportunity of witnessing them in action. Cox commented on their immense size and power, but his principal observation concerned the success of the roller bearings. (*RH*)

The tour was literally whistle-stop, taking in many centres of railway activity – both operational and construction. They were able to see and experience everything these systems had to offer from comfortable seats in the carriages to rides on footplates. Peppercorn, who had been involved in all aspects of this industry for forty years by then, would undoubtedly have been enthralled by all he saw. He must have borne in mind Gresley's well remembered visit to North America following his wife's death sixteen years earlier. Did he expect to be similarly affected by developments there?

If so, he would have seen the massive build-up of diesel engines and multiple units, ongoing experiments with turbines, the sheer scale of modernisation and much more. It was as far away from the scope for experimentation he would enjoy in Britain as the Moon is from the Sun. By comparison to life at home, America must have seemed to be a land of plenty which encouraged great developments and created great engineering freedom as a natural consequence of its industrial muscle and might. He and his compatriots must have wondered what they themselves could achieve if given access to such riches. Yet, as they would soon discover, all wasn't necessarily well in paradise. Cox captured a flavour of this on returning when he wrote:

'The intense spirit of independence produced a far wider gulf between the best and the worst than we are accustomed to. Nevertheless, it can be said that power rather than efficiency was the goal, and so great was the output required to meet operating conditions that notwithstanding a most generous loading gauge, and permitted axle loads half as much again as in Europe, the larger steam engines were reaching their physical limitations.

'Performance was much influenced by a maintenance philosophy greatly at variance with what we practice here. This was manifested in two ways. Firstly, repair programmes were not primarily controlled by engine condition and by the making good of mileage run, but according to receipts as they came in over the till from passengers and traders. Quite literally, resources for repair work could be turned off like a tap when takings fell, and we saw more than one shop silent and deserted where just this thing had happened. Many roads were labouring under the burden of deferred maintenance in consequence.

'Secondly, although main workshops were often fully equipped, they undertook a much smaller proportion of the full repair load than do ours. The bulk of the work was done at the sheds, which, although often clean and well looked after, were in general very poorly equipped, and the methods of repair were sometimes crude as to make our hair stand on end.'

The tour party spent a considerable amount of time with the New York Central Railroad and seem to have been particularly impressed by their Niagara Class 4-8-4 engines which Cox described as 'real beauties'. (*EC*)

For Peppercorn, this must have seemed a poor way of doing business. He and Thompson were experienced production engineers whose lifetimes' work had focussed on effective and cost efficient management and maintenance programmes. Even with the shortages and problems caused by war, they had not lost sight of these important issues and always went that extra mile to ensure all engines and rolling stock were in the best possible condition. As in the case of the P2s, they were also capable of taking difficult decisions when necessary to ensure engines were available and fit for purpose. Economic necessity is a central tenet of any business but for the CME and his deputy there had to be limits to ensure the railways operated as safely as possible. Clearly, in America at this time, some railroad companies had lost sight of this.

During the tour, the party spent time with the New York Central Railroad, the Union Pacific, the Pennsylvania Railroad, the Baltimore and Ohio and the Chesapeake and Ohio, but they didn't confine themselves to locomotives in service, seeing many under construction or being maintained at the American Locomotive Works, Lima of Ohio and Baldwins of Philadelphia amongst others. Peppercorn, as Bert Spencer later recalled, also met some of the leading designers of the day. These, it seems, included Albert Dean, an aeronautical engineer who designed the Pioneer and Zephyr diesel powered trains for the Budd Company, and Henry Dreyfus the industrial designer, who, amongst other things, was responsible for the New York Central's streamlined 4-6-4s. It was behind these engines that Peppercorn travelled to Chicago on the 20th Century Limited.

Olive Dennis in the 1940s when working for the Baltimore and Ohio Railroad as senior designer. There is a saying that for a woman to succeed in industry during the twentieth century she had to be smarter and more highly qualified than the men around her (and you might add 'and in America'). If this is so, Dennis is a perfect example. A talented mathematician and scientist, she went on to qualify as a Civil Engineer then rose to a very senior rank in a male dominated world, in so doing becoming the first female member of the influential National Railway Engineering Association. Her design work was cutting edge and her influence spread beyond the confines of the Baltimore and Ohio. One of the four streamlined Pacifics she helped produce is portrayed here. (JC)

Later, when visiting the Baltimore and Ohio, he met the redoubtable Olive Dennis, an engineering graduate from Cornell, who had risen to become the company's Service Engineer with responsibility for the complete design of trains. In a male dominated industry, it must have been intriguing to discover a woman who had broken the mould in such a way. He also saw a product of her work in four streamlined Pacifics and carriages for the 'Cincinnatian' service.

For many engineers in Britain such as Gresley and Stanier, the need for more effective testing of locomotives to ensure each design was as good as it could be, was a long term and frustrated ambition. There was a static test facility developed by the Pennsylvania Railroad at Altoona at which they had long cast envious eyes and Peppercorn now took the opportunity to witness the plant in action. Gresley's advocacy had led to a similar facility being approved in Britain just before the war, but the conflict had meant that it was shelved for the duration. By the armistice, work was again underway and it would open during 1948 at Rugby. The entire party visited Altoona and spent several days touring the locomotive workshops, but it seems as though only Peppercorn watched tests in progress before sampling locomotives on the road. In a brief hand-written memo, which Spencer retained, he described the centre, how it operated and the work currently being undertaken. There was also mention of the company's experimental work with the Duplex system and the performance of their streamlined T1 4-4-4-4 engines, designed by Robert Loewy. The T1 proved of particular interest to Cox as well. He later described the Duplex system, which, in essence divides the driving force on the wheels using two pairs of cylinders rigidly mounted in a single set of frames, in broad terms:

> 'It attempted to solve the urgent problem of increasing piston thrusts, which were becoming more than any normal design of crankpin could support. Although a number of three-cylinder engines were at work, the crank axles were not proving satisfactory, and a two-throw crank for four-cylinders was quite out of the question in the space available between the thick bar frames.
>
> 'Thus for the T1 power was split into two groups, each pair of cylinders driving two out of the four driving axles. Crank pin loads were halved, and the four 19¾in by 26in cylinders in conjunction with 6ft 8in diameter wheels and 300psi of pressure produced on test at Altoona a maximum indicated horse-power of 6,500. On paper, and in test plant results, it confronted the diesels.'

He and Peppercorn then rode on T1 No. 5002 from Altoona to Harrisburg and witnessed another T1 needing assistance after stalling when pulling a 930 ton load over a rugged mountain section near Jonesville. Cox commented:

> 'I would not suggest that an isolated run was representative, but there is some evidence that all this adhesion trouble remained to dog the performance of these otherwise splendid locomotives, and thus helped to make easier the eventual conquest of the diesel.'

In this statement Cox sums up the attitude of many engineers at the time. With America embracing and developing diesel and electric options their British counterparts seem to be clinging to steam's aging technology. Was it for financial and practical reasons or was it an emotional response to change and the death of a technology they had come to revere above all others? Either way, the record of Cox and Peppercorn's visit contains little to do with alternative technologies and the progress made in these fields and all to do with steam, so, perhaps, they did find the change in culture hard to bear.

Peppercorn must have returned to Britain in its winter gloom with mixed emotions and perhaps even wondering what it would be like to be a CME in America with far fewer constraints than those he would face at Doncaster. After two months or more closeted with his fellow travellers, he must also have got to know them well, especially Ernest Cox. For his part, Cox painted a short pen picture of the LNER man, which is thought provoking, especially in the light of his forthcoming promotion to CME. He wrote:

> 'Pep as he was usually called seemed to be loved by everyone, and his contributions kept closely to his prepared brief. Not for him were any excursions into the mental stratosphere, but if he himself was not a very live wire he had the inestimable ability of letting his assistants get on with it.'

The industrial designer Henry Dreyfus, whose many achievements included the streamlined Hudson Class engines for the 20th Century Limited trains (portrayed here), clocks, ships, buildings, polaroid cameras and much more. He was a new breed of engineer and scientist very much in the mould of Gresley who looked more broadly beyond the railway world. (JC)

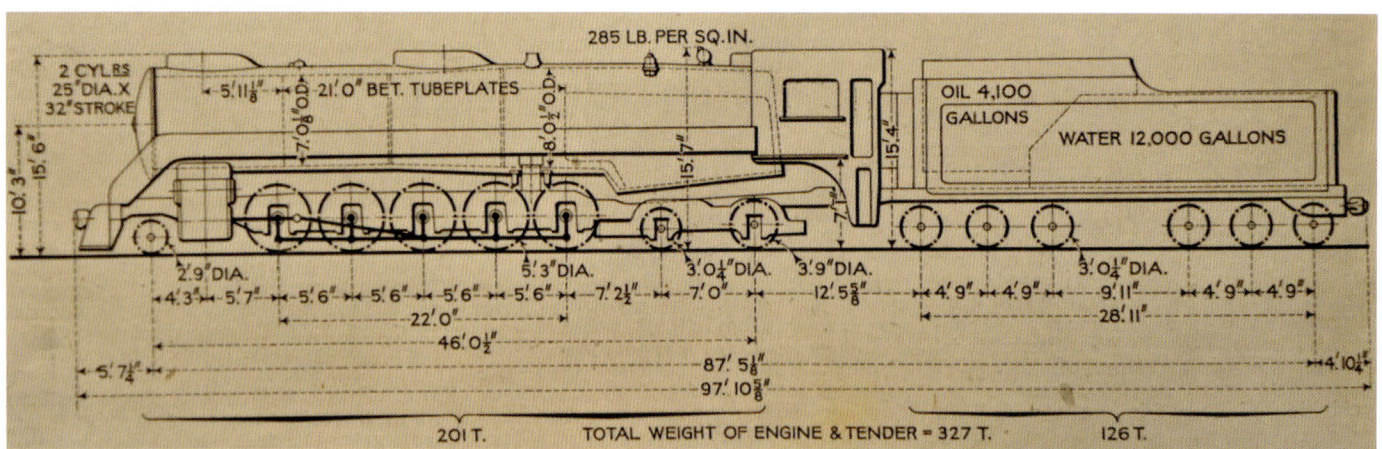

The impressive front end of T1 No. 5501 as seen by Peppercorn in November 1945. These 4-4-4-4 class engines were probably at the very limit of steam development and would soon succumb to the rapid march of alternative forms of motive power in the USA. Not so in Britain, which would cling to steam until the 1960s. (JC)

Above and opposite above: When Peppercorn returned to Doncaster he was armed with many plans, specifications, photos and brochures gathered from all those who had hosted his visit. These, according to Bert Spencer, were deposited on his desk to be followed by 'a long talk in which Pep described all he had seen and his favourable impressions of the T1s and the Canadian Pacific Selkirks'. Spencer kept much of this material including these two examples, both heavily stained and creased as though stuffed in a pocket during Peppercorn's many train rides. (BS/RH)

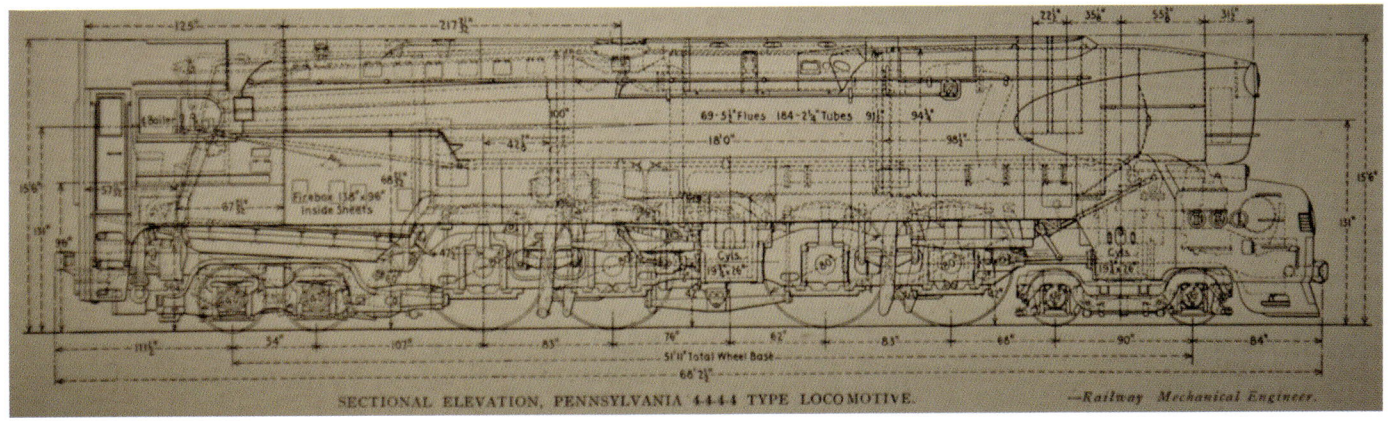

SECTIONAL ELEVATION, PENNSYLVANIA 4-4-4-4 TYPE LOCOMOTIVE. —*Railway Mechanical Engineer.*

Right and overleaf pages: Even before the Second World War advertisers in the States were trumpeting the arrival of new technologies and motive power as these three examples demonstrate. By 1945 this movement was almost eclipsing steam, although some new locomotives were still being built. However, the USA had come through the war with its industries intact, released from long term recession and oil rich so were well placed to reap the benefits of peace. Britain, by comparison, was all but bankrupt with its infrastructure in tatters, so it is little wonder that steam continued to prevail and dieselisation and electrification stuttered into existence. (*THG*)

If this is so his abilities, or otherwise, were soon to be tested. On 1 July 1946, he succeeded Edward Thompson, with the clouds of nationalisation appearing on the horizon and a huge weight of expectation resting on his shoulders.

In the aftermath of their visit to the USA, Cox produced a four-page action plan which suggested design issues that they should all consider in the months ahead. Lessons learnt are a necessary requirement of such visits, providing as it does a worthwhile return on the investment in time, energy and money. However, in its long list of actions and recommendations, Peppercorn's name is missing. This isn't to say that he found what they had observed lacking value or that he avoided Cox's efforts to create a unified response, but more probably he realised that there were much bigger fish to fry on his return. This lack of input might account for Cox's slightly caustic assessment of the LNER man. If so, it didn't bode well for the future, when Cox would quickly reach senior rank in BR and oversee development work carried out by the old companies.

ROLL OF HONOUR

WE regret to have to publish a further list of the names of members of the Company's staff who have been killed in action, have died of wounds, or have died on active service.

Name.	Grade.	Department.	Station at which Employed.	Rank, Regiment, etc.
BELL, T.	Clerk	Goods Manager's	Gateshead	Flying Officer, R.A.F.
BOYES, H. W.	Lad Porter	Superintendent's	Eastern Docks, Hull	Pte., Parachute Regt.
BUCKLE, R.	Turner	Chief Mechanical Engineer's	Darlington Loco. Works	Craftsman, R.E.M.E.
DEVANEY, J.	Labourer	Do.	Deansgate	Royal Engineers
ELPHICKE, R. H.	Lad Porter	Superintendent's	Muswell Hill	Pte., 1st Batt., Welsh Regt.
FISHER, T. L.	Clerk	Do.	Edinburgh	Lieutenant, R.A.
FRANKLIN, A. G.	Adult Oiler	Chief Mechanical Engineer's	King's Lynn	Gunner S/L., R.A.
GAUNT, E. A.	Telegraph Lad	Superintendent's	Lincoln Yard	Pte., H.Q. Sigs., 6th Batt., Lincs.
GREEN, J. A.	Labourer	Chief Mechanical Engineer's	Doncaster Loco. Wks.	Gdsmn., Coldstream Gds.
HOGGETT, S.	Relief Clerk	Goods Manager's	Durham	Sgt. Navigator, R.A.F.
MASSIE, A. F.	Clerk	Passenger Manager's	Aberdeen Joint	Sapper, R.E.
NORCOTT, S. G.	Elec. Lamp Attdt.	Chief Electrical Engineer's	Leeds	Gunner, R.A.
THOM, D. I.	Goods Porter	Superintendent's	Kittybrewster	Pte., 2nd Gordon Hldrs.
UNEY, G.	Labourer	Chief Engineer for Docks	Hull	Sapper, Royal Engineers.
WALKER, P.	Casual Carter	Goods Manager's	Hull Central	Pte., 2nd E. Yorks.
WALTHAM, W. A.	Signal Lamplad	Superintendent's	New Holland	Rifleman, Cameronians.
WHITE, G. B.	Clerk	Goods Manager's	Acklington	Flt.-Lt., R.A.F.
WILCOCK, A.	Clerk	Superintendent's	Mottram Yard	Cpl., No. 4, Liaison Armd.

PREVIOUSLY REPORTED PRISONER OF WAR, NOW REPORTED DEAD.

Name.	Grade.	Department.	Station at which Employed.	Rank, Regiment, etc.
BENTLEY, W.	Labourer	Chief Mechanical Engineer's	Ardwick	Gnr., 241st H.A.A., R.A.
BLACKBURN, L. C.	Labourer	Do.	Darlington Loco. Works	Bdr., R.A.
BLAND, K.	Clerk	Passenger Manager's	Redcar	Signalman, 48th LAAS, R. Sigs.
COATES, G. W.	Labourer	Chief Engineer for Docks	Hull	Gunner, R.A.
CORNICK, E.	Riveter	Chief Mechanical Engineer's	Darlington Loco Works	Gunner, R.A. (H.A.A.)
DAWSON, G.	Labourer	Do.	Hull	L.A.C., M.T.M., Gp. 2
DODD, J. T.	Motor/Driver	Goods Manager's	Woodburn	Fus., R.N.F.
FLEMING, F.	Motor Parcels Vanman	Passenger Manager's	Hull	L.A.C., R.A.F.
GRAHAM, W. H.	Fitter	Chief Mechanical Engineer's	Bishopsgate	Sgt., R.A.S.C.
HUME, A.	Gr. II Porter	Superintendent's	West Stanley	Driver, R.A.S.C.
McKENZIE, R.	App. Fitter and Erector	Chief Mechanical Engineer's	Doncaster Loco. Wks.	ERA. IV. H.M.S. *Exeter*.
OLIVER, G. R.	Motor Driver	Goods Manager's	Hedon	Pte., R.A.S.C.
PARTRIDGE, F. J.	Wagon Repr.'s Asst.	Chief Mechanical Engineer's	King's Lynn	Pte., Royal Norfolk Regt.
WALTON, J.	Actg. Motor Parcels Vanman	Passenger Manager's	Leeds City	A.C.2, R.A.F.

PREVIOUSLY REPORTED MISSING, NOW REPORTED DEAD.

Name.	Grade.	Department.	Station at which Employed.	Rank, Regiment, etc.
BURNS, D. P.	Fireman	Loco Running Supt.'s	Newport	Sergeant, R.A.F.
DAVIS, A. O.	Porter Gd. 2	Superintendent's	Stamford	Pte., Royal Norfolk Reg'.
DAVISON, A.	Clerk	Passenger Manager's	Ratho	Pte., Seaforth H'landers.
FROST, J. L.	Cranelad	Superintendent's	Sheffield Goods	Private, R.A.S.C.
GRIEVE, A.	Clerk	Passenger Manager's	Dysart	Sergeant, R.A.F.
GUTHRIE, A.	Plumber	Chief Mechanical Engineer's	Walker Gate Works	Pte., D.L.I.
WHYTE, A. F.	Clerk	Goods Manager's	Peterhead	A.C.2, R.A.F.

PREVIOUSLY REPORTED MISSING, NOW PRESUMED KILLED.

Name.	Grade.	Department.	Station at which Employed.	Rank, Regiment, etc.
BURBIDGE, W.	Riveter	Chief Mechanical Engineer's	Stratford	Sergeant, R.A.F.
HUNTER, K.	Clerk	Goods Manager's	Ollerton	Flt.-Sgt., R.A.F.
LAING, G.	Clerk	Goods Manager's	Leeds D.G.M.O.	Pilot Officer, R.A.F.
MILLAR, J.	Fireman	Loco. Running Superintendent's	Stirling	Sgt., R.A.F.
NICHOLSON, N.	Dining Car Attdt.	Hotels Superintendent's	Newcastle	Pte., Border Regt.
RICHER, G. W.	Labourer	Chief Electrical Engineer's	Colchester	Pte., Suffolk Regt.

Thompson and Peppercorn's war at Doncaster had been trying in the extreme and both men gave their all in trying to keep the LNER running. But both of them knew, as old soldiers themselves, the true nature of war and the terrible price paid by their many young men and women who were called to the colours. The LNER *Journal* recorded the casualties with gloomy regularity throughout the war, even, as shown here, when hostilities had ended. The two men were noted for doing what they could for grieving relatives, although, more often than not, this could only be a letter of sympathy. At the same time, they sought to help those returning from the war whenever they could. They would both have remembered the difficulties they'd faced in 1919 when having to re-acclimatise to a civilian life and so held out a supporting hand to these new veterans. Two of them were Roy Hart-Davies, who had fought with distinction in Burma, and Robert Thom's son, also called Robert, who served with the Royal Engineers. The level of sacrifice was beyond imagination. The LNER's losses were recorded as being 1,092 of the 27,000 or so who joined up, with many more severely wounded. It was this legacy that Peppercorn had to deal with along with the tired condition of locomotives and rolling stock. In comparison to these sacrifices, the debate over whether the P2s and *Great Northern* should have been rebuilt pales into insignificance in this real, severely damaged world. (*PR*)

CHAPTER 6

CHIEF MECHANICAL ENGINEER

When taking up the reins of an important post few, if any, suffer from over confidence and quite often the magnitude of the task causes a period of self-doubt. The wise take time to pause and think deeply about their work and the resources available to them. They are careful to avoid disruption as the organisation acclimatises to a change of leader. In this situation, continuity and certainty are important. When change is necessary, let it appear to evolve and flow naturally. In achieving this, it is much easier if a deputy becomes the leader. They are a known quantity and their ways of working, and their peccadilloes, are recognised and understood. And in Peppercorn they had a leader of great experience, who was also an LNER man, not some import from a competitor who might introduce different ways of working. With a secure structure and a known leader, the transition would not have been a difficult one and the phrase 'seamless transfer of power' would seem to have applied.

One of Peppercorn's first acts was to produce a booklet which included details of the management structure, showing who did what. This included a number of family trees which each member of staff could update themselves when changes were made. Bert Spencer's copy has survived intact and is updated to 1948 when BR came into existence. After that, the new nationalised body consumed the old structure, then wove its many threads into a larger corporate edifice. So whilst independent action was possible, Peppercorn set up his team as though the world wouldn't change. He had three assistants sitting around him at Doncaster, though none of them appear to have been designated deputy, as he had been for Thompson. The most senior of the three was Roy Hart-Davis, an experienced locomotive engineer, but with no obvious credentials as a designer. Then came Stanley King, who managed under the title 'Cost Control' and Ken Robertson who oversaw the Carriage and Wagon side of business. Beneath these officers came the Mechanical Engineers, a Docks Machinery Engineer, the Chief Chemist and Road Motor Engineer, all of whom seem to have reported directly to the CME.

Peppercorn enjoying the launch of the first A2/3 Pacific, No. 500, shortly before Thompson's retirement in 1946, after whom the engine was named. This photograph was thought by his widow to sum up his character; 'Intelligent, modest, shy and self-deprecating. Strongly principled, hardworking, enthusiastic and possessed of a strong sense of fun. To the end of his days he always retained a boyish interest in locomotives of any type'. Take away his hat and coat and you could easily be forgiven for thinking that he was a Top Link driver of long standing, so natural does he look in this setting. (*PR*)

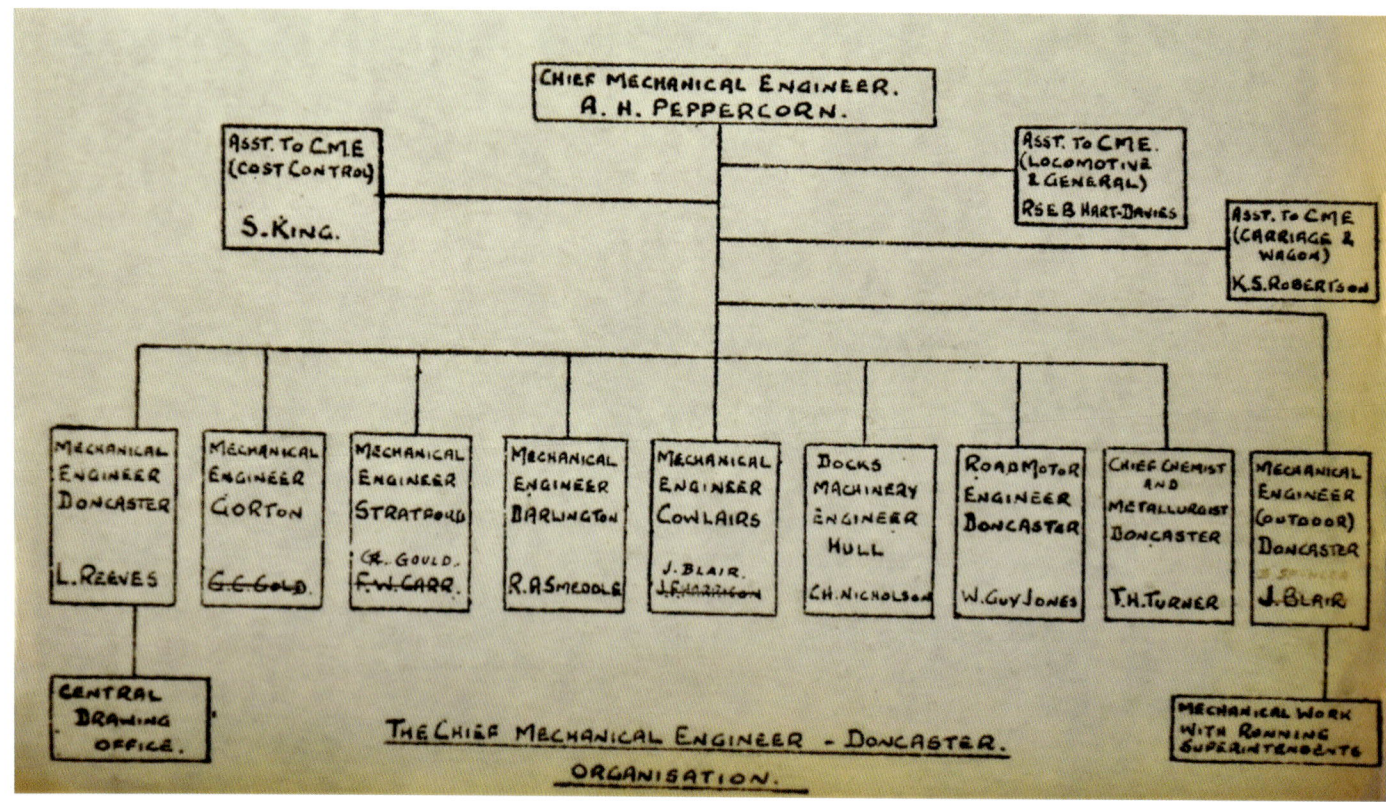

Bert Spencer's much amended family tree covering the senior positions in the CME's Department between 1946 and 1948. Most of the changes made were for operational reasons, except for Frank Carr at Stratford. He died suddenly in service on 10 November 1946. Peppercorn wrote in a short obituary, 'His wise counsel in many matters concerning the department, his fair-mindedness and considered judgement in dealing with all men made him a very respected officer in the Company and a very respected Chief of the very large staff under his control. During the very difficult days of the blitz the shops under his control were subjected to heavy air attack by the enemy, but no matter what the circumstances Mr. Carr was always with his staff giving them that quiet inspiration and guidance which endeared him to all. His passing is deeply mourned.' These words could easily have applied to Peppercorn himself. (BS/RH)

Peppercorn and some members of his senior team. A photo taken on 31 December 1947, on the last day of the LNER's life, in front of engine No. 525, the first of the CME's new A2s. In the front row sits (left to right) Edward Windle, Harper, Gresley's long serving Chief Clerk, Ken Robertson (Assistant to the CME, Carriage and Wagons), Gosling (Chief Clerk), Peppercorn, John Harrison, Roy Hart-Davies (Assistant to the CME, Locomotives and General) and Bert Spencer who had just taken over Hart-Davies' role. Of note in the back row is Robert Thom (second from the right), the son of Robert Absalom Thom, Gresley's talented and much missed Mechanical Engineer (Doncaster) who had contributed hugely to the Gresley legend. (BS/RH)

It is interesting to observe that the Chief Draughtsman reported to Luther Reeves, who remained as ME Doncaster following Thompson's departure and stayed there into BR days. In past times, Windle's reporting line had led directly to the CME, which suggests some rethinking had taken place, with Reeves so positioned to provide some sort of buffer. For a time, Bert Spencer's role in the new organisation seems unclear. According to the records that have survived, between 1943 and 1946 he advised Thompson directly on locomotive matters and had been a prime mover in forming the standardisation plan. Under Peppercorn this seems to have continued for a time. However, in 1947 he was appointed Mechanical Engineer (Outdoors) at Doncaster, in place of James Blair who moved north to Cowlairs, and made responsible for 'Mechanical Work with the Running Superintendents'. This was an interesting appointment, most crucially because its primary focus was on providing a strong link with a group of men who could, if they so wished, have exerted considerable pressure on the CME. During Thompson's time, this had proved to be a matter of some concern, so it would seem that Peppercorn considered the astute, diplomatic and talented Spencer ideal for such a difficult role. In time, Peppercorn would re-label this post Technical Assistant to the CME and in November 1947, on the eve of nationalisation, he rewarded all Spencer's hard work and dedication by making him Assistant to the CME (Locomotive and General).

Bert Spencer retained many of Peppercorn's records following the CME's retirement, these comprised a number of albums. This included a famous advert, which used a Terence Cuneo painting, and was given pride of place in this collection. It shows a new A2/3 Pacific, No. 520, *Owen Tudor*, and A4 No. 1, *Sir Ronald Matthews*, being restored to pre-war splendour, in the Paint Shop at Doncaster and given the title *Giants Refreshed*. Also included are a number of photographs that were sent to Cuneo to help him in this work, of which this is one. These pictures show A2/3 No. 519, *Honeyway* built in February 1947 and A4 No. 27, *Merlin*, which in January that year was just completing a General Repair. The artist seems to have preferred his own choice of engines. These photographs, one of which is included here, capture the look and spirit of Peppercorn's time as CME. (*BS/RH*)

John Frederick Harrison, the gifted protégé of Gresley and Thompson, who Peppercorn elevated to become his assistant in 1947. He rose to become BR's CME in 1958 and for many years exerted a strong influence on many elements of locomotive design. He was also one of the few men who reached this rank who talked extensively about his experiences and recorded his impression of those he worked with. He lived until the age of 92 and his remains are interred with those of his wife Mary near his birthplace in Settle, Yorkshire. Bert Spencer described Harrison as 'possessing great self-confidence. He was more certain of his design skills than others might have been and his part in the development of the locomotives was negligible and possibly overstated'. Strong words from someone who was usually more circumspect. (PR)

Apart from Spencer, the other name that stands out is that of John 'Freddie' Harrison, who in 1946 was Mechanical Engineer at Cowlairs. When describing his background, he recorded being born in Yorkshire during February 1904, then being educated at Malvern Wells Primary School in Worcestershire and Wellington College in Berkshire. On his family background he remained fairly silent, but recalled his early years when making his Presidential Address to the ILocoE in 1961:

'My childhood was spent at Settle, where I learnt to admire the Midland Railway in so many ways – its wonderful locomotives and its even more wonderful rolling stock, meeting on that line many members of staff in the persons of signalmen, gangers, stationmasters, who told me many stories, sometimes true, sometimes exaggerated, of the difficulties of keeping the Settle-Carlisle line open in winter. A kind of halo was added to all this by my grandfather, a civil engineer who had a Midland background.'

From early in his career, as a contemporary of Spencer, he had been considered a rising star and was nurtured and promoted by Gresley, Thompson and Peppercorn in turn. In fact, he became a Gresley premium apprentice in the early 1920s and so would have benefitted greatly from the CME's wise council and patronage. In 1926, at the end of his training, he was placed in charge of the sheds at Wigan and St Helens and became Assistant to the Works Manager at Gorton in 1930. Seven years later, he moved on to a more prestigious post at Doncaster, becoming Robert Thom's assistant, but he only stayed for twelve months or so before moving back to Gorton as Locomotive Works Manager. Here he remained for three years until Gresley's death and Thompson's succession, when the new CME promoted him to become Mechanical Engineer of the Great Central Section. He held this post through the war years with some distinction and in 1945 Thompson transferred him to Cowlairs.

Despite Peppercorn's promotion, there was no immediate transfer into the CME's new HQ team at Doncaster for him. Instead he waited until March 1947 for this to happen, with James Blair moving to Scotland to take his place. According to the few records that remain, Harrison was initially appointed Assistant to the CME, replacing Roy Hart-Davies, who was appointed Mechanical Engineer Scotland (Outdoors), and, soon after was promoted Assistant CME. It is interesting to note that he doesn't appear to have trained as a draughtsman or worked in a design office in any capacity during his career. Likewise, he doesn't seem to have written any engineering papers or expounded any thoughts on the science of design or submitted any patents which might have taken locomotive development to a new level.

Peppercorn was noted for his sense of humour and sent this cartoon, which appeared in the LNER's *Journal*, to Thompson, by then in retirement on the south coast, with a short note, which he kept, saying 'I thought you would find it amusing to see some of our old adversaries hopefully pulling in the right direction'. The picture was prepared when Pearl Wadham, the Personal Secretary to eight senior managers, was awarded the MBE. Left to Right they are – Miss Wadham, Henry Thornton, S. Parnwell, Alex Wilson, G. Thurston, Charles Newton, H. Mauldin, George Mills and Victor Barrington-Ward. Peppercorn kept in touch with Thompson and, in due course, invited him to his retirement celebrations at the end of 1949. (*ET/DN*)

The truth seems to be that he was not a design engineer like Gresley and Spencer, but, like Thompson and Peppercorn, he was a production specialist with a keen understanding of workshop practices.

When nationalisation took effect, Harrison's future was decided by the new BR management team and he became Mechanical and Electrical Engineer, a post that sat alongside Peppercorn at Doncaster for a time and absorbed many of the duties undertaken by him and Henry Richards. Two years later, he moved to Derby in a similar capacity and rose, in 1958, to become BR's Chief Officer for Mechanical Engineering, its CME in all but name. Harrison retired in 1966 and died in Cambridge on 22 May 1996. During his later years, he became a source of information about Britain's railway history and happily discussed or wrote about life at senior level in the LNER and BR; one of the few to do so. Some of his insights have come to define our view of these days, although they can appear a little combative at times. Ernest Cox described him as 'a vigorous and exhilarating personality' and 'a lifelong fighter ... humorously affecting the utmost scorn for the LMS's ways of doing things' who 'embarked upon a continuous battle with all those forces which could hinder or belittle the engineer's efforts to do his proper job'. So he is important to this story in two ways. He was a reporter of events and a key player in the last two years of Peppercorn's career as CME.

He, it must be admitted, wasn't always a huge fan of Thompson's skills as a designer and occasionally found fault in the 'dictatorial' way the CME appeared to operate at Doncaster. Criticisms, interestingly enough, later levelled at Harrison himself by several commentators, including Bert Spencer. He also put forward the view that 'Thompson had at the back of his mind a determination to undermine Gresley's reputation'. However, it is probably true to say that he was the only LNER senior manager who chose to expound this view and he did so long after the event when most of the people involved were dead and memories may have become clouded. He also viewed these events from Gorton and Cowlairs and not from a frontline seat at Doncaster, where the action was taking place, until quite late in the day. Despite many reservations, he was still able to praise Thompson for his work in converting old Great Central locomotives and improving them 'enormously', but it was a backhanded compliment. In the following sentence he added, 'but apart from the O4s there was no locomotive of any real merit in the fleet'. However, he also observed that Thompson 'without being clouded by Gresley phobia, could and did produce first class locomotives (the B1) and was well able to organize and rationalize the huge department he controlled'.

When it came to Peppercorn his views were milder but also a little self-serving and, slightly inexact, even disingenuous at times. He later wrote:

'Peppercorn felt the job was a bit too much; but I think only a few of his trusted loyal friends realised this and they certainly never let on.

As Peppercorn settled into his new job the A2/3s continued to roll off the production line, though the rate would only ever be one or two per month. No. 500 came first, but number two was 511 and given the name *Airborne* after the racehorse that won the Derby and St Leger in 1946. (*DN*)

'Most of the design work on the Peppercorn Pacifics took place following my arrival at Doncaster as Assistant to the CME. I know that both the A1s and A2s were designed with regard to Gresley's views. In other words, a continuation of what we believed he would have come to. They were in our view logical successors to his high boiler pressured Pacifics. The CME left much of their design work to Windle, Spencer and myself.

'The three of us discussed what was required and what should be done. We all, including Peppercorn, had the same object in mind, namely to produce a more reliable Gresley locomotive and we wished to eliminate from the basic Gresley design concept those things which had proved unsatisfactory, or which changed maintenance practices had made more difficult. Peppercorn took our views and digested them before passing them to Windle to turn into practical designs.

'Peppercorn was not one to interfere once he had made his feelings known and left us to get on with our work. This was the complete antithesis of Gresley who took personal control of design and construction and demanded that he be kept informed at all stages of the process. Peppercorn managed with a much lighter touch. He was liked by everyone and rarely said a cross word, even when someone was at fault. He managed diplomatically and offered support where he could as the design work proceeded.'

It seems to be a common thread of a CME's career, that their achievements are defined by the new designs that appear during their time in office. They can reorganise their departments to run more efficiently, make them more cost effective, saving the company substantial sums in the process, and meet the complicated and stressful demands of day to day life, but they still seem to be judged by the locomotives that appear on their watch.

And Peppercorn, despite all his other achievements, is best remembered for the work he and his team did on the final phase of the LNER's Pacific programme. Despite what Harrison later claimed, this work began long before his arrival at Doncaster in May 1947 and had been undertaken by Windle, Gray and Reeves working under the control of the CME, with Spencer in support. In fact, Harrison seems to have airbrushed Gray and Reeves out of the picture entirely, which does them both a great disservice. So, because this work has come to define Peppercorn's time in office, it is important to understand what happened and why and the timescale involved; basically to look beyond Harrison's recollections, self-assertions and possible prejudices to see where the truth might lie.

As one CME gave way to another, in July 1946, little appeared to change in the locomotive plan Peppercorn inherited. The A2/3 construction programme was set fair and proceeding in a slow, but measured way. By September 1947, fifteen had been built in the form set out by Windle and Gray and agreed by Thompson. Allocation across the network soon followed. With such a sizeable number in service, it was easier to assess the class in all conditions and across all routes, with reliability and economy central to the trials programme. Inevitably, this is a slow process; gathering and analysing data in a studied way will always be this way. But even so there will be a temptation to draw conclusions early in the process before testing has been completed. In this case, there appears to have been some focus on the cylinder arrangement of the A2/3s, the converted P2s and *Great Northern*. However, this doesn't seem to have emanated from the Running Department, where the Divisional General Managers appear to have been satisfied with their performance, but from elsewhere, or so Harrison and H.C.B. Rogers would have us believe. They both infer that in the last few months of Thompson's career Windle and his team began redesigning the A2/3 in secret. Rogers recorded that:

> 'He [Thompson] little knew that his drawing office staff, even before his retirement, had been thinking about these new engines [the second batch of A2/3s] and had determined to try and prevent them being built with the outside cylinders so far back, and to influence a return to the more orthodox arrangement.'

In apparent confirmation of this, Rogers reported that Barney Symes (a senior draughtman) wrote to him saying that, 'The general layout of the first Peppercorn Pacific was in fact on my drawing board, except for the front end, before Pep took over'. To me this seems to be a long way away from saying that anyone deliberately deceived Thompson. To my mind, they simply did as good designers do and prepared various options to improve and evolve a design in the light of any new evidence emerging from day to day running. Rogers' theory, that they were running a clandestine campaign to stop Thompson debasing Gresley's work, seems more suited to the pages of pulp fiction than the precincts of a tough, well-run professional organisation, with all its checks and balances. There is also the question of Thompson's own thoughts on the matter to consider. In 1948, in his interview with Brian Reed, he was quoted as saying that 'I wasn't sure if I had done the right thing [in placing the outside cylinders well back to reduce the length of the connecting rods] and later wished I had placed all three cylinders in line'. This seems to suggest that he had an open mind on the subject and could easily have been persuaded of the merits of either solution by Windle, Gray or Spencer, his experts and advisors in this field, if they had chosen to force through a change.

Where might Peppercorn have stood on this issue? Clearly, he would have approved the changes, just as he would have been party to the decisions on the earlier Pacific projects. But is it possible that he would have been so in awe or so disdainful of Thompson as to sanction any sort of deceit in seeking to change the cylinder layout of the A2/3s? It is most unlikely, if not improbable. Peppercorn was no 'yes' man and wouldn't have reached such a senior position if he had been that meek or so unassertive. The truth seems to be that in building up this story, Rogers was simply trying to sensationalise the whole issue by hinting at dark deeds. In so doing he blackened Thompson's name, which was a key ingredient of his book, and, by association, impugned the reputation of the honest and honourable Peppercorn in the process. There seems little doubt that a man such as he would have expressed his thoughts directly to Thompson and sought by reasoned argument to get his point across. There would have been no hole-in-corner business in the way he worked.

Even before nationalisation there were changes at the top of the LNER. In 1947, the stalwart Charles Newton was replaced as Chief General Manager, on a temporary basis, by Miles Beevor, the Chief Legal Adviser. Under Gresley, Thompson and Peppercorn it had become quite common for locomotives to be named after directors or other senior managers. Whether trying to exert influence or curry favour with the top echelon the flattering effect of a named engine could prove useful. In this photo, taken in early November 1947, Beevor (centre plus family) gets the treatment as A4 No. 4485 'formerly *Kestrel*' is renamed. Peppercorn looks on probably smiling at the antics of the two children, whilst Ronald Matthews, the chairman, watches the photographer. Beevor would shortly go on to work for the Railway Executive and BR at senior level. Did his 'A4' help persuade him to favour his old company? We shall never know, but politics are politics and Peppercorn must have become used to their many twists and turns as he sought to keep locomotives and rolling stock moving effectively. (*DN*)

A1/1 *Great Northern*, as she appeared in 1946, just before being re-numbered 113 and having had her unique smoke deflectors fitted. Until October 1947, the engine was based at Doncaster and participated in a number of trial runs in which she was compared to other Pacifics, most notably with the A4s. (*RH*)

Peppercorn's time as CME saw the bulk of the B1s built. Here he poses in front of the newly named locomotive No. 1249, *Fitzherbert Wright* in December 1947 (following the trend of naming locomotives after company directors). Construction of the bulk of these engines was sub-contracted to North British (290) and Vulcan Foundry (50), with sixty being built at Darlington. The programme ran from 1942 until 1952. (*DN/RH*)

There is also the importance of this work to consider. When the Thompson, Peppercorn, Windle and Gray partnership oversaw the *Great Northern* and P2 conversions, concepts which they then developed with the A2/1 and A2/3 Pacifics, the engines that resulted weren't considered poor or causing operational problems. There were signs of wear in the front frames and some muted concerns expressed about the outside exhaust ducts and metal fatigue possibly linked to the position of the cylinders. However, these were being dealt with as a routine maintenance issue at the time. In fact, all the indications are that these rebuilt and new engines were welcomed by the Running Department, where criticism of the locomotives as built by Gresley had emanated. In the circumstances, they seem to have been satisfied with the results and happy with the engines they were given. So, if they weren't pushing for more changes, there wouldn't have been pressure on Thompson or Peppercorn to produce yet another design. It seems, in the circumstances, that the cylinder issue was not a significant one and would have ranked low in Peppercorn's priorities, especially when compared to the dilapidated condition of the locomotive and rolling stock fleet after the war and the pressing need for their restoration. If it had been otherwise, it is most likely that Peppercorn would have stopped the A2/3s' production before engine No. 511 appeared in July 1946 and not wait until No. 524 left the workshops at Doncaster in September 1947. If this is the case, the relative merits of the cylinder positions was simply an issue to be considered as a normal part of business, not through some childish act of deception as implied by Rogers.

It also seems likely that Windle and his team may have been influenced by work undertaken by the LMS immediately prior to the war when designing their four-cylinder Pacifics. The first of them, the Princess Royal Class, had its outside cylinders set back over the rear front bogie, not as far back as Thompson's Pacifics, but sufficient to cause problems with their long frames. As a result, they suffered from motion flexing, which led to severe distortion of fixing holes leading to slackening between frames and outside cylinders. Metal fatigue set in and cracks began to appear in the forward section of the frames leading to increased maintenance and the need for frequent repairs. Various solutions were tried with limited success. Main stays were stiffened and extra plates added in the hope that this might eradicate the problem, but to no avail and their condition grew steadily worse, especially during the war years when the engines were worked much harder, leaving a residue of problems that couldn't be ignored indefinitely. Eventually, in 1951, BR set in hand a more radical 'get well' programme. The forward sections of the frames were cut away and replaced with new stronger pre-shaped sections which it was hoped would inhibit cylinder movement. This modification, as a June 1958 condition report revealed, 'only worked up to a point, the basic design being flawed'.

In the meantime, the Stanier/Coleman partnership produced the Princess Coronations which placed the outside cylinders further forward over the leading truck. This allowed the frames to be shortened and gave the design a better balance, reduced vibration and sought to eradicate the stress damage this could cause. It was a superior design in many ways and demonstrated how good engineers, by observation and testing, continue developing an idea. Nothing is ever truly completed, because science is a process of growth and new understandings.

It seems that the Princess Royals' motion flexing problem didn't attract much attention across the industry for many years, but this began to change as nationalisation took hold and knowledge began to be shared more freely. So, it is likely that Thompson wasn't aware of these issues when his Pacifics were being designed by Windle and Gray, but by 1947/48 the picture had changed, with lessons learnt by the Chief Draughtsman at Derby becoming common currency. We shall never know for certain, of course, but there are similarities between the LMS and LNER programmes that suggest some interesting possibilities.

Leaving this theory to one side, and ignoring Rogers and Harrison's suggestion of shenanigans at Doncaster, it seems that Peppercorn and Windle's work in taking the A2/3 design a step further was simply a way of wringing the last few drops from a long established design. It was a continuation of both Gresley and Thompson's work; a measured, evolutionary response that didn't raise eyebrows at the time because such practice was accepted as the norm. It wasn't a case of Thompson, in bitterness, needlessly trashing Gresley's philosophy or Peppercorn secretly plotting to restore the master's ideas after the pretender had departed. It was a measured response intended to improve the breed and nothing more. In any case, the changes made by Peppercorn and Windle weren't extensive. They were more in the way of an adjustment that overcame the perceived shortcomings of Gresley's conjugated valve gear, at the same time as reducing any stress damage afflicting the frames of Thompson and Windle's earlier Pacifics.

This is a view that Bert Spencer seems to have held. In 1964 he wrote that:

'The development of the A2/3s into Peppercorn's A2s then A1s was not the significant leap some later claimed and, to my recollection not surrounded, by any controversy. There is always a better way of doing things in science and engineering, which by trial and error is slowly established. Windle and Gray, as far as I can remember, were strong advocates of the cylinder layout of the Thompson Pacifics. However, with experience of these engines in service they decided to place them further forward, just as the LMS did with their Princess Coronations. I do remember that this alternative layout, or something like it, was considered amongst other propositions as early as 1944 when the P2s and No. 4470 were in the course of reconstruction. No one, if my memory serves me well, questioned the decision made, though the issue of streamlining caused some debate. These were tough, experienced hard headed engineers that both Thompson and Peppercorn respected and listened to, neither being designers themselves. In fact, both were more compliant when it came to design than Sir Nigel and tended to follow the advice they were given. Windle and Gray, who were both top notch engineers, seem to have had their complete trust.'

So in early 1947, development of the A2/3s and the A1/1 conversion moved on to their next phase, with experience gained from Gresley and Thompson's Pacifics, and possibly even Stanier's 4-6-2s, informing the debate. By mid-year, planning must have been sufficiently advanced for Peppercorn to confidently consider changing the design of the next batch of Pacifics. Would he have needed the Locomotive Committee or Board approval to do so? Their primary concern would have focussed on the number to be built and the costs involved, not the final shape or form of the engines they had commissioned. From their point of view, the specification was a broad one, containing room in which the designers could manoeuvre if they so wished.

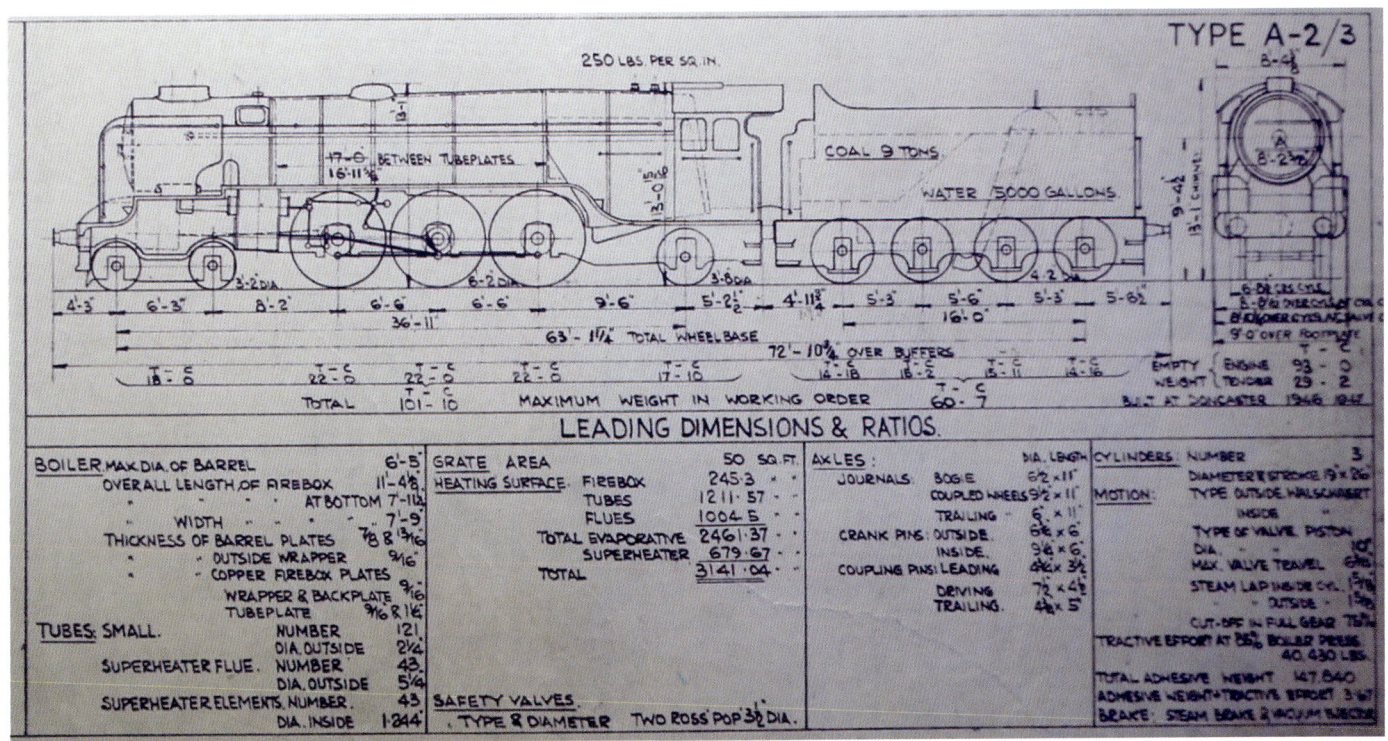

The A2/3 (above) evolved into Peppercorn's A2 (below), but each showed its LNER lineage dating back to Gresley's first Pacifics in 1922 and the ideas he espoused. Bert Spencer remembered that the cylinder layout adopted for the new A2s was first suggested in 1944, as one of a number of proposals, when the P2s and engine No. 4470 were being considered for reconstruction. Although not adopted by Thompson and Windle at the time, possibly for reasons of economy, these ideas re-surfaced two years later and became a key feature of the LNER's last two Pacific designs. This change was probably sponsored by some concerns over state of the frames when the outside cylinders were placed to the rear of the leading truck. Motion flexing was proving to be a problem requiring occasional maintenance, raising concerns over metal fatigue and fracturing. (THG)

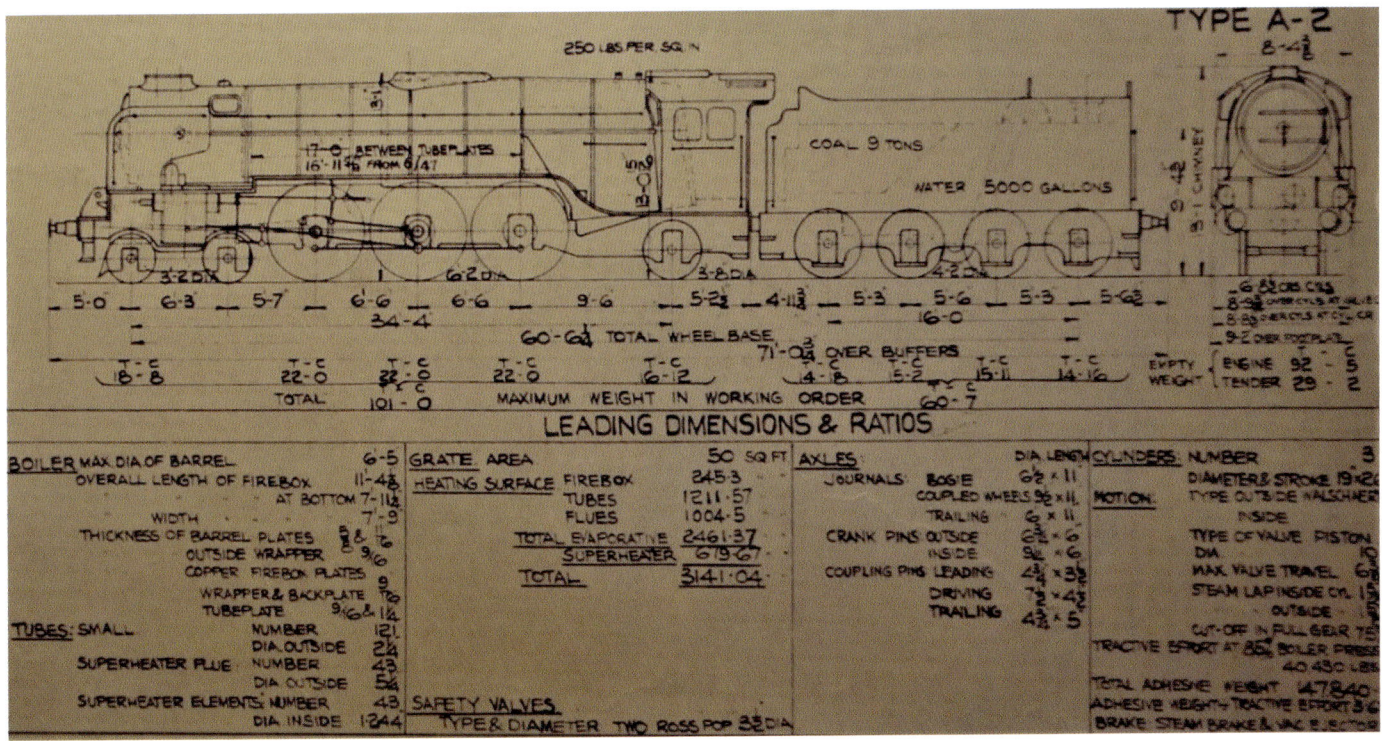

Where the cylinders were positioned or any other modifications they included would only have been of concern if costs had begun to rise, which in this case they didn't. Miles Beevor, by then ensconced as Chief General Manager having succeeded Charles Newton, and responsible for the CME's Department, would not have been qualified to comment on any technical issues involved, being a solicitor. So, he would have trusted Peppercorn and his team to produce the best possible locomotive, then carefully checked the balance sheet to make sure that the project was financially sound.

In terms of numbers of new engines, the position when Thompson retired in 1946 was that thirty Pacifics with 6ft 2in driving wheels had been ordered, with more added later. In addition, and following the comparability trials between an A4 and the A1/1, sixteen Pacifics with 6ft 8in driving wheels had also been sanctioned. However, this was increased to thirty-nine in May 1946 by the Board, with a further ten added in the months that followed. With hindsight, these seem extraordinarily large numbers, especially with so many other Pacifics already in service around the LNER's network. It was even more surprising in the light of nationalisation and the corporate management brand that would soon swallow up all independent thought and rail centres.

One wonders what the rationale behind these decisions might have been? Was it driven by concerns over the declining state of Gresley's Pacifics and the need to provide replacements? This doesn't seem likely, because they continued on until the end of steam in the 1960s. Did the company envisage a massive increase in trade requiring a build-up of numbers once the war was over? There was certainly a bounce in post-war passenger traffic, which offset the loss of military travellers. However, industry was slow to recover after the armistice and recession set in for a period as companies moved from armaments production to broader consumer needs. So trade dropped away and would only begin to recover in the 1950s. Admittedly, a locomotive programme tries to predict need in the long term and not simply the next five years, but such a large number of these new locomotives seems overly optimistic. The other option, a collective blindness to the truth of what the LNER faced, is more difficult to believe. Perhaps they genuinely thought that the effects of nationalisation would be minimal and, as with amalgamation in 1923, each company would work independently and make their own decisions regarding motive power. In truth, all these issues, coupled to uncertainty over the future, played a part in their deliberations.

So, in 1947, Peppercorn and team settled down to deliver forty-nine Pacifics with 6ft 8in driving wheels, and thirty-five additional A2/3s. As planning progressed, the two classes were designated A1s and A2s respectively to denote the differences introduced in design over their forebears. For reasons that aren't entirely clear, the A2 building programme was given precedence over the A1s. But it is probably safe to assume that their development was simply seen as an extension of the A2/3 production run at Doncaster which produced its last Thompson Pacific in September 1947. The first A2, No. 525, appeared three months later, in the last days of the company's existence, so provided a fitting end to the LNER's short life and was feted as such.

Opposite and this page: The first Peppercorn A2, No. 525, slowly takes shape at Doncaster in late 1947. These photographs were, according to Bert Spencer, kept in an album by the CME, which on retirement Peppercorn passed to him. Two pictures capture the boiler being assembled and held vertically in 'the riveter'. Meanwhile the frames, with cylinders and saddle fitted, are viewed from fore and aft, with a foreman or inspector taking an interest in the final product. (*BS/RH*)

The boiler is carefully lowered into 525's frames as final assembly goes ahead. (*BS/RH*)

When the first A2 rolled out of the workshops at Doncaster, the most obvious difference between it and the A2/3s lay in its less stretched look. This was achieved by the simple expedient of moving the outside cylinders forward over the leading truck and by amending the steam ducts. In doing this, the wheelbase was shortened and the smokebox reduced in length. However, it retained the cylinder and valve gear arrangement introduced when Thompson was CME; divided drive with the middle cylinder acting on the leading coupled axle and outside cylinders the middle axle. This could only be achieved in the space available on the A2s by discarding the Kylchap exhaust or the self-cleaning device in the smokebox. Windle and team decided that the former could go, and this, apparently, had the added benefit of improving the passage of smoke over the cab so improving the footplate crew's forward visibility. However, Spencer later wrote that:

> 'This was a false economy. The Kylchap double blastpipe and chimney, which Gresley strongly advocated, had proved its value when fitted to some of the A4s in the 1930s and some of the A3s. Thompson had seen the wisdom of this and his Pacifics were so fitted also. However, Windle was not a strong supporter of this design and his view prevailed when the A2s were being designed, although five were equipped with a double chimney. Consequently, they tended to steam poorly and only at the end did my advice prevail and the last A2 was fitted with a Kylchap.'

Received wisdom would have us believe that Windle was more likely to follow Gresley's principles than Thompson, but this issue suggests otherwise. If indeed Spencer's advice did prevail in 1948 it proved to be the right decision and the mistake wasn't repeated in the A1s.

The cab itself reverted to a 'V' shape and a 'banjo dome' steam collector was restored, both of which had been discarded in the A2/3 design. In addition, a new style of smoke deflector was fitted. But apart from these changes, which shortened the wheelbase by slightly more than 2½ft and reduced the engine's weight by 10cwt, a lot else appeared to remain the same as the A2/3s. There was the 6ft 5in boiler producing 250psi, a total heating surface of 3141.04sqft, a hopper ashpan, a 50sqft grate area, a tractive effort of 40,430lb, 19in by 26in cylinders, 22 ton maximum axle loading, steam brakes and the same type of tender was attached.

However, within this framework there were embedded some subtler variations to reflect changed thinking. Although ostensibly adopting Thompson's cylinder and valve gear arrangement, the outside connecting rods were in fact increased to 10 feet in length, but the inside rod remained unchanged at 7ft 2in. By retaining divided drive, it proved necessary to move the inside cylinder further forward, so creating a slight, 9in, overhang at the front. The boiler, although appearing the same as the A2/3s, was modified by using 2 to 3 per cent nickel plate for the barrel. This allowed the plate to be $\frac{1}{8}$in thinner without compromising its integrity, and reduced its overall weight by 7cwt. The cab, although 'V' shaped, again contained other changes. It conformed to a new standard

Engine and tender are complete and painting is underway at Doncaster. Within days, No. 525 will make her first appearance and be photographed for publicity purposes. At this stage, it is likely that the locomotive's name has been chosen by the Chairman, Ronald Matthews, and the plates have been prepared, but *A.H. Peppercorn* was not be officially unveiled until December 1947. (*BS/RH*)

gauge announced in 1947. This meant that the sides were tapered towards the corners of the cab roof, the front of which was set at an angle of 45 degrees across its sides to give the footplate crew a better view. The absence of the Kylchap exhaust system meant that a double blast pipe was unnecessary and was replaced with a single chimney.

In the past when a railway company launched a new class of express locomotive, they could usually guarantee considerable interest and items in the national press. In the post-war years, this changed. The reasons for this were only too apparent. Steam locomotion, although still in widespread use across the country, seemed increasingly out of place in a modern nuclear world, where science was making many leaps forward. Having fought and sacrificed in another long war, personal aspiration demanded something more than vague promises that life would eventually improve. Such assurances had proved false post-1918 and there was a consensus building that it wouldn't be repeated the second time around. Better housing, improved living standards, better pay and better working conditions plus the welfare state now became key issues and demands. The grimy, tired, soot impregnated railway system reflected the old world and car ownership had become a symbol of the new. The heady days of the 1930s, when Gresley's Pacifics had attracted headlines, were now over. So Peppercorn's new locomotives slipped into service with barely a whisper let alone a shout. It didn't help that the LMS launched its first main line diesel at the same time and the LNER's electrification programme was being revived. That month, its own main line loco, built years earlier and placed in store, was undergoing tests in Holland and it was expected that the programme would soon be revived. The world was certainly changing rapidly and steam's early demise seemed quite likely.

Above and opposite above: The caption beneath these two photos in the CME's album simply records that 'Engine No. 525 is steamed and leaves plant for trials – 9th December 1947'. (*BS/RH*)

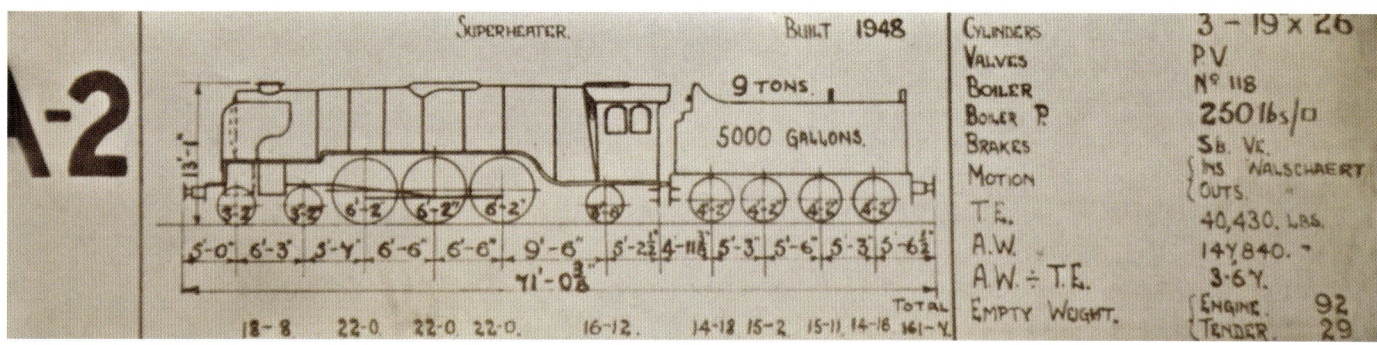

Bert Spencer's personal diagram containing the basic details of the new A2s. (*BS/RH*)

A number of articles did appear in the railway press, with the most expansive of these provided by the *Locomotive Magazine* in their February 1948 edition. However, the main thrust of this report focussed on Thompson's work in developing the Class A2/3. Only in the final two paragraphs does the new A2 get even a brief mention:

'The new A2 differs considerably from the previous engines and has the outside cylinders further forward. Apart from alterations in the layout of exhaust and steam pipes, resulting from the change in cylinder position, other differences are in the centres of the hind bogie axle and leading coupled axle, now 5ft 7in instead of 8ft 2in. The radius and eccentric rods have been considerably lengthened and the gear as fitted on No. 525 closely resembles that employed on the B1 Class. The boiler is generally similar, but the dome has given place to a steam collector of the LNER pattern and the use of 3% nickel alloy steel has enabled the barrel plates to be reduced in

Before being officially named, the engine's new plates were attached for this photograph taken at Doncaster on 31 December 1947. It shows some of the men responsible for No. 525, and much of the LNER's earlier history, with Peppercorn the central figure in the front row, before BR came into existence on 1 January 1948. There would have been few who didn't view the future with uncertainty and, according to the few memoirs written, many mourned the LNER's passing. Doncaster would still have a future under BR but never again enjoy the same premier status. (*BS/RH*)

Above and opposite: For anyone, no matter how modest they might be, and Peppercorn was a very modest man, having a locomotive with your name emblazoned on its side must be a pleasant experience. When Ronald Matthews pulled down the cover over engine No. 525's new nameplate, on 18 February 1948, the normally unassuming CME must have been delighted to be presented with this living memorial. It was, after all, in recognition of his considerable contributions to the company throughout his career and his country during two world wars. With cigar in hand admiring the nameplate and then standing on the footplate he maintains a phlegmatic air. (*RH*)

thickness . . . Electric lighting is provided for the cab and head lamps, current being derived from a Stone turbo-generator on the front right-hand side of the footplate. A rocking grate and self-cleaning smokebox are incorporated.'

It is highly unlikely that Peppercorn would have cared a great deal if the publicity was muted or not. With its brand name soon to disappear, the LNER's directors and Chief General Manager perhaps cared even less. Of greater significance at the time would have been the scramble for power and influence in the new BR organisation. By contrast, the arrival of another locomotive paled into insignificance, a moment to celebrate the ending of an exciting period of railway history but no more.

With this, the first A2 entered service, remaining locally at Doncaster shed for the first twelve months of her life as the design was evaluated. However, she was soon joined by more of the class until the last of them, No. 60539, *Bronzino*, was turned out of the workshops during August 1948, with the Kylchap double blastpipe and chimney fitted as an experiment, which meant that the self-cleaning apparatus had to be discarded. Five more of the A2s were similarly modified in 1949.

By this stage the plan to build another twenty had been placed on hold by BR, conscious of the array of building projects they had inherited and the sheer volume of locomotives on their books. In an article dated May 1948, the editor of the *Locomotive Magazine* gave the total numbers as 12,490 tender engines and 7,536 tanks of 34 different wheel configurations, let alone 448 types. Of these some 6,500 were LNER engines. There was clearly a need to rein in much of this diverse, uncoordinated effort and produce a new master plan that drew the old companies together in a practical way in order that the fleet could be rationalised.

A sunny day in 1948 and No. 525, to be renumbered by BR as 60525 in August 1949, stands at King's Cross soon to head north. 'LNER' remained emblazoned on the tender for a while, to be replaced by 'British Railways' in bold white lettering before receiving BR's first style of crest. (*RH*)

A simple record of 60525's short life. After only fifteen years of service she was condemned, or as Bert Spencer put it 'when barely run in'.

The task was a daunting one that would not be resolved quickly or cheaply, let alone the longer term need to introduce other forms of locomotion. And hovering in the background was the residue of wear and tear inflicted by the war that still had to be corrected.

The first evocation of this came when a set of locomotive comparability trials were commissioned by BR in 1948. In due course these became known as 'Interchange Trials'. The concept was a simple one. Take the best of all the engines then in service and match them, by group, in a series of tests over each region's main routes.

Then assess lessons learnt and incorporate best practice and the most effective elements of each design into a new standard group of locomotives. Despite this all-encompassing ambition, the trials didn't seek to assess new technologies, choosing instead to focus solely on steam. With the benefit of hindsight, this seems remarkably blinkered; nevertheless, it was understandable when considering the country's dire financial position and the importance and size of its coal industry.

Each company was represented in these trials and Peppercorn delegated a co-ordinating role to Bert Spencer, who then became chairman of the Locomotive Testing Committee. It was a wise choice considering his wide experience, his exemplary engineering skills and knowledge of testing processes, which Gresley had encouraged over many years. Whilst this was happening, BR selected the locomotives to be tested, with input from each company. In the LNER's case, three classes were chosen. These were the A4, which would run in the express passenger group, Thompson's B1 in the mixed traffic category and Thompson's 2-8-0 Class 01 as the freight representative. The choice of individual engines for this task was left to the CME and his staff to decide, but conditions were applied to this process by Ernest Cox, who had recently been appointed to BR . He directed that engines selected should not undergo any 'special preparation' and be 'taken direct from traffic having run between 15,000 and 20,000 miles since their last general repair'.

A4 No.33, now renumbered 60033, on 1 June 1948 about to set out on a familiarisation run for the crew prior to beginning the Southern phase of Interchange Trials pulling express trains from Waterloo. Before the first run proper, on 8 June, *Seagull* had 'run hot' and was replaced by her more famous sister, No. 22 *Mallard*. This loco developed a similar problem on the 9th and was herself substituted by *Seagull*. Originally A4s Nos. 21, 25 and 26, all single chimney engines, were selected for these trials. But, in his role as chairman of the Testing Committee, Bert Spencer suggested that they be replaced with engines fitted with Kylchap exhausts and twin blastpipes. This was agreed and three King's Cross engines, *Seagull*, *Mallard* and No. 34, *Lord Faringdon* replaced the original trio. During the trials, the A4s produced the best coal and water consumption figures of the five classes used (Princess Coronation, Merchant Navy, Royal Scot and the Western Region Kings). (*BS/RH*)

B1, No. 61251 *Oliver Bury*, gets in on the act and is seen outside St Pancras Station on 18 June 1948 pulling a trials train from Manchester to London. This engine and locomotives Nos. 61163 and 61292 appear to be the only B1s used during the Interchange Trials. Their performances compared most favourably with their three mixed traffic competitors – LMR Black 5s, WR Halls and SR West Country Class locomotives. (*RH*)

The choices made by Peppercorn are certainly interesting. The A4 Class was an outstanding design and had tremendous prestige so its selection is easily understood. The B1 and O1 are a little harder to fathom, especially if Peppercorn did harbour any concerns about Thompson and his work. The truth would seem to be that in selecting them, he confirmed this wasn't necessarily so and chose them as the best the LNER had available at the time. In addition, he was also involved in their development and inclusion in the LNER's standardisation plans, so must have had trust in their capabilities. However, the absence of the later Pacifics is noteworthy. As the company's most up to date product, and, presumably, the ultimate in what the LNER could offer, they should have been an obvious choice. One can only assume that they were deemed too new and untested, so a riskier proposition than the long established A4s. Clearly the same argument wouldn't have applied to their other B1s or O1s, both of which had been in service for some years by then.

Whilst the trials were being discussed, Harrison arrived at Doncaster from Cowlairs and was soon working as Assistant CME. He appears to have been directly involved in this exercise for a time, but soon other duties took over and Spencer was again in sole charge, answerable to Peppercorn, judging by contemporary correspondence. By March, the programme had been agreed and suitable locomotives identified. However, it seems that some doubts were by then expressed over the benefits of the whole exercise. The official report touched on this issue:

'From the outset it was realised that these indications [of the most desirable features of each locomotive] would be of a very broad nature... It was also realised that inequalities which are liable to be experienced in any variable speed testing on the track would be present and affect some locomotives more than others.'

Nevertheless, the trials went ahead and ran from April to September, with some tests over Western Region

A Thompson O1 2-8-0, No. 63773, leaves Acton Yard on a test run to South Wales on 31 August. Only one other member of the class was used, No. 63789, in the trials and this engine was measured against LMR 8Fs, WR 2800s and Austerity 2-8-0s and 2-10-0s. The O1s turned in the best figures for coal and water consumption of the five classes used. (RH)

metals being repeated in November and December. It was suggested by the committee that it might be beneficial to undertake 'further testing on the Rugby and Swindon Testing Plants and with Mobile Testing Plant' to supplement or confirm the earlier results.

In early 1949, the final assessment was being mulled over by all participants. For those who doubted the validity of the exercise they would have found ample ammunition to support this view. The overall tenor of the report was probably summed up in the opening pages, which recorded that the trials 'provided valuable and interesting information'. But the nine conclusions that followed this brief assessment were, with few exceptions nebulous, to say the least. Spencer probably caught the general feeling at the time when he wrote that:

'the trials were useful up to a point, but did not really tell us anything we did not know already. Each class had its own strengths, but the variables involved in such trials made such a broad comparison most difficult and speculative in nature. By this stage the new Test Centre at Rugby was finally opening and it was hoped that this facility would soon provide more information. But it was not until January 1950 that serious testing of any of the Interchange engines took place, by which time standardisation plans had been formulated by Cox and his design team, which included Windle.'

Nationalisation was the responsibility of the British Transport Commission under which sat the Railway Executive, which took functional control of all day to day activities. As Cox later wrote, 'thus any thought that the CMEs would continue to exist with their powers unmodified, and could pursue their own locomotive and rolling stock designs without reference to the centre, was killed stone dead at the start.' Riddles became the first head of BR's new Mechanical

In 1949, with BR now fully in control, responsibility for design passed to Ernest Cox, who recruited representatives from each region to oversee the new organisation's dictates. Here the locomotive group are gathered together to consider the future. It was a select group of men with wide experience of design within their parent companies as Chief or Senior Draughtsmen, who would bring their own views and prejudices to the standardisation programme. Cox recorded that they worked for him, suggesting that each CME would face resistance if they tried to claim ownership. However, each of them would remain at Doncaster, Derby, Swindon and Brighton, which meant any tribal loyalties would be difficult to break. Left to right they are – Clifford Cocks (ex-LNER, SR and now LMR), Jimmy Caldwell (LMR), Gilbert Scholes (WR), Frank Mattingly (Chief Draughtsman WR), Ernest Cox, Edward Windle (Doncaster), Ron Jarvis and Wilfred Durban (both SR). (*BS/RH*)

COAL AND WATER CONSUMPTION - SUMMARIES.

COAL.

The following summary shows comparative figures of $\frac{\text{all coal}}{\text{all work}}$ for each of the Owning Regions' engines and covers the performance of all engines in the complete series of tests for all applicable routes :-

$$\phi = \frac{\text{COAL. TOTAL WEIGHT LBS.}}{\text{WORK DONE. HORSEPOWER HOURS.}}$$

Regional Design.	Passenger Type Engine	ϕ	Mixed Traffic Type Engine	ϕ	Freight Type Engine	ϕ
W.R. ƒ	'King'	3.57	'Hall'	3.94	'2800'	3.42
E.R.	'A.4'	3.06	'B.1'	3.59	'O.1'	3.37
L.M.R.	'Duchess'	3.12	'5'	3.54	'8F'	3.52
L.M.R.	'6P'	3.38	-	-	-	-
S.R.	'Merchant Navy'	3.60	'West Country'	4.11	-	-
-	-	-	-	-	'Austerity' 2-8-0	3.77
-	-	-	-	-	'Austerity' 2-10-0	3.52

WATER.

The following summary shows comparative figures of $\frac{\text{all water}}{\text{all work}}$ for each of the Owning Regions' engines and covers the performance of all engines in the complete series of tests for all applicable routes :-

$$\phi = \frac{\text{WATER. TOTAL WEIGHT LBS.}}{\text{WORK DONE. HORSEPOWER HOURS.}}$$

Regional Design.	Passenger Type Engine.	ϕ	Mixed Traffic Type Engine	ϕ	Freight Type Engine	ϕ
W.R. ƒ	'King'	28.58	'Hall'	29.97	'2800'	26.80
E.R.	'A.4'	24.32	'B.1'	27.64	'O.1'	25.73
L.M.R.	'Duchess'	27.08	'5'	27.99	'8F'	27.26
L.M.R.	'6P'	25.81	-	-	-	-
S.R.	'Merchant Navy'	30.43	'West Country'	32.64	-	-
-	-	-	-	-	'Austerity' 2-8-0	28.75
-	-	-	-	-	'Austerity' 2-10-0	28.05

The Coal and Water Consumption Summaries for each class of engine on each route are shown on Pages 4 to 7.

For additional tests on the Western Region using Welsh coal, see Appendix.

ƒ Note. Western Region locomotives were not tested over all routes.

The summary of the Interchange Trials. Although this work may have proved of little value, when trying to establish which bits of which designs might feature in the new standard locomotive designs, Peppercorn and his team probably took some comfort from the performances of the three LNER classes involved. Bulleid less so, when it came to his Southern Pacifics. (THG)

and Electrical Engineering department, assisted by two Chief Officers; Roland Bond for locomotives and Ernest Pugson carriage and wagon construction and maintenance, both LMS men, as was Riddles. Cox, a product of Horwich Works, was appointed Executive Officer for the design of all forms of rolling stock, including locomotives, so would have reported to both Bond and Pugson. Such an obvious LMS bias raised a few eyebrows, but in formulating locomotive design policy, Cox was quick to recruit members from each of the new regions: Cocks and Caldwell from the London Midland; Scholes and Mattingly from the Western; Jarvis and Durban from the Southern; and Windle the sole representative of the Eastern and North Eastern, as Peppercorn's new region was called. Wings being clipped seems an apposite phrase in this situation and the four CMEs probably struggled to make the transition from relative independence to being a medium cog in a much bigger wheel.

At the same time as this was happening, a new Locomotive Testing Joint Sub-Committee, chaired by Cox, came into being, taking over the role of the Spencer-led Testing Committee. Spencer became Peppercorn's representative on this new group, but it doesn't appear

As the railway world underwent profound change the A2s continued to roll off the production line at Doncaster. In this case it is engine No. 527, *Sun Chariot*, in the early days of 1948, here being 'wheeled' for the first time. On completion this locomotive will be based at Gateshead for seventeen months before becoming a permanent feature at sheds in Scotland for the rest of her life. (*DN*)

to have met for the first time until early 1950, by which time the CME had retired.

It didn't take long for the new management team to flex their muscles. In short order, the four railway companies received new names, with any vestige of the old LNER being swept away in the process. It disappeared to re-emerge as the Eastern Region, with its base at Liverpool Street Station, the North Eastern, operating from York, and the Scottish Region, which combined both LMS and LNER teams north of the border. Each team was led by a Chief Regional Officer, which in Peppercorn's case meant dealing with Charles Bird, Charles Hopkins and Tom Cameron. However, they were all LNER men so would have been known to him, so perhaps less of a threat. Nevertheless, this would have been small compensation for his rapidly diminishing authority and freedom of action.

The Interchange Trials and the drive for standardisation seem to have been used as a reason or excuse, I'm not sure which, to review current building programmes. This led to the last twenty A2s being moved from pending to cancelled. In due course, their place would be taken by BR's new standard Pacifics. However, the argument applied here didn't include the A1 programme which remained intact. This seems a little surprising when considering the size of the programme and the nature of the new organisation. Forty-nine Pacifics on top of the hundred plus already in service seems excessive. Nevertheless, construction began in October 1948 and by December 1949 all were in service. Did they fill a necessary gap in the fleet or was this programme simply a means of keeping workshops at Doncaster and Darlington in operation until new, standard engine construction programmes could begin? Without this work it seems likely that there might have been short time working or even redundancies. Neither were palatable options, especially if they led to a haemorrhage of skilled workers before new tasks arrived. Undoubtedly, Peppercorn, who understood workshops better than most, would have voiced his concerns and sought reassurances. In this situation, allowing the A1s to go ahead may have seemed a small price to pay for continuity and stability.

Whilst all this was happening and the future of the railways was being decided, Peppercorn had to negotiate his way through a new system over which he had little control. A man of such integrity would undoubtedly feel honour bound to protect the thousands of workers who had served him and his predecessors so well. Assuring their future would have been important to him. But this could only be achieved by actively participating in all the new HQ organisation did and seeking to attract as much work as possible to his workshops. In his book *A Lifetime With Locomotives*, Roland Bond described these difficult days, the way each CME responded and how they were slowly stripped of their powers:

'The Mechanical and Electrical Engineering Committee, with Riddles in the chair, and with his senior officers at headquarters and the regional Chief Mechanical Engineers as members, surveyed and discussed the policies which it was Riddles' responsibility to dictate, subject in certain cases, to confirmation by the Railway Executive in their corporate capacity before instructions were given. Riddles went out of his way to accord to the CMEs the precedence to which the positions they had held before nationalisation entitled them. He did his best to enlist their support in all he and his officers intended to do, and to make the diminution of their powers of independent action as painless as possible.

'Reactions at the monthly meetings were fascinating to watch. Ivatt, who had been Riddles' chief in former days, quietly exerted more influence than his brethren. He invariably brought common sense and wisdom to bear upon our discussions. He was content in the knowledge that so much of what he had done, particularly in the Works organisation and practice on the LMS, would continue unaltered. Of the other three CMEs, Peppercorn from the LNER and Hawksworth from Swindon, who had never been through the same kind of upheaval as the others at the 1923 amalgamations [with Gresley in charge the changeover had been smoother than the LMS], accepted the inevitable. The greatest sense of frustration must have been felt by Oliver Bulleid whose ideas as to the future development of locomotives were so manifestly different from Riddles'.

'All four of the CMEs retired during the first five years. As each one went the new organisation in the Regions separating carriage and wagon activities was put into effect.'

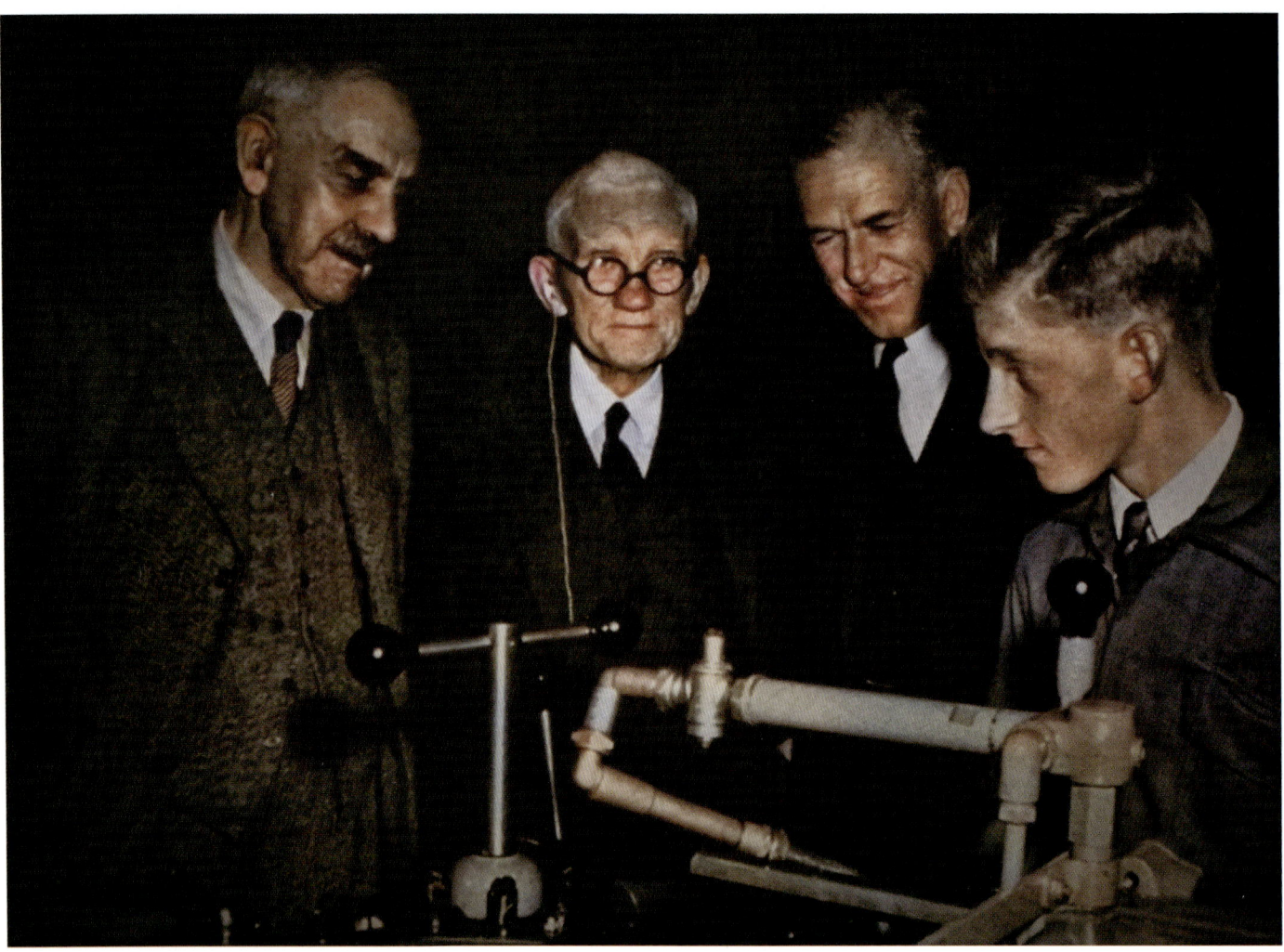

Robert Riddles (second from the right), BR's first CME, admires the work of a young apprentice accompanied by two distinguished 'old boys', William Stanier and Fred Lemon, who had both played significant parts in his rise to prominence. Lemon, as Works Superintendent at Crewe for twenty years, played an important role in the successful completion of many of Stanier's locomotive projects and ran these huge works with great energy and efficiency. Riddles was his one-time Principal Assistant, but it was Roland Bond who replaced him when deafness and poor health intervened, by which time Riddles had joined the Ministry of Supply as Director of Transportation Materials. It was with Riddles and Bond that Peppercorn would have to forge some sort of working relationship. (*ML*)

Ernest Cox later added his own thoughts on the matter and how each CME adapted to change and Peppercorn in particular. He wrote:

'It says much for human adaptability that they (the CMEs) adapted as well as they did, only shadowed by an often wooden demeanour when they faced us across the table at the monthly M & EE Committee meetings, and punctuated by occasional bouts of naughtiness.

'As regards locomotive design, their attitude was conditioned both by temperament and by circumstances. On the E & NE lines an already big stud of large engines was being supplemented by 49 A1 and 15 A2 Pacifics either built or authorised, and Peppercorn was not one to become much agitated by the passage of events.'

Riddles remained mute on this point, but in his authorised biography, written by H.C.B. Rogers and published in 1970, allowed the following line to remain, which suggests that it reflected his thoughts:

'The erstwhile CMEs at this time were variously engaged . . . Ivatt was busily occupied with his diesel

Although the maintenance and construction of steam locomotives and rolling stock was Peppercorn's primary purpose, he still had some limited involvement in the electrification programme led by Henry Richards. Completion of the Shenfield to Liverpool Street commuter line was delayed by the war and it took until March 1949 for it to even be partially opened. The construction of new A6M EMUs was also completed post-war, although a few had been built whilst Gresley was alive and stored for the duration. It fell to Thompson and Peppercorn to oversee the completion of this programme. The line opened fully in September 1949, with a ceremony attended by Peppercorn, and drew an interested audience as this photograph bears witness. (*RH*)

locomotives. Bulleid was trying to make a success of his controversial 'Leader' class steam engine . . . the amiable Peppercorn was happily turning out lots of the last LNER Pacific; and Hawksworth watched approaching events in the comfortable knowledge of Great Western superiority.'

Did Peppercorn accept the inevitable and back away from confrontation or did he play a more astute game? Keeping some new construction work going at Doncaster and Darlington in this interim period, alongside a myriad number of maintenance tasks, suggests a degree of judicious planning. In doing this, he kept his staff busy, whilst confusion over the future created disharmony and hoped to let the quality of their work speak for itself when future programmes were being discussed and agreed.

Design of the A1s proceeded alongside the A2s, which is hardly surprising considering their similarities. But there were additions and lessons to be absorbed. One of these was a proposal for streamlining, a concept never far away from the minds of Gresley's disciples and the harbingers of public relations and good headlines. As already recorded, in 1945 Thompson allowed some modelling to go ahead with a view to streamlining some or all of the new Pacifics and in 1947 some of these examples were photographed and given wide circulation, presumably with Peppercorn's agreement. According to Peter Townend, in his masterly book *East Coast Pacifics At Work*, the estimated cost of these locomotives included £500 to provide air smoothed casing of the pattern and style fitted to the A4s. During 1948, when final proposals for the A1s were being considered by Riddles and team, the idea was dropped in favour of a more traditional outline. Who knows if they were right or wrong to do so, but as Townend observed, having been shed master at King's Cross and so knew a thing or two, 'Although these were years of austerity it is wondered if the REC were fully aware of the problems due to exhaust beating down and all Doncaster's efforts to overcome this.'

In his mind it was clearly a false economy, but ease of access for maintenance seems to have been the main reason for the change. However, Riddles and Cox do not appear to have been fans of streamlining, even though they had participated in the LMS's efforts in this field. Now they were now able to wield their authority to support or terminate anything similar happening within BR. As a result, external streamlining wasn't to feature in any steam design produced during their tenure.

When the first A1 appeared, it would have been difficult to tell them apart from the A2s, but there were some differences other than in the size of the coupled wheels. Townend, who observed these engines from close quarters, probably provided the best description when he wrote:

'The wheelbase was 1ft 11in longer [to accommodate the 6ft 8in diameter driving wheels] and the cylinders were inclined at 1 in 50 instead of 1 in 30. Although the inside connecting rod was still 7ft 2in long, as on all the post-war Pacifics the outside rods were lengthened to 10ft 9in (the A2s being 10ft exactly). The boiler and cab were identical but the smokebox was increased in length by 1ft 9in. At the last minute it was decided to fit a Kylchap double chimney and as a result the whole class were free of steaming problems (unlike the A2s which had gained a reputation for poor steaming).'

There was one other significant difference but it only affected five of the new A1s, as John Harrison recalled when addressing the ILocoE in 1961:

'In 1949 Doncaster produced, under the guidance of the late A.H. Peppercorn, five Pacific locomotives having boiler pressures pressed at 250lb. per square inch, roller bearing axle-boxes, and with separate valve gear drive to the middle cylinder. They were intended to give better performance than any previous Pacific, to be cheaper to maintain, and to run increased mileages per annum and between general repairs. These five locomotives, Nos.60153 to 60157, have now been in service for twelve years and run 4.8 million miles, or 228 miles for every calendar day. The total miles run by all these locomotives

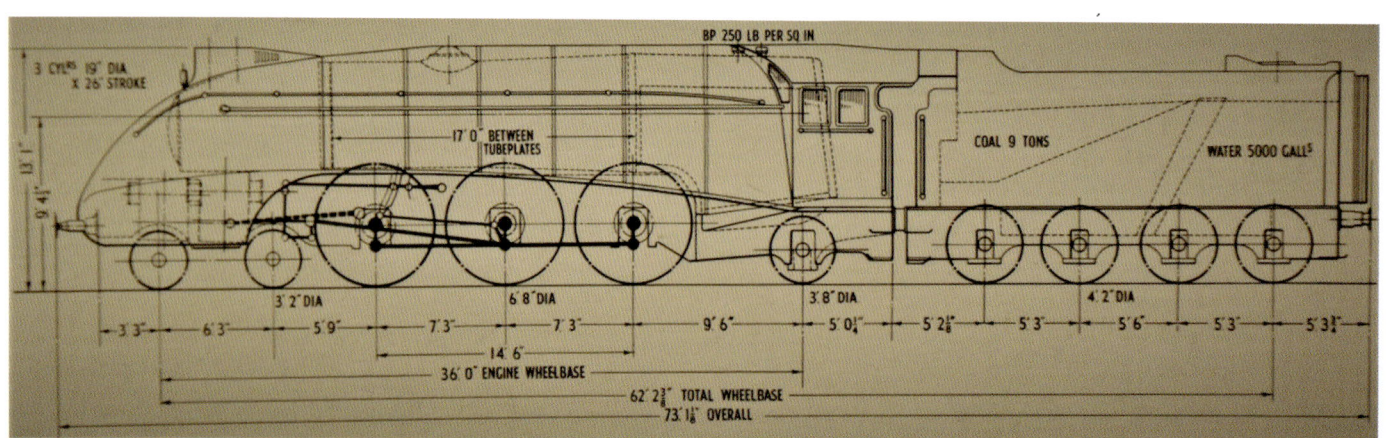

How the A1s might have looked if proposals to streamline them had passed muster with the LNER's new masters.

since new is approximately 48,000 million, an average of 202, figures which I know cannot be approached by any steam locomotive in this country.'

Leaving to one side Harrison's undoubted pride in these engines and the debate over comparable performance, it is the addition of roller bearings which is of interest. During his tour of the States four years earlier, Peppercorn had observed the New York Central 'Niagara Class' 4-8-4s fitted with roller bearings on rods and axle boxes. Ernest Cox expressed great admiration for their design, including the Timken designed bearings. So it is likely that Peppercorn felt the same way. Timken's, in fact, had a long history in this field having been established in 1899 and grown quickly on the back of the rapidly expanding automotive industry. Their first venture in the railway business took place in 1930 with an ALCO built 4-8-4. And from there this side of their business gradually expanded. In 1935 Stanier adopted this concept for use in his turbine Pacific locomotive with some success, but other designers in Britain appear to have been slow to take note. With the A1s in production, Peppercorn, possibly encouraged by Windle, Cox, Harrison or Spencer, concluded that now was the time to test these roller bearings so that the benefits might be gauged.

In due course, roller bearings were introduced by Cox and team into BR's standard locomotive programme and were fitted to the coupled wheels of Class 5,6,7 and 8 engines. Due to cost considerations, they weren't fitted to the coupled wheels of the other classes, but were adapted for use in bogies, two wheeled trucks and tenders where necessary.

The first A1, No. 60114, made its public appearance at Doncaster in August 1948, but like the first A2 it attracted little attention outside the industry. The *Railway Magazine* probably best caught the flavour of this muted reporting in an understated article that appeared in December that year. The author simply outlined the A1s' links to *Great Northern* in 1922 and emphasized the evolutionary nature of Thompson's work on the same locomotive 23 years later. This was followed by a brief note describing the LNER's standardisation plan and the progress made on this project by Thompson and Peppercorn. When commenting on this new engine, and

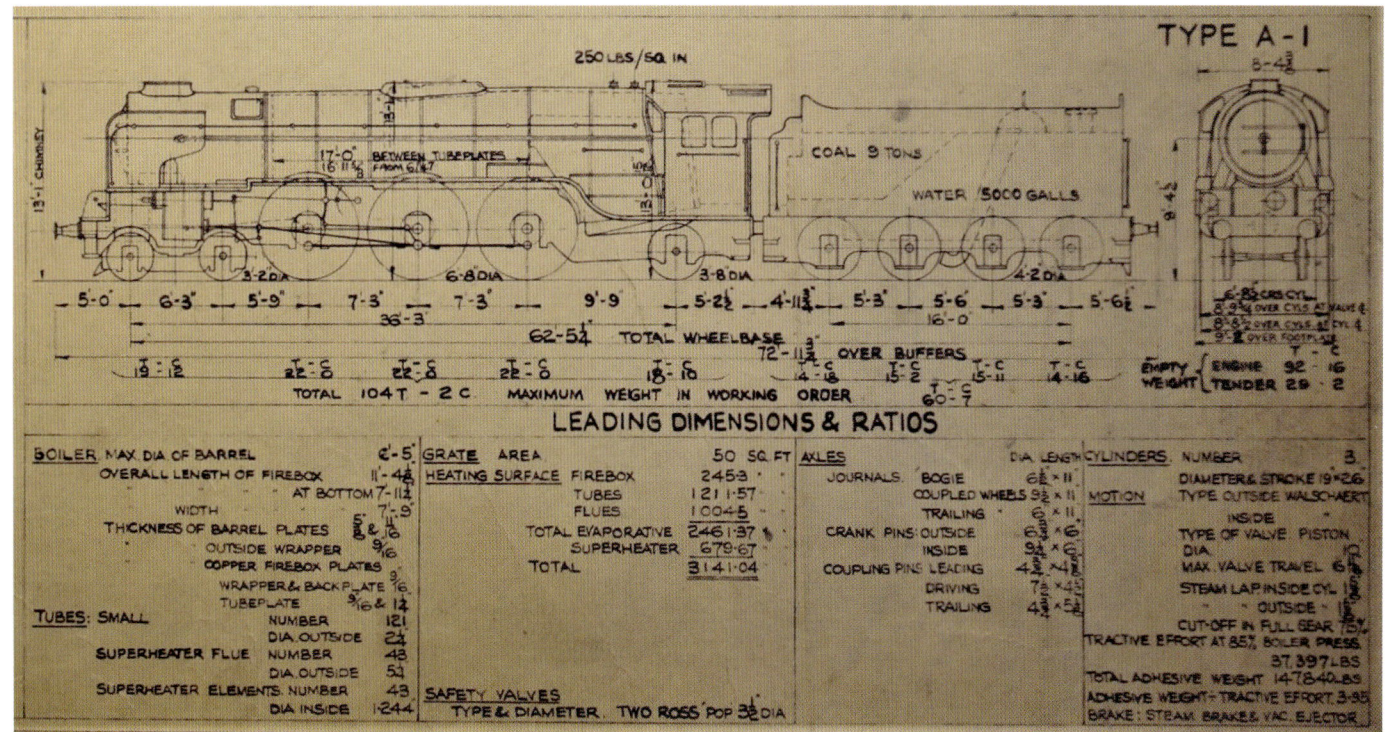

The A1 diagram. The first version is thought to have been produced in 1944, concurrently with plans for rebuilding *Great Northern*. In the intervening period the design underwent modification and this diagram is the result of all this work.

Engine No. 60114 following naming. William Allen was the Associated Society of Locomotive Engineers and Firemen's (ASLEF) General Secretary between 1940 and 1947 and had been a close associate of both Thompson and Peppercorn for many years. For his contribution to ASLEF and the war effort he was awarded a CBE in 1947 and was appointed to the Railway Executive at the same time. In due course, he would join the British Transport Commission as its Chief of Establishment. (*DN*)

the way in which ideas developed by the previous CME had been incorporated, he added:

> 'The latest Pacific is very similar to the prototype rebuild, *Great Northern*. In fact, the new A1s bear a strong resemblance to their mixed traffic counterparts... Unlike the A4s they will not be streamlined, the object being to facilitate maintenance and avoid impairing accessibility.'

At this stage, the A1's performance hadn't been assessed so a more complete review wasn't possible, but the feeling that this was just another steam locomotive hangs over the article. By comparison the LMS's new main line diesel was given very wide coverage and even ended up in newsreels to be shown in cinemas around the country, such was its impact.

When the first A1 was finally christened, there seems to have been even less interest, but the choice wasn't necessarily a headline grabber, as the *Locomotive Magazine* reported:

> 'On October 28th an interesting ceremony took place at King's Cross when Sir Eustace Missenden, Chairman of the Railway Executive, supported by General Sir William Slim, named No. 60114 *W.P. Allen*. Sir Eustace sketched the career of Mr Allen from engine cleaner at Hornsey to member of the Railway Executive, and said that the name was bestowed, not only as a tribute to Mr Allen, but also a token of appreciation of the workers in the various grades with which he had been associated [as a senior trades union official]. Mr Allen acknowledged the honour in a few well-chosen words. The proceedings closed when Mr Peppercorn presented a framed photograph of the engine to Mr Allen.'

Thompson and Peppercorn had forged a close working relationship with Allen during the war and there seems little doubt that the CME would have welcomed the opportunity to see him so honoured. Allen had been chiefly responsible for making sure disputes were settled quickly and worked hard with all the companies, but particularly the LNER, to ensure a maximum effort was exerted wherever possible. Naming a locomotive was a small price to pay for past cooperation, and potentially could help enlist the support of a man in a senior position in the new organisation when new ideas were being floated.

The first A1 was soon plying its trade from King's Cross, but in the first year of operation it spent more than ten weeks in the workshops at Doncaster undergoing repair for mostly 'non classified reasons'. Being the prototype probably meant that she attracted greater

BRITISH RAILWAYS, E. & N.E.R.
Pacific Locomotives

The illustration shows one of five Class "A1" Pacific Locomotives completely equipped with Timken tapered-roller-bearing axleboxes as follows:—

Bogie, intermediate driving and trailing coupled axles; cannon boxes. Leading driving crank axle; two independent axleboxes. Cartazzi-type trailing truck axleboxes. Tender: Dual race type axleboxes similar to those placed in service in 1937 on an A4 class Pacific tender.

TIMKEN Regd. Trade Mark: TIMKEN

tapered-roller-bearing axleboxes

BRITISH TIMKEN LIMITED, BIRMINGHAM, AND DUSTON NORTHAMPTON
Telephone: East 1321
Telegrams: Britimken, Birmingham
Subsidiary Company: Fischer Bearings Co. Ltd., Wolverhampton, makers of FBC ball and roller bearings and transmission equipment

Despite the lack of publicity for the new A1s advertisers were happy to use images of 60156 to advertise their products as demonstrated here. (*THG*)

attention and so underwent many adjustments and checks to see how each element of the design was operating. However, from their earliest months in service, concerns were expressed about the A1's riding qualities, which Peter Townend highlighted:

'It is fair to say that they were more sensitive to track conditions. The drivers complained bitterly about rough riding. I certainly recall two trips I made; the first to see for myself what one was like and I certainly got some hefty thumps in the ribs from the sill of the cab window as I sat in the fireman's seat. There was a characteristic sideways lurch at the rear end when running at speed. At the time we had twelve allocated along with 19 A4s and 11 A3s (at King's Cross). Many of the A1s were regularly manned for a time, but gradually most of the crews requested A4s, mainly because of this tendency to lurch at the cab end. Driver Hoole asked if he could change his A1 for an A4 as his mate had difficulty sometimes in getting the coal into the firehole door, but he emphasized that he had nothing against the locomotive himself, because in all other respects it was excellent and it did not worry him. Driver Arthur Davis had 60149 for many months and asked if I could stop his engine riding across the fields. He was not sure at times that it was on the rails at all.'

On the whole, these engines were happily received, which was just as well because by October 1949, all forty-nine were in service. Such a large number allowed them to be distributed around the network fairly generously. They could be found in their first few years of operation at King's Cross, Gateshead, Haymarket, York, Heaton, Grantham, Copley Hill and Doncaster sheds. Quite quickly, information relating to their performance was gathered, but by the time Peppercorn retired at the end of 1949 a complete analysis was awaited. However, such things as riding quality and steaming abilities were fairly clear, though cause, effect and solutions, where necessary, were still being considered. Earlier in the year, Peppercorn did commission a comparability study between the new A1s and A2s, but doesn't appear to have extended this work to include other Pacifics under his control. He didn't propose including any of them in the Rugby Test Centre programme either, which might have revealed much about the strength or weaknesses of their designs. Perhaps, he was just being circumspect, preferring to keep assessments in house for as long as possible and allow solutions to be found away from prying eyes.

Although the design and construction of the A1 and A2 Pacifics tends to be the way Peppercorn is remembered and assessed, there was much else of substance he dealt with. A great deal of this concerned the state of the workshops and the overall condition of the locomotives

When engine No. 60130 was rolled out at Darlington in September 1948 it was decided to photograph the engine with some of the men responsible for her construction. The engine wasn't named until July 1950 when becoming *Kestrel*. (*DN/RH*)

The A1s arrived thick and fast and, in due course, were soon seen in all parts of the network. From my view they were handsome from any angle. Engine No. 60156, *Great Central*, at rest, as is a member of her crew, with the double blastpipe clearly visible. Perhaps of greater significance were the Timken roller bearings with which this engine and four sisters were fitted. (*BET*)

Above – A gleaming 60133, *Pommern*, awaiting service on the 'North Briton' which was introduced in 1952 and ran from Glasgow to Leeds. Built in late 1948 the locomotive wasn't named until April 1950 and lasted in service until 1965. *(DN)*. Opposite – By 1948 the A2s were well established but experiencing steaming problems unlike their new sisters. Here engine No. 60533, *Happy Knight*, which entered traffic during April 1948, is seen pulling the down 'Yorkshire Pullman' on 29 July that year when based at Copley Hill, Leeds. *(DN)*

Locomotives always seem to look more powerful when photographed from a three-quarters astern position. This effect is caught well in this picture of 60124, *Kenilworth*, even though the engine is in quite shabby condition. Date and location are lost to time, but may have been taken near the end of the engine's life when based at Darlington from where she was sold for scrap and broken up by A. Draper of Hull in 1966. (*THG*)

and rolling stock in the wake of the war. A huge catch up programme, with limited resources, would help determine the success or otherwise of his time as CME. One of the key reasons he brought Harrison to Doncaster as his Assistant was to have an energetic, bustling and talented production manager beside him to oversee this work. It was a herculean task by any standards and any credit for success must go to him for this. However, there was one aspect of this task which continued to plague Peppercorn's time in office – a high number of serious railway accidents, which required his close attention.

Between June 1946, when he came to office, and his retirement on 31 December 1949, there were thirty-two in all – fifteen under the LNER and seventeen with BR in his region. It was an appalling record by any standards and many of these accidents reflected the dilapidated state of the railways. Against this, any new work on building locomotives pales into insignificance. For most of his time in office, Peppercorn was juggling an immense workload resulting from these accidents, with the need to assess the condition of locomotives and rolling stock being central to any debate that took place. Establishing whether mechanical failure, human error or simply bad luck played a part in an accident is a long and complex process, where any failures will be dealt with harshly. As CME, ultimate responsibility for the condition of rail vehicles rested on his shoulders so whilst some investigatory tasks might be delegated, accountability was his alone.

Although all thirty-two accidents were deemed serious enough to warrant Ministry of Transport investigation and public enquiries, there are five which stand out from the rest. These distressing events must have taxed Peppercorn to the limit, especially in such a short period of time. The first, at Gidea Park, on 2 January 1947, happened in dense fog when a passenger train on the 10.28 service from Liverpool Street to Peterborough, pulled by engine No.1602, a B17 4-6-0, crashed into the back of a Liverpool Street to Southend train, pulled by another 4-6-0 locomotive, Class B12 No. 1596, which was just leaving the station. The driver of the approaching train didn't slacken speed, was confused about the signals and received no warning from detonators that might have been placed on the track. So at 30-35mph, he drove into the back of the train in front shattering three carriages and only came to rest 120 yards beyond the point of collision. The station was partly demolished and seven were left dead with another forty-five injured.

The investigation that followed concluded that the cause was human error and made no criticism of either locomotive. However, the extent of the damage caused to the carriages, three of which were completely destroyed, underpinned the poor state of design. It was a long discussed issue within the LNER dating back to Gresley's time as Locomotive Superintendent of the Great Northern Railway. Even before the Great War, Edward Thompson,

The aftermath of the crash at Gidea Park on 2 January 1947. The clear up and investigation takes place. The fragility of the timber bodied carriages is only too apparent, even when strengthened with steel underframes. (*DN*)

when Carriage and Wagon Superintendent at Doncaster, had begun arguing in favour of stronger metal bodied designs, but despite improvements in the interim, wood continued to dominate in design. Could an all metal carriage have reduced the casualties at Gidea Park? With such a massive blow sustained in this collision it is impossible to say, but the force of the impact might have been better absorbed. It was an issue that the CME and his staff undoubtedly considered in some depth and would roll on into BR days.

Seven months later an even worse crash happened, this time at Balby Junction, just south of the workshops at Doncaster. On 11 August, V2 No. 936, pulling the 1.25pm from King's Cross to Leeds, crashed in to the back of the 1.10pm London to Leeds express, pulled by A3, No.50, *Persimmon*, at 40mph. The rear three carriages were crushed and split apart and other carriages were forced away sideways by the force of the impact. There were 18 fatalities and 118 injured, though not all were kept in hospital. The V2 was driven over on its side and her crew were amongst the injured. When the investigation team had finished their work, they decided that the fault lay with a signalman, who had 'improperly allowed the train to enter the occupied Balby Junction under clear signals'. Though the report contained a criticism of the long overdue modification of the signalling on this section of track, it did, at the same time, recognise that the coming of war had delayed such things. No fault was found with the V2 or its crew.

1947 proved to be an exceptionally bad year and by Christmas there had been two more fatal accidents. The first of these occurred at Burton Agnes in Yorkshire on 17 September. An Army truck containing a number of German Prisoners of War, crashed through closed crossing gates as a train was approaching. Unable to stop in time, the train wrote the lorry off and twelve men died; two NCOs and ten prisoners. But this was followed, on 26 October, by a crash at Goswick, Northumberland. Here the driver of the only locomotive involved, A3 Pacific No. 66, *Merry Hampton*, was solely to blame.

When in charge of a southbound express from Edinburgh to King's Cross, the driver missed signals and assumed he had the all clear, failed to slow down for a diversion and caused the locomotive and first eight carriages to derail. Elements of the train then rolled down

Opposite, above and right: Balby Junction disaster 11th August 1947. Being so close to the town centre and the railway workshops meant that emergency services and Peppercorn's specialists were soon on the scene to begin rescuing victims and clearing debris. Opposite – This is as Peppercorn would have seen the crash site. The V2 involved didn't have far to travel for examination and repair and is photographed at Doncaster on the 11th. Although severely damaged the engine was back in service at the beginning of October. (*DN/RH*)

Engine No. 66, *Merry Hampton,* which was derailed at Goswick on 26 October 1947, lies buried in a ditch beside the track almost fully covered with debris. This A3 Class locomotive had only recently been converted from a Gresley A1, reclassified under Thompson as an A10. By this stage most casualties had been removed and the slow process of assessing cause and raising the wreck has begun. The accident report made clear the extent of the damage caused and the driver's responsibility for the crash. The locomotive was deemed repairable and returned to traffic on 2 January 1948. (*DN*)

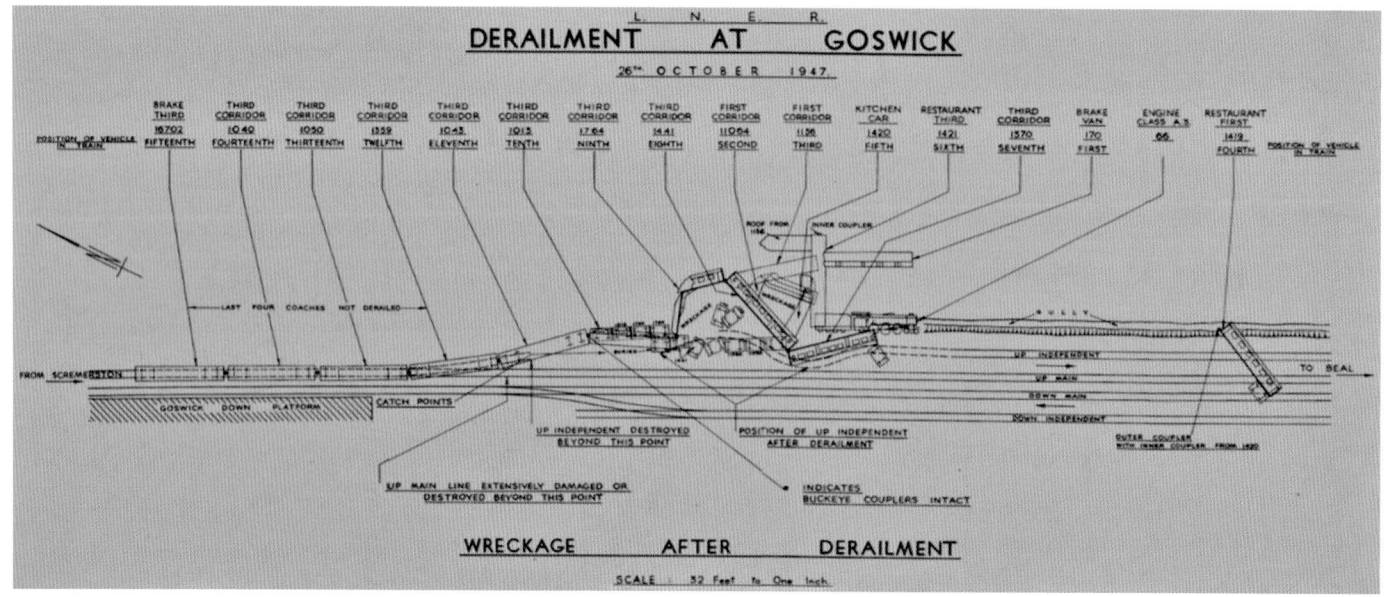

a bank into a ditch where the engine became firmly embedded. When all the casualties had been removed, it was found that twenty-eight were dead and many more seriously injured. In the investigation that followed, led by Colonel A.C. Trench and then Lt Col G.R.S. Wilson for Trench when he fell ill, condemned the actions of the driver, T. Begbie, with the words 'a grave breach of discipline' and did not 'exercise reasonable and proper caution'. In mitigation, Begbie hinted at problems with forward visibility caused by smoke and steam, suggesting a problem with the A3s' design. However, both Trench or Wilson did not find any defects with the locomotive or criticised its design. *Merry Hampton* was repaired at Doncaster and returned to work at the beginning of January the following year.

On 17 July 1948, Peppercorn and his team were again called into action when reports came in that one of Thompson's first Pacifics, now numbered 60508, *Duke of Rothesay*, had been involved in a serious accident near New Southgate at 6.00am when pulling the overnight express from Edinburgh. In the circumstances, the CME was recorded as travelling south to view the crash site himself, as he had at Goswick, Balby, Gidea Park, but not Burton Agnes where the cause of the accident was only too clear from the beginning. What he discovered in London was the engine over on its side some distance ahead of its eleven carriages, which were also derailed. With no obvious cause, attention focussed on the locomotive's condition and the crew's actions. An eye-witness, the driver on a passing parcels train, recorded seeing 'the express emerge from the south end of Barnet tunnel with sparks coming from the front bogie and as it passed small pieces of metal struck my engine'. Armed with this information, the investigation, led by Lt Colonel Wilson again, moved quickly to a detailed structural survey of the engine at King's Cross shed four days later, then at Darlington. With the engine stripped down Wilson and the CME's team could get to the root of any design problem or confirm poor standards of maintenance.

After a lengthy examination, Wilson confirmed that the engine's design was not a contributory factor and that the locomotive was in a good state of maintenance with no undue or excessive wear in any component. In fact, he described his analysis of all the wheels, leading and trailing trucks, axle bearings and springs in some detail as though some concerns over the design might have been expressed. If so, any criticism found a ready denial in his report, which simply stated that the design is 'suitable for main line duties'. Perhaps encouraged by someone in the LNER team he added 'the front bogie wheelbase is 6ft 3in with the long space of 8ft 2in between its trailing axle and leading coupled axle (reduced in later engines of the A2 Class)'. It was an addition that speaks volumes, suggesting, as it does, a depth of debate and the need for some self-justification in case there was any criticism. There was none forthcoming from Wilson.

Bad days have to be endured and during Peppercorn's time as CME there were many of them. With so many serious accidents, on average one every three weeks of his tenure, plus the weight of other problems in day to day running of his department, it was unavoidably so. Pressure from BR to conform to their new working model and fighting, with great integrity, to preserve jobs within his organisation in the face of wholesale change, would also have depleted his reserves of energy. So it is small wonder that as the end of 1949 approached he decided to pull stumps on a long career and make ready to depart for a well-earned retirement with his new wife. On marrying, she had been obliged to give up work, which was the custom at the time. It was a reflection of how far women's rights had to travel before true equality was reached, despite the best endeavours of her husband in championing their cause.

Bert Spencer caught a flavour of this time when he wrote that:

'Peppercorn seemed relieved to be retiring and had not been well for some time. However, this didn't stop him enjoying his food, a cigar and his last few months at work. He would often reminisce about our time together with Gresley and Thompson, the latter being an occasional and welcomed visitor to Doncaster especially when Pep retired.

'In 1946 and '47 Pep encouraged me to prepare a paper for the Institution of Locomotive Engineers describing all the engine development programmes undertaken by Gresley. This I did and towards the end of his time I suggested that I continue this exercise to include the years 1941 to '49. He laughed and said "No one will be interested. The war then nationalisation put paid to all our plans. It will all be diesels and electric trains from now on".

'When he went we wished him a long and happy retirement. Sadly, it wasn't to be.'

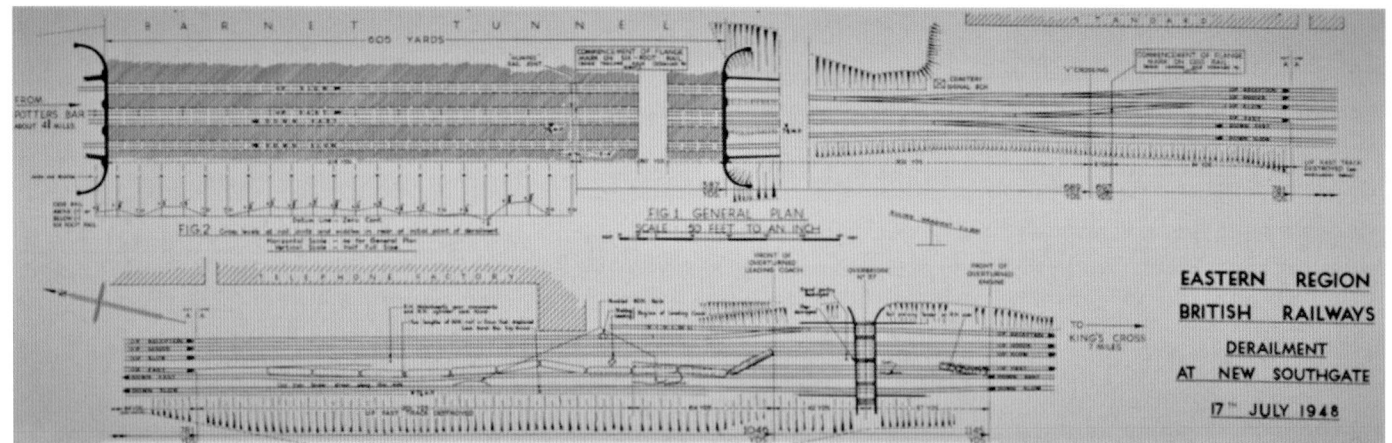

Above, left and opposite above: The accident at New Southgate, 7½ miles north of King's Cross, during the morning of 17 July 1948 as Peppercorn would have seen it later in the day and the official record of the crash site. (*DN/RH*)

Above and overleaf above: A huge part of any senior manager's work is to present a public face and be seen to lead and lead by example. Despite all other demands on a person's time and energy these requirements can never be ignored or delegated. This is particularly so in a large industrial concern undergoing huge change, as was the case during Peppercorn's time as Assistant to Thompson, then CME himself in those very difficult years between 1941 and 1949. When all his instincts shrieked 'get the workshops, locomotives and rolling stock operating effectively' he had to stand back and participate in a bigger political game. Here the ability to dodge, move smoothly through the upper echelons, make allies and play politics were all crucial, but distracting in the extreme. Peppercorn, despite a natural reserve and shyness, accomplished this with some skill, but the experience must have been draining. Here are just two examples of the many parties he had to entertain, placate, persuade, encourage or simply work with if his department was to achieve its goals. Above – Sir Eustace Missenden, front row fourth from the left, who visited the North Eastern Region at York to be briefed by Charles Hopkins, the Chief Regional Officer, front and centre and Peppercorn to his left. In the second photograph Peppercorn (second right) and Robert Smeddle (to the CME's left), Mechanical Engineer at Darlington, entertain a group of senior visitors, including Hopkins again (front row third from the right). In 1951, Smeddle became Mechanical and Electrical Engineer for the Western Region, so making him the second LNER man to go on to greater glory; John Harrison being the other. (*DN/RH*)

A fine end piece to mark Peppercorn's long career. Now in BR markings A2 Pacific No. 60528, *Tudor Minstrel*, seems to point the way to the future in a photograph that captures the power and elegance of the final two classes of LNER Pacifics. (*THG*)

CHAPTER 7

FINALE

When nearing the end of a working life, there is a tendency to look back and assess what happened and the part you played in key events. In Peppercorn's case, there was much to consider and much of which he could justifiably feel proud. However, many of his tasks would have been almost impossible to categorise or quantify because they simply involved managing an organisation in very complex and demanding circumstances. The only true measure of success in this situation would be that they kept going and kept the railways running despite the difficulties involved. But it was a time of attrition where a slow erosion of standards had set in. If the war hadn't ended when it did, the point of collapse might have been reached and become irreversible without a massive injection of capital and the restoration of a skilled workforce. Nevertheless, the damage it inflicted on the railways would take decades to overcome. Peppercorn managed his part in the restoration with great skill and dedication, as Thompson had done before him, despite stretched resources and pressure from all around him to succeed. In contrast, being allowed to develop new locomotives must have seemed a pleasant distraction from other more significant pressures he faced each day. However, it is by this work that he is probably best remembered.

In his last six months of service, there was probably an easing of pressure with BR now well into their stride and orchestrating all that happened. In Peppercorn's case, he also had John Harrison sitting at his elbow as Assistant CME, soon to become Mechanical and Electrical Engineer for the region. Although until 31 December 1949 Peppercorn was nominally in charge, the transfer of power would have been well under way by then. To be superseded is never easy but it is most likely that he would have managed it with good grace no matter what his true feelings were. Whatever he thought though, there must have been a sense of relief that the extreme burden he'd shouldered for so long was coming to an end.

By 1949, signs of ill-health had begun to appear, not helped by stress, being heavily overweight and being

Peppercorn's official retirement photograph published in 1949, though probably taken a few years earlier. By 1949, as other photographs reveal, the strain of leading his Department had taken a heavy toll and he looked much older than his years. (*PR*)

a smoker. Arteriosclerosis had been diagnosed by his doctor, H.F. Benton, and there were signs of myocardial degeneration. With treatment for such conditions still in an unrefined even crude state, with few if any drugs available, rest was the only real option and by doing this hope to avoid a heart attack. Perhaps, if he had retired years earlier and removed the primary cause of stress

King's Cross at the time of Peppercorn's retirement with BR's slow spreading influence gradually becoming more apparent with the change of insignia on tenders. Here a Gresley Pacific (name and number obscured) begins her journey northwards, whilst V2 No. 915 waits until given clearance to back down towards the station. (*RH*)

things might have been different. But he was of a generation that put personal issues and discomfort to one side if there was a battle to fight, and so he carried on well past a point of no return. According to his surviving relatives, he knew of his condition and realised the danger inherent in remaining, but wished to 'see out his time' as a nephew recalled him saying.

In his last six months of service he appears to have tied up some loose ends and enjoyed his hard-earned status in a modest way. During May he accepted an invitation from George Ivatt, son of his old mentor and a friend himself, to be a special guest on a run from Euston to Glasgow Central behind his twin main line diesels, Nos. 10000 and 10001 operating in tandem. The first of these had appeared at the same time as Peppercorn's A2 and garnered much wider publicity. This special was organised for 1 June to prove the diesels 'capable of sustained effort, with a load of 16 coaches weighing 506 tons and 520 loaded, over the West Coast main line'. Any engineer worth their salt would have been intrigued by the prospect of witnessing a new world unfold, even if they were steam exponents. Seeing into the future may carry traces of sadness over the passing of the old, but curiosity and professional instincts will always be aroused.

Peppercorn is recorded as having been present at an informal reception that evening presided over by

1 June 1949 and Ivatt's twin diesels pull away from Euston. A report appearing in the *Locomotive Magazine* a month later recorded that 'No attempt was made to attain exceptionally high speeds. Scheduled timings were adhered to, comparatively closely, throughout. Had circumstances permitted no difficulty would have been experienced in cutting the running time down by 80 or 90 minutes'. Despite such an advance, BR under Riddles and Cox didn't accelerate diesel production but instituted a major steam building programme instead, the benefits of which have long been debated and decried. (*DN*)

Riddles in Glasgow, and attended by Hawksworth from Swindon, Ivatt from Derby, but not Bulleid. According to Spencer 'Pep was on board the train and passed some of the journey in the leading cab'. Where, it is assumed, his instincts formed on many footplates since before the Great War were aroused. The contrast between steam and diesel was a stark one, with the challenge presented by an aging technology rendered obsolete by the ease of diesel power. Did Peppercorn observe this change with sadness or did he wish that he'd had the opportunity to develop a diesel or an electric locomotive himself? We shall never know, because he seems to have remained mute on the point. However, he must have seen the way the railways were moving, considered steam's demise and contemplated the possibilities presented by new technologies. But for the war he might have taken Raven and Gresley's electrification plans to a new level and been remembered for something more substantial than his Pacifics.

Nevertheless, during his time as CME he had achieved much in steam locomotive design and production, despite many restrictions. In no way could his contribution be compared to that of Gresley, but it was noteworthy nonetheless and also continued work begun by both his predecessors. Amongst other things, he took Thompson's B1, L1 and K1 programmes forward and brought the twenty-year saga of the A1/A10s' conversion to A3 standard, begun by Gresley, to a successful conclusion. His contribution to the LNER's standardisation plans was also important. With Thompson's departure, many of his ideas may have been left to die, but, apart from refining the Pacific design, Peppercorn changed very little. If the anti-Thompson feelings that prevailed in 1946 and 1947 were as deep as reported

The classic lines of a Peppercorn/Windle Pacific. A1 Pacific No. 60136, *Alcazar*, built at Darlington in late 1948, photographed at Barkston following a test run shortly after being named in December 1950. (*DN*)

by Harrison, there is every possibility that the ideas he championed would have been quietly dropped. They weren't and in 1949, Peppercorn and the General Manager authorised publication of an updated plan and an accompanying booklet. There was only one change from Thompson's time, the inclusion of the A2 in place of the A2/3. The rest remains the same. Perhaps, it was simply a case of 'what's the point of doing more, BR have taken over'. But this doesn't quite ring true because in each merged company strong views over the future prevailed and with it a determination to ensure their voices were heard when decisions were made.

As it was, some ideas developed or simply applied by the LNER did find their way into BR's plans, so their efforts were not wasted. And in Windle and Harrison's hands, holding senior rank in the new organisation, this influence was felt. Though, strangely, it was Thompson's preference for two cylinders, rather than Gresley's appetite for three, that held sway in BR's standard locomotive programme except in one case. A single prototype Class 8 Pacific, No. 71000, *Duke of Gloucester*, was built in 1954 with three cylinders, though didn't replicate Gresley's 2 to 1 valve gear but used modified sets of Caprotti valve gear instead. Although Riddles oversaw this development, Harrison is described as the 'major architect' of the project. If so, he seems to have tried to perpetuate the Gresley legacy, but the locomotive wasn't deemed a success and no more were built.

By the time Peppercorn called an end to his career he was lucky that so much that he had worked hard to achieve had reached fruition, although occasionally the degree of success may have been difficult to measure. He had survived and prospered and begun to restore the workshops, locomotives and rolling stock to their pre-war standard. At the same time, he had managed the increasing demands of industrial staff, who, after years of hardship and little influence wished for much more. But it was a difficult path to negotiate. The balance between capital and labour will always be so, especially in a country nearly bankrupted by war, where higher expectations struggled for acceptance. At the same time, he had overseen the beginning of a revolution in the employment of women. The need may have been forced on the railways by the exigencies of war, but he openly

At first glance these two Pacifics bear a strong resemblance, but the different style of smoke deflectors, the banjo dome on the locomotive in the foreground and the position of the outside cylinders give the game away. The evolutionary nature of Pacific design on the LNER through the reigns of Thompson and Peppercorn is only too apparent, with Edward Windle and David Gray providing continuity and being chiefly responsible for both designs. A2/3 Pacific No. 60512, *Steady Aim* and A1 Pacific No.60158, soon to be named *Aberdonian,* await their next turn of duty at King's Cross on 23 June 1950. (*DN*)

A1 Pacific No. 60121, *Silurian*, painted in BR blue livery, which she carried for nineteen months in 1950/51, is captured near Greenwood in June 1950. (*DN*)

embraced this change and sought to perpetuate equality when peace came, as far as he was allowed by the social restrictions of the age.

This forward view, and many others about conditions of employment, which Peppercorn shared with Thompson, were unusual for the time. It was a patriarchal society led by men born with the inbred certainty of the late Victorian age stitched into their DNA, with many wishing to perpetuate its stiflingly restrictive practices. It is interesting to note that those who had fought in the trenches and then rose to high rank were more likely to hold liberal views and sought to implement better working practices. Having suffered with their men under fire, and seen their many sacrifices, made them more sympathetic and supportive of these changes. The words 'a Band of Brothers' has often been used, but in this case it seems to be a true reflection of this altered reality. As veterans of war, Thompson and Peppercorn, judging by their actions, seem to have been imbued with this spirit and desire for greater fairness and democracy in the work place.

Yet, despite all his hard work and achievements, across a wide range of activities, it is Peppercorn's role in helping develop the LNER's Pacifics that still draws most attention. By the end of 1949, all the A1s and A2s were in service and their strengths and weaknesses were gradually being revealed. The report dated May 1949, which recorded the results of comparability trials between the two types on runs between King's Cross and Grantham, must have made interesting and satisfying reading as Peppercorn approached the end of his career. In addition, Robert Smeddle at Darlington, who took the lead in these trials, not Harrison at Doncaster, then set about reviewing the results of 1945 'standardisation' trials between A1/1, A2/1 and A4 Pacifics. In one final move, he then studied the results of the 1947 trials,

The last built A2 Pacific No. 60539, *Bronzino*, with an up express at Hadley Wood in June 1950. Although their riding and steaming qualities were criticised in certain quarters these engines could be relied upon to perform effectively, but generally not as well as the A1s. However, in this engine's case the fitting of a Kylchap double blastpipe and chimney is believed to have closed the gap somewhat. (*DN*)

which simply compared the A1/1 to an A4. From all this material he selected a range of data and presented Peppercorn with a summary on 19 August, almost as a valedictory to his time as CME.

Interestingly enough he didn't incorporate the results of the A2/1s, A2/2s and A2/3s in this short paper, but did include figures for a North Eastern Atlantic Class C6 and two Gresley A3s. The reasons for this aren't clear and Smeddle makes no reference to any debate that might have taken place beforehand. All he did in summary is let the figures speak for themselves and added:

'One very clear and satisfactory result is the ease with which both A1 and A2 locomotives worked the trains during the high power tests, proving their capacity to do so with increased economy in coal and water consumption. It will be noted that some high powers were developed and these are higher than any recorded during the Interchange Trials. It will be noted that further trials with an A4 type locomotive are suggested in order to provide additional comparable information which is now essential.'

No more work appears to have been done and the trials lapsed with Peppercorn's departure, presumably because Riddles and Cox would have seen no need to continue them. The absence of the A2/1s, A2/3s and the A1/1 is an interesting omission, especially as they had been part

A traditional and heartfelt goodbye to a much liked and respected colleague. The presentation of the obligatory retirement clock is greeted with the usual smiles at Doncaster, whilst a substantial radiogram provides something to lean on. John Harrison is master of ceremony with Luther Reeves beside him (front row second left), whilst the tall figure of Thomas Henry Turner, the Chief Chemist, towers over the group. (*DN*)

of the evolutionary process that resulted in Peppercorn's A1s and A2s. The reasons for this can only be guessed, but there is a suggestion that their performance, with Kylchap double blast pipes and chimneys, may have been equal to or better than the newer engines. If so, it might reflect adversely on the changes made whilst Peppercorn held office. Certainly the A1/1 and A2/1s had performed well when compared to the A4s during the 1945 trials. As regards the A2/3s, we shall never know. No official test data for them appears to have survived, so one can only speculate how they might have compared to the engines that succeeded them.

On 31 December Peppercorn retired. Such a popular man couldn't have just slipped away, no matter what his feelings might have been and his last few days were marked with celebrations attended by, amongst others, Edward Thompson. One evening, at a formal dinner, Peppercorn was presented with a model of his A2 Pacific No. 525, *A.H. Peppercorn*, which, as Harrison recalled, 'moved him deeply'. And with barely a ripple, as befitted this very private man, he was gone to a well-earned rest at 80 Cantley Lane in Doncaster, forty-four years after entering the works as an apprentice for the first time.

Sadly, he wasn't granted long to enjoy his retirement and his last months were dogged by ill-health. Nevertheless, he and his new wife were able to visit his old haunts around Hereford a number of times, benefit from fishing and an occasional cricket match as a spectator, a passion that had continued on from childhood. He also played the occasional round of golf, but becoming breathless and experienced chest pains, according to his family, which made these outings increasingly rare. Perhaps realising his days were numbered, he made out a new Will, which he signed on 11 November 1950, naming Florence Hebden and his solicitor, Maurice Pearson of Retford, as executors. In it, he made provision for his sisters Jane, Evelyn and Beatrice, adding the words 'no greater bequest than this as I have already helped them during my lifetime'. And apart from additional sums for his brother Charles and god daughter, Joy Atkins, the residue of his estate went to his wife. By this stage he had been predeceased by six of his siblings and would soon be followed by two more, Beatrice and Arthur.

On 3 March 1951 he suffered a heart attack and died suddenly at his home. His death was registered two days later by his brother-in-law, H.G. Lay, who travelled from St Neots to do so. He also oversaw the funeral arrangements which took place at St Wilfrid's Church in Doncaster. Here his remains were laid to

Peppercorn's house in Cantley Lane as it appears today and where he died. It seems to have been modified since he moved there in the early 1940s. His widow remained here for a short while and then remarried in July 1952. (*THG*)

Unlike Gresley's grave in Netherseal, Peppercorn's final resting place isn't graced with models of his steam locomotives. Nevertheless, he was a very worthy successor to his much admired leader and, arguably, a production engineer of far greater ability. (*THG*)

rest, a short walk from his home and a short drive from the Works, which he had graced for so long. Occasionally the sound of a distant steam locomotive working hard is still carried on the wind to his final resting place from the East Coast main line nearby, a tribute to him and the people determined to preserve this heritage.

As one would expect, his funeral, on 6 March, was well attended by family, friends and colleagues; Luther Reeves, John Harrison and Bert Spencer amongst them. It is believed that Edward Thompson journeyed north from his home in Sussex to be at the funeral, but this cannot be confirmed from the few surviving records. Alfred Ewer, District Motive Power Superintendent at Doncaster, was also amongst the mourners and later wrote:

'It was a very sad day but Pep would have been moved and probably surprised to see so many old friends gathered together to say farewell. I had come late to the LNER, but this made no difference to my feelings. In the two years before his retirement he had been a frequent and much welcomed guest in the sheds at Doncaster and Darlington, often with Bert Spencer in tow. His boyish delight at being so close to the engines was only too clear. He was a frequent presence on the footplate and had a natural affinity with the drivers and firemen, often handling the locomotives himself,

The varied and changing face of BR in the 1950s and '60s. The driver of A1 No. 60156, *Great Central*, has eased its speed in wet conditions, with a wartime Austerity 2-8-0 engine in the background and an LMS/Ivatt designed Class 4 2-6-0 sitting to its right. Post-nationalisation, eighty-seven of these engines were built at Doncaster and Darlington, taking up capacity in the workshops released by the completion of Peppercorn's A1 Pacifics. (*THG*)

though, towards the end he had to be helped up into the cab. He, quite naturally, had a preference for his A1 and A2 engines, but the other Pacifics received their fair share of his attention. When he died the footplate crew, without any encouragement, organised a collection for a wreath. Despite his seniority he was greatly respected and greatly liked. It was obvious that he had the common touch of truly great leaders.'

Several short obituaries appeared in the press, but these didn't contain the outpouring of sentiment and accolades that had accompanied Gresley's death ten years earlier. This isn't surprising, though. Gresley's work and achievements had a very public face and attracted huge publicity in the process. In fact, it was left to Edward Thompson to provide the most moving memorial to his old friend and colleague when he wrote a short appreciation that was subsequently published in the *Railway Gazette*:

'Arthur Henry Peppercorn was the last CME of the London and North Eastern Railway. From the time he started on the old Great Northern Railway to the time he set active work aside he had all the share of affection of those with whom he came into contact. Ever ready to help, ever ready to take responsibility, full of the lore of his great teacher, Herbert Nigel Gresley, invaluable in those so difficult and arduous days of war, Peppercorn rose to the highest position of his department and has surely left an indelible mark on British Railways.'

The *Gazette* supplemented Thompson's words with a brief editorial:

'His death robs the railway mechanical engineering world of a loveable personality. He was appointed to the premier position in his profession on the LNER not only in the still abnormal conditions of war, but also when the great upheaval of nationalisation was impending. Even so, Peppercorn was able to develop the ideas in locomotive design of Gresley and his successor, Mr Edward Thompson. It was his fate, however, to be in command in an abnormal and transitional era, so that his scope was much restricted; but the proof of his efficiency is the work performed in difficult conditions of maintenance by the motive power in his charge, and the remarkably good condition – again in the most difficult circumstances – of the locomotives and rolling stock which he handed over to the nationalised railway system.'

Luther Reeves added to this in a short article he prepared for the *Engineer* magazine and the IMechE journal:

'Mr Peppercorn was awarded the OBE in the King's Birthday Honours list in 1945, and visited the United States as a member of a mission from British railways in the same year. He was appointed Chief Mechanical Engineer of the LNER in 1946, a position he held through the difficult years immediately preceding and subsequent to nationalisation, until his retirement. He was responsible for the A1 Class locomotive, the first of which bears his name [in fact it was the first A2]. This was the last locomotive to be built by the LNER. His untimely death after a short retirement came as a shock to a large circle of colleagues and friends to whom he had endeared himself over a long period of years and through a long and varied career.'

At best these were modest accounts of a distinguished life and hardly likely to set in stone his work or his memory. In many ways, it fell to Peppercorn's widow, Dorothy, until her death in 2015, to remind the world of her husband's considerable achievements, her efforts receiving wider coverage in the wake of the decision to build a new A1 Pacific, No. 60163, *Tornado*, all the others having been scrapped by BR in the 1960s.

So, where does Peppercorn stand in railway history and what did he contribute, in his long career, of lasting impact? Earlier in this book I surmised that much of what he did was of extreme importance but almost impossible to measure. When the baseline is survival little else matters than continuing to fight and meet whatever comes your way head-on. And this he did, with great success, throughout his career. Yet as a designer of locomotives or rolling stock he seems to have been regarded as a promoter by members of his team and not an active player. So is it not surprising that each brief obituary barely mentioned this aspect of his work?

The words were kind and conventional but, apart from Thompson's memoriam, they conveyed little about the man or his achievements. This left me wondering if, when it came to design, that to some he was a blank canvas on which they could paint their own pictures. Thompson has been criticised for his ideas on design and his motivation for implementing change, but at least his creative efforts were recognised, but for Peppercorn there seems to be nothing.

In truth, neither controlled their own destiny or had the design skills bred into them at an early age, as would a draughtsman. Production engineering and railway operations were really their forte, which meant that both had to rely heavily on their designers for guidance. The Pacifics may be remembered as Thompson or Peppercorn locomotives, but they were really developed in the capable hands of the Chief Draughtsmen and their staff. A CME may express an opinion, set out a specification, nibble around the edges of a design and approve the final product, but it was drawing office staff who provided the fine detail and where the ultimate shape of a locomotive was determined. This meant that Edward Windle, David Gray and their like were probably the key players, providing continuity through the periodic changes of CME, from Gresley to Peppercorn. They then advised and directed their leaders accordingly, though in Gresley's case this was probably less pronounced, he being a designer of note himself.

In describing the nature of locomotive design during each CME's reign two names continually surface – Bert Spencer and Edward Windle. Both, by all accounts, were retiring individuals who preferred to remain in the shadows of the great and good. Nevertheless, they were talented designers and served their masters with dedication and great insight. Spencer's work with Gresley is well known, less so his contribution to Thompson and Peppercorn's work, which was also important. But it is Windle who seems to have escaped the historians' gaze. Yet from the 1930s through to the 1950s, his influence on design within the LNER and then BR was considerable, as Ernest Cox told me in a letter:

'He was a small but active man who reigned over the drawing office with a firm hand and did not tolerate outside interference in the work he or they did. In this he was ably assisted by David Gray. They both came to prominence under Gresley and served Thompson and

Even at the end of her life, engine A1 No. 60155, *Borderer* still looked a thoroughbred, especially when given a clean, which by 1964 was rare given the shortage of employees available to do such work. When this photograph was taken the engine was based at York and would soon be condemned. (*October 1965*) (*THG*)

Illustrated here - Three evolving solutions to an old problem – how to get the most from a steam locomotive. Thompson and Peppercorn built on Gresley's work and tried various ways of improving the basic concept. But, inevitably, it was the Chief Draughtsman and his staff who determined the results and incorporated ideas that had gradually become common currency in their industry. (Lower picture on the adjoining page) Gresley's ideas as personified by his Class A3s. Engine No. 2508, *Brown Jack*, as it appeared when built at Doncaster in 1935. By this stage Edward Windle dominated the drawing office and strongly influenced engine design. (Above) Thompson takes a hand and the A2/3s are born, with Peppercorn's assistance, but once again with Windle at the helm. Here engine No. 60519, *Honeyway*, completed in February 1947 with early BR crest, awaits her next turn of duty. (*RH*)

Nearly the final form. Class A2 No. 60534, *Irish Elegance*, completed at Doncaster in April 1948 and scrapped in 1964. (*THG*)

Peppercorn with equal skill. Windle and Thompson were similar in personality and both enjoyed a good fight, but the CME always demurred to his Chief Draughtsman. Peppercorn played a stealthier game, but did not get the better of him either and his ideas tended to be implemented. Later on Windle was just as robust when assisting in the design of BR's standard engines. I do not think that he was a great admirer of three cylinder engines, particularly with Gresley's 2 to 1 gear, despite their preponderance in the LNER. He seemed much happier with the direction Riddles took BR with a preference for two-cylinder engines.'

So, were the last two CMEs blank canvasses on which Windle and Gray painted their pictures? Not entirely, or so it seems, because they approved the final drawings and any changes made to them, but it seems likely neither would have had the time or the finely tuned skills to do more. If this is true, the locomotives weren't Thompson's or Peppercorn's but Windle's and Gray's, which probably means that there wasn't a clear division between each post-Gresley Pacific as many would prefer, but a gradual and connected evolution, with different ideas being tried and tested. However, this is only one aspect of a CME's work, there was much else to consider when judging their careers and contributions as a whole.

During their time in office, Thompson and Peppercorn had to manage problems of immense complexity in almost impossible conditions. It was here that their exceptional skills as engineers came to the fore. Both understood the nature of workshop tasks and how to review and improve efficiency and output. In doing this, they had to cope with the loss of staff and reducing skill levels, as men went off to fight, a heavy overuse of their locomotive and rolling stock fleet and the deterioration in condition this caused. And on top of this, there were the many additional production tasks laid on them by a War Office desperate to extract every last drop of industrial effort from any workshop in the country. Their task was immense and the shredding effects of stress must have been overpowering at times. In truth,

The sad cycle of great engineering endeavour was played out in workshops and scrapyards during the 1950s and '60s. All things must pass and by the mid-1960s Gresley, Thompson and Peppercorn's engines were on their way to the smelters for re-cycling. Some phoenixes did rise from the ashes to grace our modern world, but so much more could have been preserved. A2 Pacific No. 60528, *Tudor Minstrel* survived longer than most and didn't succumb until June 1966. Being a Scottish based engine from 1949 to 1966 probably gave her a longer life than her sisters. Here she is captured apparently having been stripped for spares, yet still has a tender full of coal. This engine was cut up by J. MacWilliam of Shettleston, in Glasgow's east end, later that year. (*THG*)

it is amazing that either man survived into retirement. Nevertheless, these profound experiences undoubtedly affected their physical and mental health, with both suffering from serious heart conditions following years of extreme pressure and worry.

In the final analysis, Peppercorn's many strengths are only too clear – a talented production engineer, an exemplary manager of people and resources, a diplomat with a strong political sense, a man of honour and integrity, and a man who knew when to delegate and then manage the result with perception and good sense. When assessing how he used these skills to influence events, I believe it was as a facilitator rather than initiator that he showed his true worth. I believe both roles are crucial, especially in such a large industrial organisation. He could see, as good facilitators do, a much bigger picture of need and available resources to meet them.

He seems to have had a sharp analytical mind which allowed him to stand back, observe, plan and shape his response to best meet the circumstances that prevailed.

Then, with a gift for organisation and efficiency, he brought order where chaos might easily have reigned. His lightness of touch and perception when dealing with people, also allowed him to select the right staff to fill crucial positions then get the best out of them. It was something that Thompson never quite managed and even Gresley, who would often drive not lead, as some contemporary accounts suggest, lacked Peppercorn's sure touch. However, Peppercorn could be just as tough and robust when the need arose and during his time as Assistant CME, then CME, this probably became more frequent as the pressures grew.

Locomotive design, although important, was not his true legacy, though the A1s and A2s were fine machines. It was his unerring ability to manage a complex organisation, in the most difficult circumstances imaginable, that stands the test of time. This he did without thought for his own wellbeing or comfort. He was indeed a man for all seasons and one who deserves to be revered and remembered for all time.

Timken's published a book in the early 1950s which set out the work they were doing with roller bearings and their application to locomotives. As artwork they used this stunning picture of a Peppercorn Pacific, which makes a fine end piece to this book. (*THG*)

REFERENCES AND SOURCES

The National Railway Museum (Search Engine)
Records Consulted
Corr/LNER/1 to 6.
Calc/LNER/1.
Loco/LNER/1 to 9.
Spec/Don/7.
Spec/LNER/1 to 7.
Test/LNER/1 to 10.
The E.S. Cox Collection.
The R. Riddles Collection (donated by author).
The Immingham Collection (donated by author).
The E. Thompson Collection.

Other Collections
The Imperial War Museum library.
The Churchill Archive in Cambridge.
Museum of Science and Industry, Manchester.
The National Archives (Discovery).
Science Museum, London.
Institution of Mechanical Engineers, London.
R.A. Hillier.
J. Constantine.
W.O. Bentley.
D. Neal.
T.F. Coleman/M. Lemon.
B. Spencer.
R.A. Thom.
N. Newsome.
R.H.N. Hardy.
A. Ewer.

Publications
IMechE/ILocoE Journals
The *Engineer*
The *Gazette* (various dates)
The *Meccano Magazine*
Steam World

Books
Allen and Bursley, *Heat Engines*, McGraw-Hill 1941
Bannister, E., *Trained by Sir Nigel Gresley*, Dalesman 1984
Bentley, W.O., *W.O.*, Hutchinson 1958
Bond, R., *A Lifetime with Locomotives*, Goose and Son 1975
Brown, E.A.S., *From Stirling to Gresley*, Oxford Publishing 1975
Brown, E.A.S., *Nigel Gresley. Locomotive Engineer*, Ian Allan 1961
Bulleid, H.A.V., *Master Builders of Steam*, Ian Allan 1963
Bulleid, H.A.V., *Bulleid of the Southern*, Littlehampton 1977
Bush, D.J., *The Streamlined Decade*, Brazillier 1975
Coster, P., *Book of the A3 Pacifics*, Irwell Press 2003
Coster, P., *Book of the A4 Pacifics*, Irwell Press 2005
Coster, P., *Book of the V2 2-6-2s*, Irwell Press 2008
Cox, E.S., *Locomotive Panorama Vols 1 and 2*, Ian Allan 1965/66
Cox, E.S., *Chronicles of Locomotives*, Ian Allan 1967
Cox, E.S., *Speaking of Steam*, Ian Allan 1971
Crump, N., *By Rail to Victory – The LNER in Wartime*, LNER 1947
Dalby, W.E., *The Balancing of Engines*, Arnold 1920
Dalby, W.E., *British Railways: Some Facts and A Few Problems*, IMechE 1910
Dow, G., *British Steam Horses*, Phoenix House 1950
Grafton, P., *Edward Thompson of the LNER*, Kestrel/Oakwood 1971 & 2007
Hardy, R.H.N., *Steam in the Blood*, Ian Allan 1971
Haresnape, B., *Gresley's Locomotives*, Ian Allan 1981
Holcroft, H., *Locomotive Adventure Vols 1 and 2*, Ian Allan 1962
Hughes, Geoffrey, *Sir Nigel Gresley*, Oakwood 2001
Martin, Kingsley, *Father Figures*, Hutchinson 1966
Nock, O.S., *Locomotives of Sir Nigel Gresley*, Railway Publishing Company 1945
Pope, A., *Wind Tunnel Testing*, Wiley 1947
RCTS *Locomotives of the LNER – Vols 2A & 6B*, RCTS 1973 & 1983
Rogers, H.C.B., *The Last Steam Locomotive Engineer*, Allen and Unwin 1970
Rogers, H.C.B., *Thompson & Peppercorn. Locomotive Engineers*, Ian Allan 1979
Simmons, J., *The Victorian Railway*, Thames and Hudson 1995
Taylor, A.J.P., *War by Timetable*, Penguin 1969

Tomlinson, H., *Hereford Cathedral School*, Logaston Press 2018

Townend, P.N., *East Coast Pacifics at Work*, Littlehampton 1982

Yeadon, W.B., *Yeadon's Registers – Nos 1,2,3,4,5,8,9,10 and 25*, BLR various dates

Photographic Sources/Credits

B. Spencer (BS), R. Hillier (RH), T. Coleman (TC/ML), Author (THG), H.A.V. Bulleid (HB), LNER Journal (LJ), LNER PR (PR), A. Ewer (AE), J. Constantine (JC), R. Thom (RT), D. Neal (DN), N. Newsome (NN), E. Thompson (ET), Watts Family (WF), W.O. Bentley (WB) and BR PR (BR).

Copyright is a complex issue and often difficult to establish, especially when a photograph or document exists in a number of public and private collections. Strenuous efforts have been made ensure to each item is correctly attributed, but no process is flawless, especially when many of these items are more than 70 years old with photographers or authors long gone. If an error has been made, it was unintentional. If any reader wishes to affirm copyright, please contact the publishers and an acknowledgement will be included in any future edition of this book, should a claim be proven. We apologise in advance for any mistakes. A number of documents held by the NRM have been quoted in this book. My thanks to the museum for permission to do this.

INDEX

Adams, William – 35.
Allen, Cecil – 42, 43.
Allen, William P – 224.
Allen, Jack – 107.
American Locomotive Works, Lima – 185.
Anderson, Alan – 143.
Ardsley Loco Depot – 61-64, 81.

Balby Junction Accident – 232, 233, 235.
Baldwins of Philadelphia – 185.
Baltimore and Ohio Railroad – 185, 186.
Barnham Accident – 153.
Barrington-Ward, Victor – 169.
Bazin, John – 61.
Beevor, Miles – 200, 204.
Begbie, T Driver – 235.
Bentley, Walter – 19, 25-29, 32, 50, 57, 59, 60.
Benton, H F (Doctor) – 239.
Bevin, Ernest – 147.
Beyer Peacock – 105.
Blades, Fireman – 103.
Blair, James – 195, 196.
Bingham, Colonel (US Army) – 152.
Bird, George – 37, 43, 53.
Bird, Charles – 219.
Board of Trade – 15, 57.
Bond, Roland – 218-220.
Bowen-Cooke, Charles – 25, 53.
Brampton Barracks – 7, 73.
Brown's Hotel – 95-97.
Bryant and May – 15.
Budd Company – 185.
Bulleid, H A V – 41, 82, 93, 94.
Bulleid (Ivatt), Marjorie – 28, 94.
Bulleid, O V S - 11, 28, 32, 52, 54, 58, 65, 80, 82, 84, 85, 86, 93, 94, 100, 103, 114, 119, 127, 132, 147, 164, 219, 221, 241.
Burton Agnes Accident – 233.
Bury, Oliver – 39.

Calder, James – 92.
Caldwell, Jimmy – 216, 218.
Cambridge University – 19, 21, 24.

Cameron, Tom – 159, 219.
Carr, Frank W – 119, 194.
Chesapeake and Ohio Railroad – 185.
Classes – A1(A10)/A3 (4-6-2) – 99, 101-107, 136, 138-143, 160, 161, 166, 171, 177-179, 192, 199, 200, 202, 206, 232, 234, 241, 245.
  A1 (Raven 4-6-2) – 101, 104.
  A1 (Peppercorn 4-6-2) – 198, 202, 207, 219, 221-228, 242, 243, 248, 253.
  A1/1 (Thompson 4-6-2) – 168-174, 177, 200, 202, 204, 209, 223, 244, 245.
  A2 (Peppercorn 4-6-2) – 156, 198, 202-206, 209-212, 218-225, 235, 238, 240, 246, 248, 253.
  A2/1 (4-6-2) – 148, 156, 161, 167, 168, 170, 173, 177, 244, 245.
  A2/2 (4-6-2) – 161, 162, 166-168, 171, 201, 235.
  A2/3 (4-6-2) – 156, 172-174, 177, 193, 195, 198, 199, 202, 203, 206, 207, 242, 243, 245.
  A4 (4-6-2) – 6, 89, 101, 119-122, 130, 131, 133-135, 141, 148, 149, 157, 158, 168, 169, 171, 173, 175, 195, 200, 213, 214, 222, 244, 246.
  Baldwin 2-6-0 – 62, 63.
  Big Boy 4-8-8-4 – 183.
  BR 8P (4-6-2) – 242.
  B1(4-6-0) – 177, 179, 197, 201, 209, 214, 241.
  B12 (4-6-0) – 116, 231.
  B17 (4-6-0) – 105, 107, 120-126, 141, 231.
  Caledonian 903 (4-6-0) – 53.
  C1/C2 (4-4-2) – 36-40.
  D1/D2/D3 (4-4-0) – 36, 81, 83, 92.
  D14/D15/D16 (4-4-0) – 115.
  D49 (4-4-0) – 105, 106.
  E1/E2 (2-4-0) – 36, 56, 81.
  8F (2-8-0) – 160.
  F2 (0-4-2) – 60.
  GWR 'Great Bear' (4-6-2) – 42, 43.
  GWR 'Saint' (4-6-0) – 42.
  Hudson (4-6-4) – 187.
  H1/H2(K1)/H3 (K2) (2-6-0) – 63, 64, 66.
  H4 (K3) (2-6-0) – 66, 68, 98, 100, 105, 141.
  J (0-6-0) – 60.
  J4 (0-6-0) – 81.

J7 (0-6-0) – 81.
J11 (0-6-0) – 177.
J13 (0-6-0) – 36.
J21 (0-6-0) – 46, 47.
J22 (0-6-0) – 46, 48, 80.
J23 (J50/J51) (0-6-0) – 66.
J38/J39 (0-6-0) – 105, 106, 143.
J50 (0-6-0) – 177.
K1 (GNR 0-8-0) – 43-45, 60.
K1 (2-6-0) – 177, 241.
K4 (2-6-0) – 120, 139, 141-143.
L1 (0-8-2) – 44, 45, 60, 66, 177, 180, 241.
Leader (0-6-0+0-6-0) – 132.
LMS 10000/10001 – 240, 241.
Merchant Navy (4-6-2) – 132, 147, 213.
Niagara 4-8-4 – 184, 223.
N1/N2 (0-6-2) – 45-47, 98, 99, 128, 143.
O1 (2-8-0) – 64, 177, 213-215.
O2 (2-8-0) – 64, 65, 99, 100, 105.
Pioneer – 185.
P1 (2-8-2) – 104, 105.
P2 (2-8-2) – 120, 129, 136, 143, 147, 149150, 158, 159, 161, 162, 165-167, 173, 176, 177, 185, 192, 199, 200, 202-204.
Precursor (4-4-0) – 53-55.
Princess Coronation (4-6-2) – 202, 213.
Princess Royal (4-6-2) – 166, 201.
Q1 (0-8-0) – 177.
Selkirk 2-10-4 – 182, 188.
Royal Scot (4-6-0) – 213.
Turbomotive (4-6-2) – 110.
T1 (4-4-4-4) – 186, 188, 189.
U1 (2-8-0+0-8-2) – 105.
V1/V3 (2-6-2) – 110, 120.
V2 – 138-141, 143, 160, 161, 166, 167, 232, 233.
W1 (4-6-4) – 108-110, 134.
Zephyr – 185.
Churchward, George – 33, 42, 64.
Coburg Court Hotel – 112, 120.
Cocks, Clifford – 216, 218.
Coleman Tom – 160, 202.
Coltrane, T H Lt Col – 69.
Colwick Loco Depot – 55, 56, 58-61, 81.
Cox, Ernest – 158, 180, 181, 184, 186, 191, 197, 215, 216, 222, 246, 249, 250.
Craster, S J Colonel – 74.
Creasor, Mary – 84.
Crump, Norman – 155.

Darlington Works – 109, 110, 120, 137, 139, 145, 147, 155, 156, 160, 180, 221, 235, 243.
Day, F – 166.
Day Lewis, Sean – 94.
Davis, Arthur Driver – 226.
Dean, Albert – 185.
Dennis, Olive – 185, 186.
Dreyfus, Henry – 185, 187.
Doncaster Technical College – 29, 43, 52, 60.
Doncaster Works – 19, 26-31, 35, 43, 46, 56, 57, 60, 80, 82-87, 93, 102, 110, 113, 120, 137, 139, 145, 147, 148, 151, 155, 156, 160, 186, 194, 197, 198, 200, 210, 211, 214, 218, 219, 221, 224, 230, 233, 235, 243.
Dow, George – 134, 135.
Durban, Wilfred – 216.

East Anglian – 121-125.
Elwell, Cyril – 150, 158.
Elwess, William – 30, 61, 165.
Ewer, Alfred – 247, 248.

Fleetwood, Frederick – 30.
Ford, Henry – 51.
Fryer, Driver – 124.
Furber, John & Emma – 95.
FW8 (Directorate of Fortifications) – 74-78.

Geddes, Eric – 75, 91.
General Strike 1926 – 84, 110.
Gidea Park Accident – 231, 232, 235.
Gilbreth, Frank – 137.
Glaze, Charles – 111.
Goswick Accident – 232-235.
Grantham Accident – 30, 32.
Gray, David Dickson – 161, 162, 165, 166, 175, 177, 199, 201, 202, 243, 249, 252.
Gresley, Herbert Nigel – 9-14, 21, 28-30, 40, 42, 49, 52, 60, 63, 64-66, 79-88, 91-93, 97-104, 108-110, 113-116, 120, 126, 129, 131, 132, 139, 140, 143, 145, 146, 150, 158, 161, 163, 165, 168, 169, 171, 173, 177, 182, 183, 186, 187, 194, 196, 198, 201, 203, 206, 221, 231, 235, 242, 248, 249, 253.
Gresley, Marjorie – 108.
Gresley, Violet – 108.
Groom, Isaac – 119.

Hardy, Richard – 7, 168.
Harper, H – 180, 181, 194.

Harrison, John – 57, 194, 196-199, 202, 214, 222, 230, 239, 242, 243, 247.
Hart-Davies, Roy – 192-194, 196.
Hawksworth, Frederick – 127, 132, 219, 221, 241.
Hawthorn, Leslie – 98.
Hazeldene, Fireman – 107.
Hereford Cathedral School – 19-21, 72, 83.
Hinkley Locomotive Works (Boston) – 35.
Holcroft, Harold – 99.
Holden, Stephen – 116.
Hopkins, Charles – 219.
Hudswell Clarke – 73.

ILocoE – 99, 109, 163, 196, 222, 235.
IMechE – 31, 33, 55, 60, 69, 114, 120.
Inglis, Robeet – 147, 159.
Interchange Trials 1948 – 212, 213, 217.
Ivatt, Henry Alfred – 25, 30, 33, 34, 37, 38, 40-42, 45, 48, 51, 53-55, 57, 59, 64, 66.
Ivatt, Henry George – 54, 127, 240, 241.

Jarvis, Ron – 216, 218.
Jenkins-Jones, C M – 116.

King, Stanley – 193.

Leather, Frederick – 147.
Lloyd, Roger – 134.
Lyttleton, Oliver – 147.

Mace, Driver – 125.
Marlborough School – 23.
Marsh, Douglas – 38, 40, 45.
Martin, Kingsley – 23, 24.
Mather (Louch, Peppercorn), Dorothy (Pat) – 7, 147.
Matthews, Ronald – 156, 200, 207, 210, 211.
Maudlin, H H – 124.
Middleton St George – 137, 138.
Mills, George – 116, 141, 147, 159.
Missenden, Eustace – 224.
Mitchell, R J – 50.
Musgrave, George – 117, 168, 171, 180.

Newark Loco Depot – 82.
New England Loco Depot – 67, 69.
New Southgate Accident – 235-237.

Newton, Charles – 115, 116, 121, 124, 136, 146, 149, 157, 175, 176, 200, 204.
New York Central Railroad – 185.
North British – 65, 201.

Oakes, R Lt Col – 74.
Oxford University – 21.

Pennsylvania Railroad – 43, 185, 186.
Peppercorn (Watts), Agnes – 15-18, 48, 84, 120.
Peppercorn, Alfred – 15-19, 46, 47, 49.
Peppercorn (Furber), Florence – 95, 97, 112, 120.
Peppercorn, William – 15.
Peterborough – 70, 71.
Pettigrew, F W – 60.
Pibworth, Albert – 103.

Ragg, Henry Murray – 21-23.
Railway Act 1921 – 91.
Railway Executive Committee – 147, 200.
Railway Inspectorate – 15.
Railway & Road Training Centre (Longmoor/Borden) – 72, 73.
Ransome-Wallis, Patrick – 139.
Raven, Vincent – 69, 87, 104, 165.
Reed, Brian – 199.
Reeves, Luther – 145, 156, 195, 245, 247, 249.
Retford Loco Depot – 81-83.
Richards, Henry – 132, 146, 180, 197, 221.
Riddles, Robert – 179, 215, 219-222, 242, 246.
Robertson, Ken – 193, 194.
Rogers, H C B – 57, 113, 175, 179, 199, 202, 220.
Royal Engineers – 55, 68, 71, 72, 192.

Sanders, T H – 163.
Scholes, Gilbert – 216, 218.
Sherburn, Ann & Emma – 84.
Smeddle, Robert – 243, 245.
Smith, Walter – 42, 43.
Spencer, Bert – 11, 43, 52, 65, 95, 99, 100, 102, 108-110, 114, 131, 136, 139, 143, 158, 165, 167, 172, 173, 185, 186, 188, 194-199, 203, 205-207, 209, 212, 213, 214, 215, 218, 235, 241, 247, 249.
Stamer, Arthur – 11, 111, 112, 145.
Stanier, William – 60, 110, 158, 202, 220, 223.
Stirling, Patrick – 19, 33, 59, 60.

St Luke's Church, Stoke Prior – 14, 16, 17, 49.
St Mary's Barracks – 72.
Stratford Works – 111-116, 119, 120, 194.
Street, Tom – 11, 132, 146, 164.
Strong, George – 35.
Sturrock, Archibald – 44, 59, 60.
St Wilfrid's Church, Doncaster – 246, 247.
Symes, Barney – 199.

Talbot, Ralph – 32, 51.
Taylor, A J P – 68.
Thom, Robert A – 11, 103, 112, 119, 135, 136, 164, 194, 196.
Thom, Robert – 192, 194.
Thompson, Edward – 11, 12, 21, 60, 62, 69, 82, 84, 85, 87, 89, 92, 95, 99, 102, 103, 107, 110, 113, 114, 116, 126, 135, 136, 137, 145-150, 152, 156, 158, 161, 164, 166-171, 172, 174, 175, 177, 179, 185, 191, 193, 196, 197, 201, 202, 204, 206, 209, 223, 224, 231, 234, 241, 242, 243, 246-249, 251, 252, 253.
Timkens – 223, 225.
Townend. Peter – 222, 226.
Trench, A C Colonel – 235.
Twentieth Century Limited – 185, 187.

Underhill, Fireman – 125.
Union Pacific – 185.

Vulcan Foundry – 93.

Watts (Sparkes), Caroline – 15.
Watts, Jane – 15.
Watts, John – 15-18.
Webster, F W – 28, 61.
Wedgwood, Ralph – 92, 126, 143, 156.
Westinghouse – 57.
Whitelaw, William – 103, 131.
Wilkinson, Isobel – 137.
Wilson, G R S Lt Col – 235.
Windle, Edward – 158, 161, 162-166, 168, 173, 177, 194, 195, 199, 201-203, 206, 206, 215, 216, 218, 242, 243, 249, 251, 252.
Wintour, Francis – 11, 28, 45, 55, 61.
Worsdell, Wilson – 42, 43.
Wright, Fireman – 124.

Yarrows – 109.
Yarrow, Harold – 109.
York Works – 87, 95-97, 109, 112.